MW00782421

Beyond the Violation
of the Self

Getting Your Soul Right

To Andrew
from Uncle Bill

by
William M. Jump

Beyond the Violation of the Self: Getting Your Soul Right
Copyright© 2008 by William M. Jump. All rights reserved.

No part of this book may be reproduced or transmitted in any form
or by any means, graphic, electronic, or mechanical, including photo-
copying, recording, taping or by any information storage or retrieval
system, without permission in writing from the publisher.

MAYFAIR BOOK PROMOTION, INC.
PROFESSIONAL PUBLISHING SOLUTIONS

For information contact the publisher:

Mayfair Book Promotion, Inc.
P.O. Box 91
Foresthill, CA 95631

www.mayfairbooks.com
prospct1@foothill.net.

ISBN: 978-1-934588-37-6

Printed in the United States of America.
Distributed by Reality Press for Mayfair Book Promotion, Inc.

Acknowledgments

I am indebted to my client S who has gone beyond the call of duty and allowed her Spiritual Guide to share the wisdom of the universe so that others may heal and achieve a greater Spiritual balance. S also gave of her time and energy to help me with a number of complicated cases so that these individuals could rise above the tyranny of their past. I maintain the dream that some day we can work together to help others to heal. S is a once in a life time gift that I will never take for granted. Her contribution to this book is invaluable.

This book is dedicated to my parents who were always there for me and my siblings. They modeled that love is about giving and sacrificing and taught me the importance of being humble and considerate to others. Because of them I carry a special reverence for life.

A special thanks to my beautiful daughter for her technical and emotional support throughout this project. More importantly, because of her, I know the deepest love a human being can feel.

A special thanks to my clients who trusted me in helping them through their childhood wounds. I have learned so much from them.

I want to thank the handful of mental health workers who had the courage to rise above the psychological dogma and political correctness to make the appropriate referrals so that trauma victims could get the proper treatment.

I would also like to acknowledge my lifelong friends for just being there. Having loyal friends is something to cherish.

Contents

Beyond the Violation of the Self

Foreword

We live in possibly the most uncertain age of human existence. In spite of our increased knowledge, we as a species have started to deteriorate from within. Reliance on quick access to information has had the reverse affect of diminishing our ability to listen to our intuition as we blindly accept what others – especially in the mass media – propagandize through our televisions, printed material and computers. We have become the victims of our own designs. Religions are failing to guide us towards serenity, as the extremists on all sides still do not understand that beliefs are extremely personal experiences that cannot be dogmatically thrust upon others. At the same time, the age of 'political correctness' has led to mounting controls on our bodies and minds in a futile attempt to appear to manage our environment and selves. If one questions this statement, all one need do is look at the increasing amount of mistrust of others, laws that seek to limit our behaviors and personal freedoms, and swelling prison populations. All these things are culminating in an increasing sense of hopelessness that is almost palpable in the air in around us. Everything appears to be a 'cause' these days and getting a message heard that needs telling is becoming increasingly difficult. We, as a species, principally in highly developed countries, would rather entertain ourselves with trivial pursuits than work hard to earn what we deserve and, more importantly, to face what lurks beneath the skin. The gulf between the rich and poor is widening yearly as we are constantly under threat of 'losing everything'. We live in a most uncertain time and it appears that it will only get worse as people attempt through either violence or legal means to place stopgaps on the situation.

These statements perhaps seem drastic but we as a species need to wake up as we are in the midst of a confusing and demoralizing paradigm shift that is uncovering so much angst and guile that our ability to harness the inner peace we all crave is more difficult to attain. Practicing yoga, holistic health care, meditating and 'paying it forward', among other ideas for achieving happiness, all appear to be creative ways to increase our karmic goodness. However, with pervasive negative news, fascination in destructive outlets such as aggressive video games, insidious addictions, self-medicating with drugs, alcohol, or food or simply wasting time watching a cathode ray we are rapidly becoming the most redundant generation that has inhabited this world. More and more of us encounter those who give off a sense of entitlement, disconnection or are abusive in some fashion and it is increasingly rare to meet others who are shine with real tranquility, are altruistic towards their neighbors and have found a balance and harmony between themselves and their environment. Most of us feel confused, lonely, depressed or maybe even scared of what the future holds. Life is easier on us with all our gadgets, yet more of us feel that we have less quality time and happiness in our lives than our antecedents. Do we have faith in our neighbors or ourselves any longer or do we see each other as labels? Can any of us truly look any deeper than the surface? So many people try to love and fail that estrangement, divorce or break-ups seems almost banal. Our society seems more interested in the actions of so-called celebrities than in those we live near and work with daily.

This all appears to be a blueprint for disaster but there is still hope and a great deal of good in our world if we choose to seek it. Anger can be transformed into love, disillusionment can become inspiration and we can select how to frame our lives with quality and meaning. It all starts from within. I came to understand that in order to heal from my own painful past, I needed deeper work – a spiritual cleansing of sorts. I had tried religion, counseling, psychiatry and the ensuing medications only to realize that most of what was hampering my efforts lay somewhere deep in my subconscious and the only way to repair my inner well-being was to turn off the noise in my mind. How to do this seemed impossible for a single mother in the midst of an undergraduate degree but the answer came to me through a research study on hypnosis. What I experienced in the study allowed me to be outside my own 'presence' and I finally had the ability to tap into something amazing that I thought could heal the wounds I carried internally. That time finally came several years later when I started working with Bill Jump. We were able to establish a dialogue and I was literally able to transform myself from underachieving doormat to someone who at least was able to recognize destructive impulses and leave many bad habits behind. It is still work to maintain equilibrium, but the power that I experienced through the hypnotherapy sessions finally allowed me to get beyond mental struggles that were holding me back and emerge as a strong, benevolent person able to help others. By turning off my conscious self, I was able to 'defrag my hard drive' and return to a more positive, peaceful and functional state. It can be done by anyone who is willing to dig a little deeper and can accept a new way of thinking. I know that things can truly become better for us if we just take that first step.

I am pleased to be a part of the effort that Bill has worked on for so long and am proud to have been of assistance to him with some of his clients. I realize that I have an extraordinary gift of sensitivity to others and am hopeful that our times will change as more of us accept that there is something beyond what we see in our chosen reality connecting us all. Perhaps the first step is realizing that hurting inside our mind and heart achieves nothing but destruction to all inhabitants of what is a truly beautiful planet. A healing process is available if only we choose to find it.

Client S

Preface

"There is a new collective consciousness in the minds of people, and a new spiritual awareness is spreading throughout humanity."

Wayne Dyer

There is a flood of new information associated with the current paradigm shift. We've been asleep for 2000 years, and science has turned a blind eye to spirituality. As Denise Breton and Christopher Largent explain in *The Paradigm Conspiracy*, "**We're knee-deep in the dynamics of transformation and we're shifting paradigms in the direction of greater soul connectedness.**" They go on to say that, "**We can't wait for science whose premise is to discount the invisible unmeasured to support and validate a spiritual psychology.**"

A new paradigm of mental health treatment is emerging that will combine psychological healing and spiritual growth. It has been called Spiritual Psychology as well as Transpersonal Psychology. This new paradigm looks beyond the symptoms and addresses the underlying source of the system's imbalance. Old notions of hypnosis must be dismissed because the new paradigm will require the use of hypnosis (used the correct way) to access and resolve childhood wounds safely and tolerably. Our childhood wounds keep us living in the past and continue to manifest in symptoms, triggers and behavior re-enactments. All efforts to deny the past, avoid current triggers, and to self-medicate do little to alleviate our symptoms or improve our quality of life. Medicine alone only perpetuates the denials. A paradigm of healing that combines psychology and spirit helps the individual move toward wholeness and authentic power. In *The Seat of the Soul*, Gary Zukav reminds us that Psychology means Soul knowledge. "It is supposed to be the study of the Spirit but it remains the study of the five senses." The reality is that healing is at the Soul level. As Denise Breton and Christopher Largent point out in *The Paradigm Conspiracy*, "Through our inner lives, we have access both to the wisdom of the universe and to the wisdom embedded within our own consciousness and bodies." The trance states align us with the forces that bring things to us.

Each of us has a guiding force which we call out Spirit, Spirit Guide or Higher Self as well as all the power and resources within ourselves to heal. Sadly, even though it is not the fault of my clients who bring a Host of symptoms and manifestations from their childhood traumas to the sessions, they must ultimately take responsibility for their healing. Every one who carries childhood wounds wants to alleviate their symptoms but fear usually keeps them from healing. The hypnotic/abreactive work is not easy. To revisit childhood feelings and sensations takes courage. I respect those clients who over the years have chosen this difficult journey toward wholeness. I have learned the most from my clients and continue to be inspired by those who have taken the path toward authentic power. What is on the other side of resolving child-hood wounds is alleviating triggers, compulsions and phobias; placing the childhood traumas in their proper perspective, i.e. something that happened in the past; and ultimately feeling alive.

The title and subtitle of the book are quotes from S's Dominant. (You will come to know S's Dominant in Parts III and IV.) In Part III, S's Dominant stated, "THEY will continue to force the system to go within to find their purpose, mission and vision. Otherwise the Host will continue to repeat situations. The consciousness has to move **Beyond the Violation of the Self.**" The subtitle comes from another quote in Part IV. "You are not going to be happy if you don't have your SOUL RIGHT. The soul can't be right if blocked off traumas are allowed to surface and triggers are allowed to play a role in creating bad life choices."

Hopefully this book will inspire those individuals who know that their childhood wounds are affecting their current reality, to commit to healing. It is difficult to move ahead as long as you hold on to your childhood wounds. You have all the power and resources inside yourself to deal with those things that you need to deal with. Choose to move toward Authentic Power.

"*Each day more and more people begin to understand and accept the forces of which there is no tangible hold.*"

S's Dominant

Introduction

"The wounding and painful shafts do not come from outside, through gossip which only pricks us only on the surface, but from the ambush of our own unconscious. It is our own repressed desires that stick like arrows in our flesh."

Carl Jung

The essence of this book is expressed in the following quote: "Human beings have so much pain that they are carrying around with them when they were a child and they are not letting go of it and not realizing their full potential. That's what hypnosis is, that is what the trance work does; it releases that ... To get a grip on your feelings you need to 'disconnect' the conscious mind in order to get to the root of the problem in the sub-conscious mind." This quote comes from the main subject of this book who you will come to know as S's Dominant.

I wrote this book not to impress academia or the scientific community, but to give hope to those who know or may not understand that their current problems are because of their childhood wounds and to share a treatment process that has been effective in healing childhood stressors and traumas. Many individuals who experience childhood traumas and continue to experience problems have lost faith. I always try to convince my clients that despite their problems, they have all the power within themselves to heal. As they work hard to resolve their childhood wounds, the clouds are removed and the sunlight begins to shine through. On the other hand, denying, avoiding, and failing to face our fears will certainly never move us toward a sense of wholeness that our systems are seeking. It is interesting how we tend to avoid the very thing we need to do to heal, and continue to be drawn to situations that perpetuate our problems. Believing that there is an underlying source for your symptoms and that resolving these feelings can help you move away from a life of perpetual problems and toward a path of integration, is the message being brought forth. Otherwise the unresolved childhood wounds keep you living in the past and replaying the old movies in your relationships. This book is not about recovering memories. It is about releasing and resolving the negative energy associated with traumatic memories. *(You will come to understand that certain aspects of the trauma will be accepted into consciousness as a memory of something that happened in the past.)* Carolyn Myss expressed this so profoundly in the *Anatomy of the Spirit* when she wrote, "The 'wounded child' within each of us contains the damaged or stunted emotional patterns of our youth, patterns of painful memories, of negative attitudes, and of dysfunctional self-images. Unknowingly, we may continue to operate within these patterns as adults, albeit in a new form. These patterns can damage our emotional relationships, our personal and professional lives, and our health. Loving ones self, begins with confronting this archetypal force within the psyche and unseating the wounded child's authority over us. If unhealed, wounds keep us living in the past."

This is my contribution to a Transpersonal/Spiritual perspective of healing. As Gary Zukav writes in *The Seat of the Soul*: "**Spiritual psychology will support the choice to learn through wisdom, the choice to release patterns of negativity, of doubt and fear, that are no longer appropriate to who we are and what we are becoming. It will make clear the relationship between the personality and the soul, the differences between them, and how to recognize those differences.**" We can no longer deny the spiritual component of the psyche. From a psychological perspective, Dissociation theory and the research that has come from Harvard over the last number of decades gives the best explanation for trauma and all of its manifestations. The research continues to validate my clinical observations about the nature of childhood trauma. My concern is that the research is not getting out of scientific journals and into the mindsets of the mental health community as well as to those individuals impacted by trauma who could benefit from this invaluable research. When I share a dissociative viewpoint with my clients, they seem to understand their symptoms and behaviors for the first time. From the Spiritual perspective, S's Dominant has been my gift from the non-physical realm. The inspirational writings from Gary Zukav, Eckhart Tolle, Wayne Dyer, Brian Weiss Roger Woolger, and Caroline Myss, to name a few have served to reinforce what S's Dominant as well as other Dominants and non-spiritual helpers have taught me with regard to healing at the soul level.

The reoccurring theme within a Transpersonal perspective is the resolving of childhood wounds, not containment or suppression through medication, although, medication may be needed at times to take the edge off of the symptoms as the traumata is being resolved. For psychological healing, Dissociation research emphasizes the resolution of trauma. In *Traumatic Stress*, Bessel van der Kolk stated that, "**As long as memories of the trauma remain dissociated, they will be expressed as psychiatric symptoms that will interfere with proper functioning.**" For Spiritual growth as stated by Ceanne DeRohan in *The Right Use of Will*, "**Only seeking and healing the cause in the consciousness will produce true healing.**" S's Dominant stated the following, "**You have to let go of the negativity and realize that it is your past.**" Simply stated, we can not move on until the inner work is done.

For almost two decades I have utilized a combination of hypnotic/abreactive and cognitive restructuring techniques for the healing of childhood wounds with rewarding results. This approach balances the uncovering of past trauma and ego strengthening. During the course of doing this work, the non-physical world of helpers and protectors emerged. It involves a realm beyond conscious reality, a world of soul helpers, guides, teachers, incarnates, who as a team come together way before we are born and enter the physical body when we take our first breath. You quickly learn that the

Spiritual presence in each client knows exactly what to do and knows how to help you heal. Again, the work is humbling because I realize that I am just an external helper. Many in the psychology field who wish to keep psychology secular and scientific have, and will, criticize those who have crossed over to a Transpersonal perspective. I certainly have been criticized, ridiculed and have been called a witch doctor. Assistant directors would recommend to supervisors not to refer to me because of the hypnosis. I don't mind playing the fool. It has been said that the fool can speak the truth. The fool also knows that holding on to old worn out beliefs is dangerous. I understand that people need to dismiss the truth to preserve their current view of the world. Those who maintain a narrow view will probably not survive the current paradigm shift. Those in power will all too often attempt to suppress the emergence of absolute truth.

I remain mystified that hypnosis can continue to have such a stigma in our western culture. As S's Dominant proclaimed, **"Hypnosis will have to be rediscovered as a natural state of mind that allows both healing to occur as well as giving us access to the power and resources that are available to us."** Again, it's the state of mind in which the universe brings things to us. Remember that Pierre Janet, who coined the term Dissociation at the turn of the century, believed that hypnosis was necessary for the resolution of trauma. The Shamans have been doing hypnotic ceremonies for thousands of years. In *The Healing Wisdom of Africa*, Malidoma Patrice Somè speaks of a radical ritual that involves repairing a broken psyche or spirit by pushing out the unwanted "energetic debris" that is keeping the individual trapped. It is interesting that the Dagara tribe understands that healing is about releasing negative energy through a hypnotic ritual and that our high-tech society still thinks that hypnosis is voodoo, witchcraft and even the work of the devil. The bottom line is that on both psychological and spiritual levels, healing is about releasing the negative energy and balancing our systems. It's using our natural God given states of mind to heal our psychological wounds.

None of us escapes the reality that we come to this life with lessons to learn and parts of our self that need to heal. I want everyone who could benefit from what has come to me to have the chance to clear up any childhood wounds that are slowing them down. I often tell my clients that carrying the baggage of childhood wounds is like driving up the hill of life with only three cylinders and a trunk of cement. The negative emotions we carry are heavy and they slow us down both psychologically and physically. The healing approach that I am talking about allows you to drive up the mountain of life with all six cylinders and no extra baggage.

I also want to affect those therapists who resist the emotional encounter with their clients because they are concerned about being sued, so they just avoid dealing with survivors and trauma victims. Hypnotic/abreactive healing involves an interpersonal connection with the client, particularly at the soul level where healing truly takes place. I urge these therapists to get out of your "mind-dominated" perspective and catch up with the paradigm shift and understand that we need to help clients at a deeper level or refer them to someone who can. What I am seeing is that those seeking to heal are looking into psychics and shaman ministers for answers because they know that their problems go far beyond the five senses. Utilizing trance and abreactive work to safely and tolerably help clients extinguish childhood wounds is not that far out of the box. I don't deny that people may need to sit and chat with a therapist and that many aren't ready for the deeper work. This is not some new age alternative approach but an expanded approach that allows the deeper dissociated material to be brought to the surface to be healed.

Hopefully this book will awaken more individuals to a healing process that has always been available but not desirable for most because it requires the stark reality of confronting our anxieties, fears and despair. I'm getting a sense that more and more people are realizing that they don't want to be pumped up with medication and that they know that they have to confront their emotional pain. I have had teenagers tell their parents that they think that they need hypnosis because something is blocked off and that sitting and talking about how their week is going isn't helping them. If one in four females and one in five males have been abused as children, then there are quite a few people walking around with a lot of blocked off material that has been and will continue to affect their lives. Again it's not only about trauma and severe abuse. Many of my clients grew up in dysfunctional families with daily arguments and a lot of emotional abuse that they witnessed and experienced.

Many of us would rather have a psychic tell us what is going on inside of us rather than to go into our own quiet darkness in our minds and find your own truth and face our fears. Psychological healing at this level means working through often painful experiences. In our Western culture, we are so attuned to the healer, the doctor, the therapist doing something to us, fixing us, making the pain go away so we don't have to deal with it. I often have to convince my clients that hypnosis is not something I am doing to them, rather it is a special state of mind that allows their own power within to help them work through the underlying emotions that are causing their symptoms. The abreactions that my clients have are often difficult. Bits and pieces of the original feelings and sensations are being released through the trance state. These feelings and sensations are the same intensity as they were when they were blocked off. To feel like a scared five-year-old or to have the sensation of being held down is not pleasant. As I tell my clients, the choice of going through these abreactions in a safe setting over time versus living with the symptoms and manifestations the rest of their life becomes the choice. I know for sure that the clients who have courageously worked through their painful experiences have made incredible strides in their lives. As Caroline Myss states in *Anatomy of the Spirit*, "**We end up living in a seemingly endless cycle of mentally wanting change but emotionally fearing change at every turn. Admittedly it is frightening to leave the familiar contents of one's life, even though one's life is often desperately sad. But change is frightening, and waiting for that feeling of safety to come along before one makes a move only results in more internal torment because the only way to acquire that** feeling of security is to enter the whirlwind of change and come out the other end, feeling alive again."

We are in the midst of a changing paradigm, a shift in consciousness, a new way of thinking. What has opened up for me is a deeper process of psychological healing that, however scary or difficult, allows that which is unconscious, dissociated and blocked off, to be brought to the surface and healed. Again, to accept that the trance state allows us to connect our personality to our soul, our conscious mind to our unconscious mind, our physical reality to our non-physical reality, and through a safe and tolerable process, we can release, extinguish, and resolve painful emotions, thus alleviating symptoms, manifestations, triggers, and behavior reenactments in order to feel alive and whole. There is nothing new here but rather an awakening to a healing process that recognizes both psychological and spiritual perspectives. Be careful about any nifty new technique that doesn't address healing at the soul level. Be leery of any quick fixes. Healing at the soul level takes time. Most importantly, understand that this is a natural healing process, and through your commitment, it utilizes your own power and resources to guide you toward a greater psychological and spiritual balance.

"What is most important in this life is your spiritual evolution."

S's Dominant

What you will learn in **Part I** is that this is not even a new idea in psychology. John Watkins has been doing abreactive work with dissociative clients for decades. Pierre Janet coined the term Dissociation at the turn of the century and believed that blocked off memories from trauma would return as nightmares, physical sensations and behavioral reenactments and that the blocked off feelings could only be released through the hypnagogic state.

Part I combines my clinical observations with the Dissociation research to explain the nature of trauma and its impact on the psyche. This section covers the symptoms and manifestations of trauma. You will learn that symptoms are the red flags that are telling you that there is something inside that needs to be healed. If not addressed, the blockages will continue to manifest in compulsive behaviors and intrusive emotions. You will learn that hypnosis is not the work of the Devil but actually a God given state of mind that connects you to all the power and resources you have to help you heal. In fact the trance states allow the abreactions to occur. Case studies will show the importance of the combination of hypnotic/abreactions and cognitive/restructuring techniques in the healing of childhood wounds.

In **Part II** it is my intent to show that we need to expand psychology and to connect psychological healing and spiritual growth. Some call it Transpersonal Psychology, others Spiritual Psychology. Part II identifies the non-physical helpers, teachers, and guides and their roles. In this part, I will share the incredible schema of helpers who opened up to me from the trance work and who operate within us at the soul level. You will learn how they emerge to protect us from overwhelming childhood experiences and then work hard to help us heal and move toward integration and wholeness. Here you will understand that not only unresolved painful experiences from this lifetime manifest in symptoms, but that sometimes your soul chooses to allow an unresolved story from your ancestral line to be incarnated within you for purposes of healing and resolution. Part II will become a glossary for understanding the roles of the non-physical helpers, which will be helpful in following the case studies presented in this book.

Part III is S's case study from beginning to end. I chose S's case for a number of reasons. Primarily, S has a complex system, a system that includes both trauma from this lifetime as well as two incarnates from her ancestral line who were allowed to come into S in this lifetime for healing purposes. The fact that S's Dominant (Higher Self) was able to communicate verbally through the trance state, can allow the reader to understand how that the Dominant truly guides the healing process. Also, I was able to communicate directly with the child helpers. As you follow the case, you will clearly see my role as the external helper.

Part IV is a transcript of six, one hour conversations with S's Dominant. S was put in trance just like in the therapy sessions. Her Dominant emerged, responded to my questions and free associated with, what I think was, the purpose of relaying important information that needs to be understood on a conscious level. Understand S did not hear these conversations. During the therapeutic sessions, S's Dominant informed me that my Dominant wanted me to write a book. I responded in saying that the book would be about S. The Dominant and S agreed to come to my office after the therapy sessions had been completed for the purposes of taping conversations with S's Dominant. (I will refer to S's "Higher Self," "Spirit" and "Spirit Guide," as the Dominant throughout this book. This is clarified in Part II.)

Part V reinforces the Transpersonal perspective that is emerging during the current paradigm shift. Arguments for choosing to heal one's childhood wounds and the consequences for not healing them, are discussed. The hypnotic/abreactive process for the healing of childhood trauma and overwhelming stressors is described. A plea for those who are experiencing a spiritual imbalance to take responsibility for their psychological healing and spiritual growth is also presented.

The message is clear. Your Spirit will not allow you to continue to deny those parts of the self that need healing. Let go of the old emotions that are holding you back so you can grow, evolve and live a more fulfilled life.

"Traumatic events overwhelm the ordinary systems of care that give people a sense of control, connection and meaning."

Judith Herman

Part I

"Kids need support guidance and wisdom not jealousy, anger, hatred and fear."

S's Dominant

The stark reality is that the majority of child abuse starts under the age of eight. Unfortunately, these are the formative years, during which children have to conquer major developmental milestones. We finally understand that there are long lasting consequences for child abuse. My clients are teenagers and adults who bring a Host of symptoms and manifestations from their adverse childhood experiences. We must understand that it is not just that the individual is carrying the bad memory, but that earlier experience forced the victim to establish blueprints to cope with the stress often resulting in heightened aggression and hyper vigilance, and or constriction and withdrawal. In a 2002 article, *Scars that Won't Heal*, Martin Teicher explains how the brain is being sculpted by the traumatic experience. **"The impact of severe stress can leave an indelible imprint."** Defense mechanisms have to go on a heightened alert in order to cope with the deeper primary emotions of despair, rage, and panic that arise during the trauma. Some or most of the experience is dissociated/blocked off, only to show up later in triggers and behavior re-enactments. This early adaptation to trauma and overwhelming stressors explains the extreme reactions that manifest long after the threat is gone.

I don't want this book to be focused on sexual abuse although many of my examples involve this trauma. I want to emphasize that one does not have to experience a horrific sexual or physical abuse for dissociation to occur. Family stressors, family disruption, harsh punishment, parental conflicts, being bullied and or teased, can all have an affect on the developing ego. Certainly those who experience severe neglect and abuses within their family seem to have the most devastating psychological consequences.

State agencies have estimated that over a million kids are neglected or abused in this country each year. And we wonder why so many small children and adolescents are displaying such extreme, aggressive and anti-social behaviors. I will argue that all too often the kids are given an ADD diagnosis and the adolescents are given a bi-polar label and pumped up with psychotropic medicine as the solution. Assessing small children and adolescents as victims of early trauma and overwhelming stress, and recognizing that specific symptoms are red flags for a deeper problem that requires specialized treatment, is critical for the healing of these experiences.

Child Development 101

In an ideal world, all children would grow up in a safe, secure, nurtured, and protective environment with no trauma or overwhelming stressors. The parents' leftover childhood wounds wouldn't be displaced and projected onto the child. The parents would balance active listening with clear rules and expectations and would follow-up with non-punitive consequences: getting the child to earn back privileges through improving their behavior and attitude over short periods of time. (Grounding for a week doesn't work.) Parents must do what they say they are going to do in regard to consequences. The parents would live the values they are purporting to their children. They would help their children learn frustration tolerance as well as to delay gratification. They must learn after age one that they don't get what they want when they want it. Children do live what they learn. Parents would understand that discipline means to teach, versus punishment which means to cause physical harm. Spanking doesn't work. Even if the parents separate and divorce, they would quickly provide a predictable environment for the child. The parents would separate spousal issues from parent-child issues. Ideally, parents would protect their children and know who to trust and not to trust with their care.

Certainly children need to experience some adversities, face challenges and learn to conquer some frustrations of life as they progress through developmental stages. Our struggles give meaning to our lives. The child who is protected and spoiled grows up to be filled with narcissistic rage. The child who receives strict and harsh punishment grows up carrying fear and anger. Again, parents need to set clear rules and expectations in the categories of school, curfew, chores and attitude. Know the leverage you have with your child and respond to broken rules with natural and logical consequences. Children need to EARN back their privileges over a short period of time by improving on specific target behaviors. Remember, don't give the child treats and then tell them to behave. Treats and fun times have to be earned. Don't let guilt keep you from denying a bike ride or pool time. There is a bigger guilt down the road for not doing what I am describing when your children become undisciplined, inconsiderate young adults. Always pleasing the child perpetuates the child's irrational need for pleasure and comfort. If you don't take things away and get the child to earn things back when they are four, five, or six, don't complain that your ten-year-old is acting like a four-year-old when they don't get their way. Don't complain if your teenager is out of control if you didn't set and follow through with rules and expectations when they are were younger. The sheep herder didn't beat the sheep with his rod, but guided them. Remember, to discipline means to teach and guide; to punish means to cause physical harm.

Erikson's Stages of Development

Let's take a look at Erik Erikson's psychosocial stages of development that starts in early infancy and carries through to late adulthood. For the purposes of this book let's look at the childhood stages up to the adolescent stage.

We go through a series of stages of development in order to gain a sense of security, adequacy, competence and sense of power which are the components of our self-esteem. Each stage is a polarity of success and failure, psychological opposites. The first four stages occur in the first eleven years of life. The success or failure of these four stages determines our sense of identity, our self concept that we take into our adult stages of life. For example, the first stage from birth to one year, involves the issue of TRUST. The child receives affection and need satisfaction. If a child is neglected or abused, mistrust emerges. It is important to point out that the child needs to develop a balance between the two dimensions. One develops a sense of trust for things one should trust, and a bit of mistrust for things they should mistrust. If the child develops an extreme mistrust because of abandonment, neglect and/or abuse, it jeopardizes success in the second stage which is AUTONOMY. If a child develops trust, they move toward a sense of AUTONOMY, a sense of independence and self-control. During the next stage, ages four to five, the child develops INITIATIVE. The child uses his imagination and learns to do things on his own. Remember, each stage builds on the other. Between the ages of 6 and 11, the child develops a sense of industry. The child develops a sense of accomplishment and feels competent. All of these stages trust, autonomy, initiative, and industry, build toward a sense of identity, a sense of self-concept.

What is important to understand is that failure at one stage makes it difficult to succeed in the next stage. If a child experiences abandonment or neglect in the first year of life, it would be difficult if not impossible for them to develop a sense of autonomy. If a child is made to feel inadequate in the autonomy stage, shame and doubt is carried on to the next stage which is the initiative stage.

Again, it is important to point out that a majority of child abuse occurs under the age of seven or eight. Consequently, their sense of autonomy and initiative are often seriously threatened. Most of the work with my clients involves the blame, shame, and guilt they bring with them from their childhood wounds. The integration work is always about helping the client acquire the ability to use their personal power to assert themselves, and to speak up for themselves. Also, when abuse occurs at an early age, the industry stage is stifled. Many children who have experienced some form of abuse often have difficulty in school performance. Many of the children I see have some difficulty either in a specific area such as reading or just struggle in general to complete their work. They have trouble paying attention, often feel inadequate, have a sense of failure that may manifest in being the class clown, the class bully, or the ever popular, "if he or she would just apply themselves," child. When this happens, both the parents and the school become frustrated with the child, adding to his sense of inferiority.

Success or failure at each stage either promotes or jeopardizes success in the next stage. The first four stages build to a sense of identity during early adolescence. Failure at one or more of the stages leads to what Erik Erikson called identity confusion where the adolescent may feel isolated, anxious and indecisive. This identity confusion is carried into adult life and can affect personal and intimate relationships as well as the ability to perform and succeed in the work place.

Your Foes Will Be Of Your Own Household

Unfortunately, we all too often bring our childhood wounds into our personal relationships. We project and displace our unresolved feelings, unknowingly, onto our spouses and children. We too often treat our children as we were treated despite our belief that we would never do so. We draw ourselves unconsciously to relationships that trigger our childhood wounds. These wounds can not be resolved through the relationship. We expect our spouses to meet our unmet needs and when they don't we withdraw and or get angry. The essence of this book is about resolving our childhood wounds so we don't continue to violate ourselves and others.

This book is not just about trauma. The mind also blocks off overwhelming stressors. I am glad to see that the latest research includes the term "overwhelming stressor" versus a previous emphasis on "trauma." Too many of my clients minimize their childhood experiences such as parents fighting, yelling, physical punishment, post divorce tension and squabbles, and don't connect their current personal and interpersonal conflicts as related to the past. Remember, many clients are amnestic about their childhood conflicts.

Studies have shown that over 50% of inpatient, outpatient, and psychiatric emergency patients have a reported history of childhood trauma. The reality is that children do experience physical abuse, sexual abuse, emotional abuse and neglect. Children do witness their parents yelling and fighting. Children go through divorce and get caught up in post divorce double-bind situations. Children do experience the abandonment of a parent or at least inconsistent and disappointing visitations. Interestingly, we fail to realize that medical procedures and hospital stays for children can be frightening and are often blocked off only to manifest later in fears and triggers.

I need to point out that obviously not all children are mistreated and abused by their parents. In fact, a majority of my sexual abuse victims were abused by individuals who may have been known and trusted by the family or who were related in some way such as step-parents, cousins, baby-sitters, older siblings of friends, not to mention the "nice" man up the street. Some of my clients were also physically mistreated or bullied by siblings and both teen and adult sitters.

Remember, the primary emotions felt by children in these situations are very intense. Again, it doesn't have to be a trauma for the child to be overwhelmed emotionally and for feelings to be dissociated from these experiences. We can accept that traumas such as sexual abuse and physical abuse will certainly have an impact on the child. In fact many of my case examples are about sexual abuse because of my specialty in this area. However I want to emphasize the fact that children are vulnerable and can have long-lasting consequences for other overwhelming and stressful experiences. Again, under ideal conditions children have to conquer major milestones as they pass through these stages. How the parents treat each other and how they treat their children has a great influence on the developing child's sense of self. When the child is overwhelmed by stress and trauma the ego is threatened and experiences are blocked off which results in alterations in emotions, perceptions, self-esteem and interpersonal relationships. Because of the ego's need to turn internal threats to external projections, the child will adapt to the stress and traumatic material by displacing their disowned anger and frustrations onto others. Understand, as long as we deny our childhood wounds, we will all too often treat our children as we were treated. Believing that our discontent is caused by other people or other things is to live in external power.

"Your children are not your children. They are the sons and daughters of Life's longing for itself. They come through you but not from you, and though they are with you yet they belong not to you."

Khalil Gibran

DISSOCIATION THEORY

"Many traumatized people expose themselves, seemingly compulsively to situations reminiscent of the original. These behavioral re-enactments are rarely consciously understood to be related to earlier life experiences."

Bessel van der Kolk

Psychology was grounded in the belief that symptoms and manifestations were related to repressed or blocked off traumatic experiences and that through the hypnagogic state, the trauma could be accessed and healed. The theory of Dissociation is not a new one. Over the last one hundred years, much attention has been paid to past trauma's continuing affects on people. Pierre Janet developed the theory of Dissociation at the turn of the century. The theory purported that one part of the mind can function separately from the others. He recognized that in the hypnotic state that the client could recall things which had been forgotten. He recognized that people did not often have memories of things that were associated with **"repressed desires and unpleasant events."** These dissociated memories would return as nightmares, physical sensations, and behavioral re-enactments. Janet believed that hypnosis was a way that could bring these dissociated memories back to consciousness. In doing this, the client would get relief. If the dissociated material was not integrated, the blocked off thoughts, feelings, and perceptions would continue to be repeated as a contemporary event.

There is overwhelming evidence that early trauma is related to the development of psychological problems. Children who are neglected, emotionally, physically, and or sexually abused, dissociate these experiences from their conscious mind as a protection and or a defense. It is important to point out that the conscious child does not choose to dissociate the trauma, but as you will understand later on, the unconscious mind makes this choice not to allow the unpleasant, overwhelming material to enter the child's psyche. This material is siphoned off into various parts of our unconscious mind. Unfortunately these dissociated experiences will show up in a variety of symptoms and manifestations that make it difficult for the individual to successfully move through their developmental stages.

Children will display bed wetting, nightmares, and changes in school performance. During the early teen years anger will manifest as defiant and rebellious behaviors, running away, as well as drug and alcohol experimentation. With adults whose childhood wounds go untreated, panic attacks, depression, relationship conflicts, and somatic problems will manifest.

Frank Putnam defined dissociation as an ongoing process in which certain information such as feelings, memories, and physical sensations, are kept apart from other information with which it would normally be associated. The unconscious mind blocks off overwhelming, and traumatic experiences as a protection when we are children. (Certainly in adult traumatic situations, we can dissociate from the experience as well.) These experiences are divided into thoughts, feelings, and perceptions. Pierre Janet proposed that traumatic memories are split off from consciousness and instead are stored as sensory perceptions, obsessional ruminations, and behavioral re-enactments. Again, the dissociated aspects of the trauma will show up in a Host of symptoms and manifestations such as depression, compulsions, self-destructive behaviors, rage, panic attacks, phobias, drug and alcohol problems, as well as physical symptoms. Unless the original dissociated material is released, cleared up, worked through or extinguished, the symptoms and manifestations will continue to be a problem throughout the individual's life.

MANIFESTATIONS

Your unconscious mind blocks off unpleasant, scary, overwhelming, painful and traumatic experiences, and then subdivides them into their separate components as a protection and or means of survival. The feelings, sensations, and perceptions, start to emerge as symptoms. Symptoms are about letting us know that there is something going on inside that needs healing. Assessing symptoms becomes extremely important in the cases where there is no reporting of (or in many cases, no recollection of) an original overwhelming or traumatic experience. Most of the juvenile offenders in my case load had no memory of their original trauma. Even when a client has a cognitive memory of a trauma or overwhelming experience, the dissociated emotions from that experience will continue to intrude upon their current reality. Overwhelming experiences, emotional, physical and or sexual abuse, witnessing acts of violence, family disruption, all have an impact on children who are affected by one or more of these issues. The impact is seen in often long term and persistent symptoms and manifestations on one's life.

Lenore Terr reported four characteristics in individuals who have experienced trauma. They include, **"repeated visualizations or other returning perceptions, repeated behaviors and bodily responses, trauma specific fears, and revised ideas about people, life and the future."**

In *Trauma and Recovery*, Judith Herman describes three categories of symptoms associated with trauma.

Hyperarousal is described as a permanent alert that the individual goes into, after a trauma. It is thought once the trauma occurs, the antennas go up and the individual is always on guard. It is typical for young victims to worry excessively when their parents go to the store that something bad is going to happen. Even years after the trauma, the individual is often filled with anticipatory anxiety as well as specific fears and sleep disturbances.

The second category that Herman describes is **Intrusion**. "Long after the danger is past, traumatized people relive the event as though it is continually recurring in the present," Judith Herman. These individuals have flashbacks and vivid dreams. The blocked off trauma can be triggered spontaneously. For example, a young adult survivor in my case load was triggered by an innocent hug around the neck, which sent her off to her room filled with powerful upset feelings. It is important to keep in mind that when anxiety and fear is triggered in the present, the individual often does not make the connection to the original trauma. Again, the feelings feel contemporary and the individual often looks for something in their current reality to explain them. Blocked off feelings can manifest in phobias and panic attacks. For example, a client who drove successfully for years developed a phobia about driving in her thirties. She would slow down and often have to pull over when the panic set in. What is emerging is the panic related to a childhood trauma. Remember, the primary emotions that are blocked off in early trauma are so powerful that when triggered years later can result in intense feelings and anxiety reactions.

The blocked off trauma is often acted out in behaviors. These feelings which are primary emotions propel the behavior. The juvenile offender, who could be amnestic for his original sexual trauma, is acting out what happened to him. When you uncover his victimization, the feelings that he remembers are the same feelings that he experienced during the acting out behavior. The juvenile will describe the moment of his acting out behavior as surreal, as though he was standing next to himself watching the behavior occur. On occasion, the individual is amnestic for his acting out behavior. Children who have experienced trauma will display behaviors that even when they receive a consequence, they will compulsively repeat that behavior whether it is bothering a younger sibling, or being aggressive with classmates.

The intense emotions from trauma will manifest when we are awake through intrusive thoughts, panic attacks, and compulsive behaviors, as well as during our sleep in nightmares and vivid dreams.

The third category, **Constriction** that Judith Herman describes is a "state of surrender." It is about avoiding, shutting down, feeling numb, detached and withdrawn. Many of my clients who have experienced overwhelming childhood stressors and traumas have difficulty in expressing feelings, using their personal power to assert themselves and make decisions, and tend to avoid new situations that trigger emotions. Herman reports the traumatized people who cannot spontaneously dissociate may attempt to produce similar numbing effects by using alcohol or narcotics.

"In avoiding any situations reminiscent of the past trauma, or any initiative that might involve future planning and risk, traumatized people deprive themselves of those new opportunities for successful coping that might mitigate the effect of the traumatic experience. Thus constrictive symptoms, though they may represent an attempt to defend against overwhelming emotional states, exact a high price for whatever protection they afford. They narrow and deplete the quality of life and ultimately perpetuate the affects of the traumatic event," Judith Herman.

An important argument for recognizing symptoms and getting help, is that the symptomatic child gets yelled at, becomes the black sheep of the family, and can typically get labeled the problem child. Important in this regard is the school problems that emerge which are usually looked upon as the child not living up to their potential, or that the child is not applying him or herself. So the child can be traumatized unbeknownst to the parents, display symptoms, particularly behavior problems and get criticized and put down for acting out which only adds to the child's confusion and self-blame. Many of these kids get labeled ADHD and are pumped up with medication. My concern is that a possible earlier stressor or trauma is not explored and consequently not addressed and healed.

Clients often put themselves in Catch-22 situations. A part of them that holds the anger may drink or do drugs to self-medicate, but the drugs and alcohol serve only to weaken the internal controls making it easier for the traumatic feelings to be re-enacted. (You will learn more about the roles that the unconscious parts play in dealing with the traumatic feelings in Part II.) So it's not the alcohol or drugs that make the person go off but that the alcohol and or drugs that weaken the internal controls allowing the rage that is already there to emerge. "Disinhibition resulting from drugs or alcohol strongly facilitates the occurrence of such reliving experiences, which may take the form of acting out violent or sexual traumatic episodes," Bessel van der Kolk.

TRIGGERS

Important to dissociation theory is that the reliving of blocked off trauma is experienced as real in the present moment, as a contemporary event. Few people realize in their current behavioral and emotional re-enactments, albeit in relationship disputes, fits of rage, and self-destructive behaviors, that the feelings that they are experiencing are rooted in the past. Only when my clients get to the original source of their problem do they make the connection to the feelings they relieved in the healing process are the same feelings that they were re-experiencing in their current reality.

It is important to point out that the blocked off feelings can be triggered by a spouse, co-worker, the smell of alcohol or cologne. Also important, the blocked off feelings do not need an external source to be triggered. Remember, these feelings can be so powerful that they just break through without a precipitating event. Often individuals will subconsciously provoke a situation in order to have a stage to project and release their anger. Keep in mind that when the anger is expressed in these situations, the anger is not diminished despite the illusion we have of a temporary relief. If the anger was diminished each time we went off, our anger should get better after a number of outbursts. In fact, the blocked off emotions that are expressed in behavioral and emotional re-enactments only seem to become more reinforced and often more intensified.

Often one spouse will subtly say or do something that triggers the other, not being aware that the powerful feelings that are felt and often acted upon are really feelings from a negative childhood experience or experiences. The person who is being mistreated by their spouse is instantly thrust back to the powerful feelings from their original abuse. The person who goes on a cocaine spree finds himself in dangerous and frightening situations as a reliving of his original childhood fear from a violent father. I remember reading a case example of a woman who fainted at her son's wrestling match because of the smell of sweat. She was abused by her heavyset, perspiring stepfather. One teenager in my case load was triggered by the smell of leather because the perpetrator wore a leather jacket. Many of my teenage boys who were abused by males were triggered for example in gym class during a wrestling match. Many of my survivors are triggered by an innocent touch on the neck or a hug.

Keep in mind that the blocked off feelings don't have to be triggered. Often the feelings will surface and the person will subconsciously provoke a situation, the "picking a fight syndrome," and coerce another into an antagonizing situation. Many of my clients will admit that they did push their partner's buttons until they got the negative response that they were subconsciously seeking. Out of all of our emotions, I believe that anger tends to manifest in external reality through projections and displacement. If you have triggers, you still have blocked off emotions.

"Compulsive repetition of the trauma usually is an unconscious process that, although it may provide a temporary sense of mastery or even pleasure, ultimately perpetuates chronic feelings of helplessness and a subjective sense of being bad and out of control. Gaining control over ones' current life, rather than repeating trauma in action, mood, or somatic states, is the goal of treatment. It is important to keep in mind that the only reason to uncover the trauma is to gain conscious control over the unbidden re-experiences or re-enactments."

Bessel van der Kolk

VICTIMS BECOME VICTIMIZERS

In his article, *The Compulsion to Repeat the Trauma*, Bessel van der Kolk discusses three ways in which blocked off trauma is manifested. I have seen this profile time and time again in my practice. In fact, I began utilizing hypnosis with offenders almost two decades ago with success in uncovering and resolving an underlying trauma. In the behavioral re-enactment of the trauma, the self may play the role of either the victim or victimizer. The re-enactment of victimization is the major cause of violence. The research is clear that most criminals have been physically and or sexually abused as children. The case example discussed before is a good example of the victim becoming the victimizer. Most of my juvenile offenders in the years of doing this work have uncovered an original sexual abuse trauma. Studies used to indicate around a 50% rate of abuse for juvenile offenders. These relied on self report and did not recognize the amnesia factor that I have addressed. I believe that all juvenile offenders have been sexually abused and the treatment needs to be focused on uncovering and releasing the feelings from that original trauma. Certainly external controls need to be established early on.

Why victims become victimizers will be discussed in Part II when I cover the role of the different part of the self on an unconscious level. The simple explanation is that the part of the self that holds the memory of the trauma can hold a desire to get back at someone for what happened to them, victims becoming victimizers. There is an identification with the perpetrator, the aggressor. Most of the adult males who expose themselves were abused by teenage girls, interestingly, girls at the same age who abused them. Juvenile offenders tend to act out with children who are at the same age that they the offender was when they were abused. Let's keep in mind that all victims have the potential to act out their abuse. Not all do. Perhaps historically men have expressed their anger more overtly and we saw more male perpetrators. As social norms change, we are seeing more women expressing their dissociated rage in overt acts. (Just watch the news.) I have seen an increase in the number of survivors in my case load who were abused by females. I am also seeing an increase in female juvenile offenders.

A simple example of victim becoming victimizer is that the bully in the school yard is usually the kid who was beaten by a parent and or witnessed acts of violence in the home. Studies show that a percentage of juveniles who have committed serious crimes and even murder were extensively, physically and or sexually abused in childhood. *(Remember, the theory gives reasons, not excuses.)*

Manifestations of trauma aren't gender oriented. The powerful blocked off emotions are going to manifest in often intense and destructive re-enactments to the self and to others. Again the importance of recognizing the symptoms and getting help for the trauma early on is tantamount so that the child doesn't become a juvenile delinquent and then perhaps an adult criminal.

The bottom line is that anger against the self and others is a central theme with those who have been abused. We don't tend to see the aggressive behavior as being connected to an earlier experience. My first juvenile offender who I did hypnosis with, became aggressive in third grade. He was never physically punished nor witnessed his parents fighting. The blocked off anger from his abuse began to manifest even before his acting out sexually with his sister. His case example is described in this section. **Identification with the aggressor** is a major defense that permits feelings of powerlessness and helplessness to be replaced with feelings of power and omnipotence.

VICTIMS REMAIN VICTIMS

One of my male clients who was both physically and sexually abused said that he would pick on the biggest guy in the bar and get the crap beat out of him, a good example of victim remaining a victim. It's not only females who can remain in victim roles. Most of my sexual abuse victims have been in numerous abusive relationships. Bessel van der Kolk reports that twice as many women with a history of incest report physical violence in their marriages. Any effort to help battered spouses needs to include treatment for the victims. This is not to say that victims are asking to be raped or battered, but at an unconscious level, the blocked off memories do continue to replay themselves in behavioral re-enactments as well as with many other symptoms and manifestations that we have discussed.

"Look closely at the dynamic in which you are involved and you will see that when one soul seeks to prey upon a weaker soul, and a weaker soul responds, both souls are the weaker soul. Who preys upon whom? The logic of the five-sensory personality cannot grasp this, but the higher-order logic of the heart sees it clearly. Is there truly a difference when two consciousnesses are trying to link into a dynamic that ultimately will lead to balance when both have identical missing pieces? What causes the need to dominate for example, is the same that causes the need to be submissive. It is merely the choice of which role the soul wishes to play in working out the same identical struggle. We create our experiences..."

Gary Zukav

As long as we remain fragmented, parts of our self continue to seek others to allow the unresolved feelings to find a stage to be acted upon. We match up with others at the same level of differentiation. Particularly in relationships, stop blaming your spouse for your woes and turn to yourself and ask, what is it about me that draws me to this kind of person? Leo Busgalia said, **"We can only give what we have."** If we are needy, selfish and insecure, then that is what we give to others. Our missing pieces can not be fulfilled by another. The parts of our soul that need healing can only be healed through facing our childhood wounds and resolving them. Only then can we move from powerlessness to a sense of authentic power. Otherwise, we unconsciously continue to draw ourselves to situations that perpetuate our sense of being a victim.

SELF DESTRUCTION

A third way that blocked off emotions manifest is through self-destructive behaviors. The following is an excerpt from a client.

"There isn't one act of self-destructiveness that I haven't tried on for size. Sometimes the behaviors would come individually, sometimes in clusters. But I never got a break. It was always something. Some would go away for a while just to return a couple of years down the road. For example, when I was a child, I had gained a lot of weight. Then, as a teenager, I flipped over to being compulsive about my weight and nearly anorexic. Now, I'm fat again. Smoking also has been the same way. I was drinking heavily during high school and college. Now, I hardly touch the stuff. The same with drugs. I haven't used at all since I've been in therapy. That's pretty good. My worse acts of self-destructiveness were the suicide attempts and self-mutilation. I'm pretty sure that they were more a method of stress management rather than serious attempts to harm myself. Relationships were also a form of self-punishment. I got involved with some really bad people and allowed them to hurt me. I put myself in situations where I was taken advantage of and where I was used sexually."

Client

Self harm is a common manifestation of childhood trauma. Studies indicate that many physically and sexually abused victims have a history of self-mutilation. Many children and teenagers have a history of wrist cutting, head banging, and burning to name a few. One of my clients reported that she used to drop the bed post on her foot. Also in the category of self-destructive re-enactments are alcohol and drug abuse, as well as eating disorders. Certainly painful childhood experiences can be linked to later life behaviors of self-destructive behaviors and addictions.

As I will later discuss in Part II, the part of the unconscious mind that holds one form of the dissociated anger tends to be the part that can deal with the pain through self-medication, drugs and alcohol, as well as through the abuse of prescription medication. This is the part of the self that can sabotage and get back at the self and cause the conscious Host to feel the pain that is being held by that part of the self. (*A more detailed explanation of the parts of the self and their roles will follow in Part II.*)

SYMPTOMS

"Only through emotions can you encounter the force field of your own soul. Feelings are the means through which we discern the parts of itself that the soul seeks to heal."

Gary Zukav

Symptoms are telling us that something is going on inside of us or our child. Particularly with children, we need to get more sophisticated with recognizing the symptoms and manifestations that are being expressed as red flags to an underlying problem. Remember, the unconscious mind blocks off feelings, sensations, and perceptions from negative experiences to protect you, but those blocked off feelings will soon break through in fears, anger, nightmares, behavior re-enactments, and often self-destructive behaviors. Understand that the experiencing of these feelings is one way that your unconscious mind can let you know that these feelings are there and need to be addressed. If ignored, the symptoms will continue to persist. Medicine can subdue the symptoms and give you the illusion that you are better, but if you stop the medicine the symptoms will surely return.

"When dissociated experiences return to consciousness, their form will be determined by the way they were encoded in the memory," James Chu. The emotions we experience as children are primary emotions that are much more intense than the emotions we feel as an adult. Children experience deeper emotions for protection and survival. Anger is rage, sadness is depression, and fear is panic. This explains why the blocked off emotions are so intense when they are triggered in the present moment. An adult who experiences a panic attack is actually feeling the panic from a scary experience from childhood, an experience that is usually not remembered or at least connected to the present situation. My survivors who are triggered by their spouses and go into a rage are feeling the rage from their earlier childhood abuse.

During the years that I worked on the sexual abuse team, a number of signs and symptoms would typically be present in many of the children and adolescents that we interviewed who had been or were suspected of being emotionally, physically and sexually abused. Hopefully through case examples, the correlation between the nature of the trauma and the symptoms and manifestations will be clear.

The complexity of how a trauma manifests varies from individual to individual. The research supports what I have observed, which is that children who are abused at an early age by family members, and for long periods of time, seem to have more severe symptoms and longer lasting affects. Why does one child around the age of six who was abused by the teenage son of the baby-sitter, seem to be able to talk about what happened to him where another client at the same age, who was abused by the lady up the street, has no recollection of his childhood abuse until abreactive work helps him remember fifteen years later? I have worked with brothers and sisters who were close in age. The sister remembered details of dad coming home and being verbally abusive to the mother, while the brother had no memory of such events. Not all victims become victimizers, but all victimizers have been victimized.

I am not limiting the discussion to severe trauma such as sexual abuse —although many of my case examples involve such a trauma. It is important to keep in mind that as a child we can be overwhelmed by stressful situations in our lives and subsequently dissociate these feelings only to have symptoms emerge at subsequent stages.

Recognizing that a profile of symptoms can be a red flag to a serious underlying problem, and that the child needs to get the proper treatment to address these symptoms, is extremely important. It is often tricky because the symptoms can be very subtle. The symptoms can be misconstrued as a stage. The child can be misdiagnosed with a learning disability, or quite often with an attention deficit disorder, when in fact more often than not the child may be experiencing symptoms and manifestations related to a dissociative disorder secondary to overwhelming physical, emotional, and or sexual experiences. Many kids who have been abused or have experienced overwhelming stressors have trouble focusing, concentrating, and paying attention in school.

Again, it may or may not be abrupt changes in the child that indicate a problem. Suzanne Segroi's list of stress related behaviors in children and adolescents (listed below) remains a very good list of behavioral indicators. Children and adolescents in my current case load tend to display many of the behaviors listed below.

- Sleep disturbances - nightmares, night terror, fear of the dark or sleeping alone, trouble falling asleep and/or frequently awakening during the night, or excessive sleeping.

- Changes in eating behaviors - loss of or sudden increase in appetite with resultant weight loss or gain.

- Regressive behaviors - this may include clinging and separation difficulties, thumb sucking, bed wetting and bowel control problems (after child has been trained).

- Hyperactivity/hypervigilance/insecure behaviors.

- Excessive and/or inappropriate fears - fear of a particular person or place.

- Hostile, aggressive or acting out behaviors.

- Varied and repeated somatic complaints with no physical etiology.

- Change and decline in academic performance, school avoidance, and poor peer relations.

- Excessive crying, feelings of hopelessness, withdrawn behaviors, decline in personal appearance, suicidal ideation and/or gesture, and substance abuse.

Suzanne Segroi

Other important considerations in assessing behavioral changes, are the severity and the pervasiveness. Certainly a child who has just had their tonsils removed may have some nightmares and or some regressive behavior. These symptoms usually subside rather quickly. Children may experience some sleeping disturbance after the family moves into a new community. Not to minimize family disruption ie., separation and divorce, but children may display somatic complaints, become sad and withdrawn or even become Hostile. However, if the parents quickly establish a predictable environment for the children, these symptoms can often diminish. Certainly if a child who is going through a family separation continues to be symptomatic, then that child should be placed in counseling.

Remember, symptoms that persist are red flags and clues to the nature and extent of a more serious trauma. We tend to see symptoms falling in the following categories: emotional, interpersonal, cognitive/perceptual, behavior, and physical. **Emotionally** children may display blame and shame, guilt, anxiety reactions, phobias, and depression. On a **cognitive** level children may experience nightmares, hallucinations, and school performance problems. On a **behavioral** level, children may experience enuresis/encopresis lying, stealing, fire setting or self-mutilation.

On the **interpersonal** level children may display regressive behavior, aggressive behaviors, and a hyper-maturity *(acting older than their age)*. The deeper anger and rage from childhood wounds tends to manifest in early adolescence in defiant and rebellious behaviors as well as depression. Remember, depression is anger turned inward. **Physical** symptoms particularly with sexual trauma present in urinary and bladder problems, bowel complications, and stomachaches.

The misdiagnosing of dissociative reactions and post-traumatic stress syndromes continues to be problematic. Many children, adolescents and adults often receive numerous diagnoses before being identified as a trauma victim. Children continue to be labeled ADHD, and in increasing numbers, teenagers are being diagnosed Bipolar. Underlying trauma and stressors are too often overlooked and ignored. Thankfully the Dissociation research is producing comprehensive lists and scales for dissociative reactions so that an accurate diagnosis is obtained and the proper referral for specialized treatment of trauma and abuse is given. Frank Putnam has compiled a list of *Signs and Symptoms of Dissociative Reactions in Children*. This list is paramount in assessing children for possible trauma.

"Child abuse fosters the development of abnormal states of consciousness in which the ordinary relations of body and mind, reality and imagination, knowledge and memory, no longer hold. These altered states of consciousness permit the elaboration of a prodigious array of symptoms, both somatic and psychological."

Judith Herman

AMNESIA

"Those who cannot remember the past are condemned to repeat it."

Euripides

Many clients are amnestic for childhood events. Note that many people including some mental health professionals don't believe that one can be amnestic for a child-hood trauma. The unconscious mind has the ability to block off portions and or the complete trauma. Traumatic experiences when blocked off are separated into thoughts, feelings, and perceptions. Many individuals have the pictures of their trauma in their mind, but the feelings are dissociated. Typically I have found, and the research supports, a developmental cutoff point, where under the age of six or seven, more aspects of the trauma tend to be dissociated. All but one of my juvenile offenders was completely amnestic for their original trauma. The exception was a teen who had been abused by a teenager when he was 10. This teen remembered the pictures but had little memory for how he felt about his own abuse. The fact that this teenager acted out would preclude that his mind blocked off the emotional aspects of his abuse. Remember, you only act out or have intense feelings if there are blocked off feelings. Even though you may have a conscious memory of your trauma, if you are symptomatic, you still have blocked off feelings. It's the blocked off feelings that propel the symptoms.

I worked with a young woman in her twenties who came to therapy because of tumul-tuous problems with her boyfriend. During the assessment phase, she reported that she had been sexually abused by her grandfather around the age of nine. She believed that because she had a cognitive memory of her childhood abuse, that the abuse wasn't related to her relationship problems. The reality is that her unconscious mind blocked off the feeling/emotional aspect of her abuse and that these feelings would emerge and be reenacted in her relationships. She was "matter of fact" in talking about her childhood abuse which gives credence to the fact that the emotional aspects were dissociated and that she only had a cognitive memory of her trauma.

Often a client will remember for example that her older step-brother began to abuse her at age ten. Upon further assessment, you see that there are many dissociative symptoms that were present prior to the age when she remembers the abuse starting. For example, the client is amnestic for much of their childhood; they had bed-wet-ting problems, nightmares and problems with their school performance. During the course of the trance work, the client remembers and re-experiences the abuse that actually started when they were five or six. This is an example of how the uncon-scious mind can block off the complete experience under that seven or eight-year-old range and then allows the child to have a cognitive awareness as they get older. The exception to this is that the unconscious mind will block off experiences after the age of seven or eight if there was an earlier trauma or set of overwhelming experiences under the age of six or seven.

I worked with a teenage boy who acted out with his sister. What was uncovered through the trance work was that he experienced a sexual trauma at 13 for which he was amnestic. I concluded that there were prior unrelated emotional traumas in his early childhood. When the unconscious mind sees that the system is vulnerable and already fragmented, it tends to block off subsequent trauma even when the individual is older. It comes down to being a continued protection to an already fragmented system.

Another exception to the under six or seven rule is when the perpetrator is an older kid in the neighborhood, such as a teenage baby-sitter, that the younger victims can remember and be able to disclose the abuse, particularly if the symptoms that emerge are recognized and dealt with very carefully. Usually these kids are symptomatic which again means that portions of the trauma were blocked off. A young boy I am working with began to show symptoms of nightmares, encopresis, and anger. It emerged that he acted out with a same age friend. When confronted, he disclosed that the teenage son of his baby-sitter had abused him over the course of a year. More an exception, this young boy was able to talk about the details of his abuse. I believe that much of the emotional side of the abuse was dissociated and thus was worked on in therapy. Perhaps his acting out with his friend, not to discount the effects on the friend, was a blessing for my client in that it was an announcement to the outside world that something was going on inside.

Again, the individual can be completely amnestic for the original trauma. The client has no memory of their parents fighting, of being physically, sexually or emotionally abused. The emotional aspects, the feelings, blame, shame, sadness, anger, will emerge in current life situations. The reliving of childhood trauma can be very pervasive and overwhelming as well as immobilizing and confusing for the person who is often doing compulsive, self-destructive behaviors to themselves (as well as causing harm to others) without understanding where these behaviors are coming from. **"The inability of the individual to communicate the true origins of their behavior once again set them up to be blamed by themselves and others for what they are experiencing,"** James Chu.

Perhaps the most confusing and hardest to believe aspect of amnesia occurs when the person is amnestic for their acting out behavior, whether the behavior is directed to themselves or toward others. Please remember, not everyone who acts on previously dissociated feelings are amnestic for their behavior. Most of the men who expose themselves remember doing that behavior. However, juvenile offenders have varying degrees of recall about their acting out behavior. They usually always report feeling dissociated from the experience. Many of the spouses of my survivors report that the client had an episode of rage which they do not remember. An eleven-year-old got up and literally attacked her younger sibling in the waiting room. Later in the privacy of the therapy office, this young girl did not remember attacking her sister.

When people are reacting to their original trauma, they feel what is termed depersonalized. They report feeling out of their body, in a dream like state, and often not themselves. "There is an involuntariness about the behavioral re-enactments," Judith Herman. Many of my clients report that they were beside themselves as though they were watching themselves go off. Again, when the dissociated material is relived or reenacted, it can become overwhelming and confusing as well as making the person feel that they are going crazy. The unconscious mind has the ability to shut down the person's consciousness to a point where they are not aware of their reliving of the traumatic feelings. Remember, dissociation is about protection of the conscious person. When powerful traumatic feelings are being triggered and re-experienced in the present moment, the unconscious mind can shut down the conscious Host so that they are not aware of how these feelings are being reenacted. We seem to understand that when a Multiple Personality (now referred to as Dissociative Identity Disorder) has one personality take over for hours, days and even months, and the conscious Host is not aware of what is going on during that time frame. This opens up a can of worms with the person's responsibility with regard to his actions, particularly if that individual is amnestic for the acting out behavior. I even argue for example, that juvenile offenders who do recollect their acting out behavior, can not overcome the powerful compulsion to reenact their blocked off feelings until they resolve their original trauma. In these cases, the individual and or the parents are responsible for getting help. Again, recognize that symptoms are red flags for deeper problems. The theme of this book is that if we can help an individual resolve their trauma when they are younger, then perhaps we can prevent any future acting out behavior.

On Frank Putnam's list of *Signs and Symptoms of Dissociation*, he lists "Children who continue to lie or deny their misbehavior when the evidence is obvious and immediate." One boy who I was working with, denied setting toilet paper on fire, even though his mother saw him doing it. It is difficult for us the observer to believe that when a child or teenager is acting out, that they aren't aware of their behavior at that moment. I am not discounting the powerful defense mechanisms of denial and projection. Under stress, these primitive defenses can easily kick in and motivate the person to lie, deny or minimize their actions. I'm not denying or minimizing the fact that many of the offenders in the group that I co-led were denying and minimizing their acting out behavior in order to cover their butts. Certainly parents and school personnel often perceive children and teenagers as liars and great manipulators. We have to understand that this is not so much a conscious action but a reaction and response to the powerful feelings and experiences that people have when they are reliving dissociated feelings. It is more of a justification, a covering of the tracks of confusing and overwhelming feelings and impulses that pervade the conscious mind. In keeping an open mind I began to see much of the same dissociation phenomena with the offenders that I was observing with the victims, that is the experience of depersonalization, derealization, amnesia for childhood, and often memories of childhood trauma. I came to the same conclusions in working with teenagers who had acted out. As you will understand, my work with juvenile offenders is about releasing and resolving the feelings and sensations from their original trauma. Certainly early on in the therapy I work with the family and the teen in establishing external controls.

CASE EXAMPLE

The following is a case example of a teenage boy who was not only amnestic for his original trauma, but also amnestic for his acting out sexually with his sister.

B, age 15, was referred to me after his sister 13 disclosed that B had for about two months been coming into her room at night, lying on top of her and humping her. She reported that he didn't say anything and that he had what is described as a trancelike stare about him. The trancelike stare is a symptom of dissociation. When confronted about these allegations, B vehemently denied that he had done that to his sister. I quickly gained the parents' trust and tried to get them to believe in the possibility that B was not aware of his acting out behavior. I had come to believe by this time that juvenile offenders have been victimized and that we need to uncover their trauma in order to extinguish the compulsive acting out behavior. This was actually the first juvenile offender with whom I had attempted to do the trance work. Prior to this I had been trained and had done trance work with victims.

As always I did an assessment of B's background and childhood. B began to have problems in the third grade with anger at home and at school which had not been a problem before that year. At age nine the parents reported that he had displayed low self-esteem and signs of depression. He also had dark circles under his eyes, perhaps related to his sleep disturbance that B reported for, but which his parents were not aware. He was assessed for Attention Deficit. This case is a good example of a child being diagnosed with Attention Deficit disorder when actually his symptoms were more about his blocked off trauma. Around this time he had gotten into eight fights at school. At age 10 he was seeing a psychologist for his rage. B was amnestic for under the age of seven. He had a problem with headaches. An interesting symptom was that B had a phobia of girls which will make sense as you follow the case study. I continued with a gentle, noninvasive, unconscious process of allowing his unconscious mind to prepare B to remember what he needed to remember to heal. What emerged from the trance work was that B was abused by the baby-sitter's eleven-year-old daughter at age five. It occurred in her bedroom. She played with his genitals, laid on top of him and humped him. She asked him if he liked it. She got him to touch her private places. She told him not to tell because he would be in trouble.

This case study shows how through the trance work, the blocked off material can be released very safely. The release of the blocked off pictures, feelings and sensations is what is referred to as an abreaction. There will be a further detailed discussion of this process later on.

This is a good example of the compulsion to re-enact your original trauma by acting out the same thing that happened to you. The sister reported that B asked her if she wanted bubble gum during his acting out with her. What emerged in the trance work was the baby-sitter's daughter coerced B into her room by giving him bubble gum.

33

When B's trauma was remembered, it was learned by the parents that the baby-sitter's daughter had also been abused as a child.

In this case, the teenager is acting out the thing that happened to him but not on a conscious level. Again it's difficult to understand that we can act on feelings from a trauma that we don't remember. I believe that even though many juvenile offenders remember aspects of their acting behavior, it is still an unconscious process and their behaviors are involuntary. We will get into the conscious responsibility debate.

Amnesia is an important aspect of dissociation. Most of, if not all of, my clients who have been abused have periods of amnesia say for age six, or a general amnesia for childhood events under the age of seven or eight. Again, there are exceptions in that the amnesia can extend further into the teens. Remember you can have a cognitive memory of your trauma, but it is the dissociated feelings that fuel the emotional triggers and behavioral re-enactments. For many of my clients there seems to be a relief when I talk about the amnesia. It is usually something that they haven't discussed with anyone.

It is often difficult to get spouses, parents and the legal system to understand that Johnny is not consciously choosing to misbehave or to be cruel to his sister, just as he is not choosing to bed wet or to have nightmares. This is not to say that the child or teenager's behavior goes undisciplined. I spend a lot of time with the parents of the kids I see teaching them very specific discipline techniques as well as working on external controls particularly for those kids who are at risk for acting out sexually.

The blocked off feelings are very powerful, and when the child is displaying symptoms and behavior problems, we need to know that these are red flags telling us that something is going on inside. One of the main goals of this book is to get parents to recognize the signs and symptoms of childhood trauma so that specialized treatment can hopefully prevent this child from becoming the teenager who kills school mates, abuses his niece, or becomes hooked on drugs as a way of self-medicating. We can no longer look for five sense explanations for multi-sensory problems. I believe we cannot resolve deep blocked off emotions that manifest in compulsive and destructive behaviors through conventional five sense psychology.

Only when and if the blocked off feelings are cleared away, can the powerful symptoms and manifestations be conquered. As mentioned earlier, Bessel van der Kolk states in his article, *The Compulsion to Repeat the Trauma*, that "**The only reason to uncover the trauma, is to gain conscious control over the unbidden re-experiences or re-enactments.**" When the teenager in the above case study resolved his original trauma, there was no further acting out behavior. If one doesn't clear away the original traumatic feelings, he/she will continue to relive the trauma. Again, these behavior re-enactments are not consciously associated with childhood experiences.

Freud thought that his repetition compulsion was about conquering the feelings, but we know that acting out blocked off feelings probably goes further to perpetuate the re-enactments. The compulsive re-enactments only give a temporary relief of that emotion. It doesn't go toward extinguishing the feelings or stopping the compulsive behavior. Through the hypnotic/abreactive process, the unconscious mind can safely and tolerably resolve the blocked off trauma.

THE H WORD - ALL HYPNOSIS IS SELF HYPNOSIS

Despite the controversy that remains with the phenomena of hypnosis, the research shows that hypnosis, particularly in the areas of trauma and abuse, can be a productive tool in helping clients uncover and integrate blocked off memories. Masud Ansari states that, "Hypnosis is a valid scientific phenomenon which can help people overcome mental problems." In *Traumatic Stress*, Bessel van der Kolk states that, "Hypnosis is no longer a novel approach, but it represents of the oldest and possibly one of the most effective ways of helping people revisit past trauma without becoming overwhelmed." *(I will utilize the terms hypnosis and trance interchangeably.)*

I explain to my clients that hypnosis is not something I'm doing to them but that I'm helping their unconscious mind to relax and reach the trance state so that their unconscious mind can do the work that needs to be done in preparing and carrying out the process of releasing blocked off feelings, sensations and perceptions in a safe and tolerable way. When you are in trance, all of the power and resources you have within yourself become available to you. This is why it is important for us to meditate. When we are awake, the frequencies of our left and right brain do not match up. Only in the two trance states, Alpha and Theta, do the frequencies of the left and right brain match up. Only then are we in balance. Famous people like Mozart, Einstein, Edison, and Cayce tapped into their creative intelligence through trance.

What I want the reader to understand from my approach with hypnosis is that the unconscious mind wants the client to be in a trance state so that the blocked off material can be safely and tolerably released through the abreactions. This process is completely controlled by the unconscious mind. I believe as the therapist that I am an external helper and that I can not force any memories to come out that are not ready to emerge, nor do I believe that I can, or ever would, plant false memories into my client.

Certainly as you come to understand in reading about abreactions as well as in Part III, S's case study, that the feelings, pictures, and sensations that emerge through the trance are powerful, primary emotions. The hypnotic/abreactive process allows these feelings and sensations to be released safely and tolerably over time.

I always tell my clients who are a little skeptical of trying the trance work that we experience trance everyday. Trance is a naturally occurring state of mind. Trance can be as simple as focused attention. I prefer using the word trance in my work because I believe that most people associate trance with something that happens internally and unconsciously within themselves versus that the therapist is in some way taking control of their minds. Daydreaming is trance. When we are focused on our work or play, when time seems to pass quickly, we are in a trance state. Half falling asleep on the sofa, but you still hear the television is being in trance. Some people walk in their sleep and even perform tasks without any recollection.

The Work of the Devil

Before utilizing trance, I spend time getting the client to understand its purpose and trying to dispel the various misconceptions that often scare people off. In all the years of doing trance work, I have only had one parent not permit me to use trance with their child.

After hundreds of years of modern hypnosis, many still think that hypnosis is the work of the devil and that it comes from magic, and superstitions. At the turn of the century, Pierre Janet recognized that one part of the mind could function separate from the others. Janet believed that hypnosis could be used to bring back, **"repressed desires and unpleasant events, subsequently giving relief to the client."**

Hypnosis is not therapy. It is a natural, God-given state of mind that allows healing to occur. We need to understand that any healing comes from the client's own higher powers and internal resources and that the trance state allows the blocked off experiences to be released safely over time.

Hypnosis is not sleep. When my clients are in the Alpha state, they tend to hear what I am saying and can usually talk to me. Sometimes it is important for the client to be able to share with me what they are experiencing as well as having the sense of security and connection with me, particularly if they are dealing with scary feelings for example. Theta is the trance state where the client reports that they are either in a favorite place or just in the darkness in their mind. In this state they do not hear the conversation. This is more of the suspended state of mind that was discussed earlier. Many clients feel as though they fell asleep. I know that the unconscious mind makes the decision to send the client to this deeper state of mind. Even though the Greek word hypnosis means sleep, this deeper state is not sleep. Sleep is known as the Delta state.

Masud Ansari reports that our cardiac and respiratory action during hypnosis is nearer to that of the waking state than to normal sleep. Blood circulation during hypnosis resembles that of the waking state rather than sleep. People often report an anticipated fear of losing control while under hypnosis. Actually you are in more control while in trance. The therapist does not control the client's mind. I always remind clients during the induction, while they are still hearing the conversation, their unconscious knows how to protect and take care of them. I also tell them that the unconscious mind knows exactly what to do and that their unconscious mind is more powerful than me and their own conscious mind. It is a myth that you won't wake up from trance. With my approach, the client is always returned to their favorite place, and then safely returned to consciousness. Once the deeper work begins, the clients often feel exhausted after the sessions. The process of releasing negative energy is emotionally draining.

Most of my clients respond to trance quite well. In fact most of them, after about three formal sessions, begin to go into trance by themselves. Many clients don't remember me talking about going down the steps which is part of the induction that I talk about fairly early in the process. I know that the unconscious mind, particularly with kids and teenagers, starts to shut down the system before they ever get to the therapy session. One young teenager would almost have to be helped from the waiting room to the therapy room, because of being so tired and out of it. One teenage girl would go into the therapy room by herself while I was talking to her mom in the waiting room, and when I joined the teen, she was usually in trance. Some of my clients will even tell me that they can't keep their eyes open and that I should start the trance work. The therapist is only another external helper that the unconscious mind needs to help the conscious client receive and process the feelings, perceptions and sensations that are being worked through in the trance.

An Idea Whose Time is Overdue

Many of my clients come to therapy with a long history of intense symptoms and manifestations which are typically rooted in unresolved childhood experiences and or unresolved past life experiences which will be explained in detail in Part II. Many of my clients have had years of conscious talk therapy as well as years of taking psychotropic medication, often with little symptom relief. I'm seeing that many people are recognizing that they need a therapy that goes beyond the conscious work. People are calling me up and requesting hypnosis for their teenager, or asking whether hypnosis works for anxiety, or compulsions. I certainly have not had any problems over the years convincing the parents of juvenile offenders, as well as teenage survivors, to let me try the trance work. I have been pleasantly surprised that the parents of the teenagers that I work with seem to have an inherent understanding of dissociation theory and have generally supported my efforts. I am shocked by how many mental health professionals (who I guarantee have not read the literature and who have not done extensive work with trauma victims) are discounting the notion of dissociation and all of its components. Not to mention the court system and Juvenile Services who seem to be making decisions based on outdated theories or without a theory at all, particularly with regard to children and teens who act out sexually. Wake up and join the paradigm shift! There is a body of enlightening information out there!

More importantly, we are at a time in history when more and more people are in need of deeper work because survivors are coming out of the woodwork, teenagers are killing their parents, mothers are drowning their kids, children are making bomb threats at their schools, teenagers are blowing away their peers, people are going to their jobs and killing their bosses ... and on and on. Insurance companies want the mental health system to pump clients up with medicine and utilize short term treatment techniques to fix complex psychological problems.

A Word to the Supposedly Wise

A word to therapists who claim to be "experts in sexual abuse" is that in utilizing any kind of trance work, you don't have to go and try to dig up the old stuff. When the client is ready, their unconscious mind will bring to you - in a logical sequence - those aspects of the system that need healing. Again, know your place, you are an extra external helper that your client's unconscious mind needs. No matter how many problems your client has, their unconscious mind, and all the power and resources contained therein, is much more knowledgeable than you the conscious helper. Also, know the dissociation literature in and out.

The process should not be about "recovering memories" but providing the setting that allows the higher unconscious processes to release and work through the blocked off emotions, sensations and pictures, thus alleviating the symptoms and manifestations.

I don't take a client back to specific childhood people or places. Early on, I sometimes suggest that the client remember a childhood home and then get them to see it from the perspective of a child and to see the people who influenced them. Then if it is appropriate, I get them to share their hurt, upset, angry feelings with that person. That exercise is only done if the unconscious mind feels that the conscious person is ready to do so. With the affective bridge technique, I ask the unconscious mind to take the pervasive feelings that the client is feeling in their present life back to the time where these feelings originated. So you see, the unconscious mind knows where to take these feelings, to what place, to see what person and so on. Intense feelings, sensations, and perceptions only emerge when the unconscious mind choices to release them.

Pierre Janet recognized that one part of the mind could exist separately from the others. He believed that hypnosis could be used to bring back **"repressed desires and unpleasant events,"** subsequently giving relief to the client.

We are vulnerable as children. Our unconscious mind blocks off overwhelming and traumatic feelings to protect us. Later on these dissociated feelings and sensations begin to show up in a Host of symptoms and manifestations, which will persist and continue to pervade that person's life. Through a natural state of mind, these feelings, thoughts, and perceptions can be erased, extinguished, resolved safely and tolerably, however you want to understand it.

Look at the trance state as a natural state of mind that allows your Higher Self and all of the other power and resources that you have, to come together to help you heal. The blocked off emotions are very draining, and the symptoms and manifestations that are felt and played out in the lives of those who have been traumatized are very confusing and often immobilizing. The thought that individuals who have suffered with symptoms all of their life will not be open to a healing process that uses the natural state of trance, is quite astounding.

"Hypnosis is of unparalleled assistance in this process because it enables the patient to enter the psychological and biochemical state in which state-dependent learning originally occurred and permits activation of individual ego states for therapeutic work. We endeavor to help personality parts tolerate uncovering and abreaction without re-traumatization, to master, renegotiate, and integrate the recollected experiences, to become strengthened, and to mature to such an extent that inner harmony can be restored."

Maggie Phillips & Claire Frederick

ABREACTION

If not resolved, blocked off feelings will continue to surface in a variety of symptoms, manifestations, and behavioral re-enactments. The symptoms may change from overt expressions of anger to somatic problems such as stomach problems where doctors can't seem to find a cause. I have spent a lot of time talking about how the unconscious mind blocks off overwhelming and traumatic events, or certain aspects of those events, to protect the conscious Host from overwhelming feelings. Over time these blocked off emotions, perceptions, thoughts, and sensations begin to surface as symptoms and manifestations that usually persist, confuse, and overwhelm as well as immobilize us.

The question becomes, how does your system alleviate your symptoms and resolve this blocked off stuff? The answer is through what is called in psychology **Abreaction**. I define the abreaction as the process that the unconscious mind uses to systematically release dissociated feelings, thoughts, sensations and perceptions from overwhelming and or traumatic childhood events. It usually involves bringing these aspects of previous events to the conscious level. Again, the argument shows the need for the client to be in a trance state in order to receive this unpleasant material safely and tolerably.

The American Psychiatric Association defines abreaction as "an emotional release or discharge after recalling a painful experience that has been repressed because it was consciously intolerable. A therapeutic effect sometimes occurs through partial discharge or desensitization of the painful emotions and increased insight." *(I prefer the term "dissociate" vs. repress. Repressing something has a connotation that we consciously have a choice in not remembering something unpleasant.)*

Again, we need to understand that when we are triggered by something that causes us to feel panicky and angry and we react to these emotions, this is not an abreaction. The feelings that are felt when we are triggered by someone or some event are not extinguished. Perhaps there is a temporary feeling of relief when blocked off anger for example is expressed, but those feelings remain in our system just as powerful as before. Only when the feelings, sensations, and perceptions are released through the abreaction do they lose their power. The abreaction is a systematic release of the blocked off material. It is controlled by the unconscious mind, not the therapist. The therapist is an external helper. Only when the client is ready to receive the unpleasant body sensations or upset feelings, does this material enter the client's awareness. Remember, this approach is not about recovering memories but providing the setting that the unconscious mind needs to safely release the dissociated feelings and sensations which results in the alleviation of the pervasive symptoms.

The blocked off trauma is stored in an altered state of mind in fragments of **thoughts, feelings and perceptions.** A more comprehensive SIBRAM model has been introduced by Peter Levine. His model emphasizes **Sensation, Imagery, Behaviors, Affect, and Meaning.** During the abreactions, the clients will experience separate aspects of the trauma. A client can experience an abreaction that only brings forth the body sensations, without pictures or feelings. For example, they may feel that they are being held down. Most abreactions are about the "feelings" that were blocked off from the traumatic event. Many individuals remember the cognitive aspects of their childhood stressors and or trauma. It is the blocked off feelings that cause most of the symptoms and manifestations. Most of my clients who were abused as children feel a "scared, got to get away feeling" during their abreaction. An abreaction may present a childhood view of an upsetting experience. Most amazingly is when a client sees the childhood trauma from a bird's eye view. During this experience, they may feel the feelings and or a compassion for the little hurt child. Understand, the feelings and sensations felt during these abreactions are not a recollection of how the individual felt, but an experience as though the feeling or sensation is occurring right now. The client may report that they were lying down or that they were the physical size of a five-year-old. Through a series of abreactions over time, your unconscious mind can uncover and release the blocked off trauma safely and tolerably.

It is probably best to describe how abreactions occur through case example. Keep in mind that the third part of the book is a detailed case example that will be clear if what you have read so far has been understood. It is important to understand the abreaction.

CASE EXAMPLE

The following is a case example of a teenager who was amnestic for her sexual abuse which occurred approximately at the age of six. J was referred by a therapist who felt that there was something blocked off.

J was amnestic for specifically second grade. When questioned, J had no recollection of any childhood abuse. J displayed the trancelike stare as reported by the mother. She showed episodes of anger. The mother reported that she would often get mad as a child. She reportedly was very manipulative, even as a child. In the seventh grade she took an overdose of aspirin. By the time she engaged in therapy with me, she had run away numerous times. She was sexually active around the age of twelve. J reported that she had little recollection of her sexual experiences with boys.

The mom agreed to allow me to utilize trance in order to get to the source of J's symptoms. J responded well to trance. I established communication with her unconscious mind through ideomotor signals. As I describe other cases, you will see that sometimes the parts of the unconscious mind can communicate verbally and in this case, can only communicate through signals which are called ideomotor signals. I usually establish three signals with the lifting of fingers. For example, the first finger is a yes response. Another finger could be a no response, and the third finger is a "not ready" so as not to interpret a no response as never.

This is an example of a case where I knew through the communication with her unconscious mind that J had been abused around the age of five or six by a relative and that it happened at the grandmother's house. Most of the time, particularly when the unconscious mind does not want the conscious Host (the client) to know or to hear the communication, the Host is placed in Theta trance. I let the mom know for example that I had learned some important information from the trance work and that in time J would clear away and resolve the dissociated material that had been the source of her symptoms and manifestations.

What emerged during the process of therapy, after much unconscious planning as well as J being prepared to receive the information, was a series of abreactions that brought forth dissociated anger, fear, sensations, and perceptions. I would get a yes response from the unconscious mind for the question, "Are you preparing J to remember what she needs to remember?" Each week for a number of weeks there was a No response to whether J was ready during that session to remember or feel something while in the trance state. Keep in mind that much of the preliminary work is done unconsciously without the client feeling and seeing much of anything. Only when the unconscious mind has prepared the Host, are the dissociated feelings released.

When the Yes response came to the question of J being ready to remember something, a series of abreactions related to her trauma began to emerge over the next number of sessions. J is an example of a client who would receive the information in the Theta state of trance. Remember, this is the deeper trance where J would not be able to talk to me during the abreactions. The fragments of feelings, sensations and pictures would be processed through J in the suspended trance state. Once the feeling was processed, it was turned off. When the client returns from the trance state, they describe what they had experienced. Yes, sometimes there is what I call residue which occurs when the client still feels a little bit of the feeling or sensation that was processed. However it quickly subsides, usually before the client leaves the session. After coming out of trance, she would describe what she experienced. Sometimes the client can describe to me what they are feeling or seeing as it is happening even though they are still in a trance state. The unconscious mind makes the determination of how the blocked off material is most safely and tolerably cleared away.

J's first major abreaction with regard to her sexual abuse was an out of sequence bird's eye view (first place dissociation) of herself as a child. She saw herself lying on the sofa at her grandmother's house. It is important to understand that the viewer feels the feelings of the child. In other words, the viewer is seeing themselves as a child from an objective viewpoint but feeling the feelings that the child is experiencing. The unconscious mind does this as a protection particularly when you are seeing the trauma in pictures. Most abreactions of intense feelings that are experienced as being in the body are exclusive of pictures. You feel the feelings usually in the darkness of trance. Most body sensations if experienced as being the child are felt in the dark. Once in awhile the client will switch from having an abreaction in the body without pictures to being outside of themselves watching themselves as the younger person.

Think about this, your unconscious mind has the ability to show you a movie of yourself in a childhood situation that you don't remember experiencing. Just as amazing, your unconscious mind can let you experience just the body sensations of being held down, without the pictures or the scary feelings. This tells me that our system has the amazing ability to separate the thoughts, perceptions, feelings and sensations from a trauma into separate compartments or frequencies ... however you want to look at it. This is important in that as you see in this example, the abreactions are partial, bits and pieces of the trauma that are released separately, systematically and often out of sequence. This is the argument against "recovering memories." The work is about clearing out the components of the trauma, not one big rush of reliving and remembering the trauma so that it haunts you for the rest of your life. This is what some people believe and perhaps this is why some people are reluctant to remember what they need to remember in order to heal. Remember, what you are trying to forget is causing the problems that you want to get rid of. By releasing the feelings through the abreaction, they lose their power and you gain more of your potential and alleviate your symptoms.

J's second major abreaction was another bird's eye view of herself at her grandmother's house. (This is where she would stay to visit her dad) Her father was about to go to work and she felt upset perhaps a little fearful that something was wrong. Sometimes that is the complete abreaction for that session.

In the following weeks, J would have a number of sessions where she felt that she was in her body and feeling the feelings. These feelings were upset, scary, lonely and something is wrong. J also experienced a sense that mom was going to be mad at her for what happened. The client often reports that they feel as though they are five-years-old both mentally and physically.

Certainly when the client is reliving the feelings or body sensations from a perspective of being in their body, this kind of abreaction can be somewhat uncomfortable.

Usually this type of abreaction occurs without pictures. So imagine in the darkness of your mind that you are feeling the scary feelings of an unpleasant childhood event for the first time, not remembering but actually experiencing the feelings or sensations for the first time, from a trauma that you don't remember.

Often during an abreaction where the client is experiencing feelings in the dark, they may have a sense that there is a person there, but they can't see them. Again, the unconscious mind is protecting the client from knowing the perpetrator at that time. Sometimes they never know and sometimes the client will have a perception of the perpetrator.

J had another type of abreaction that allowed the unconscious mind to release the actual physical act of what happened to her through a dream. J reported that she had a dream that a man was chasing her around the room and then a vague recognition that he stuck an object into her private places. The dream didn't seem to bother J that much. Her unconscious mind was able to release the memory of the physical aspect of the abuse through this metaphoric dream.

Abreactions are often metaphoric in that the pictures or the visual story that is seen is not real but the feelings associated with the metaphor are real feelings. The unconscious mind needs to trigger scary feelings, for example, through a scary story. Often feelings are released long before the pictures can be seen, so the mind uses metaphoric stories to trigger the feelings. Remember, feelings can be triggered without pictures. If my client has an abreaction that a Pterodactyl is chasing them down the street, this obviously did not happen to them, however the fear that they are feeling is real fear from a real experience.

During the abreactive work, clients often report that they had vivid dreams during the week. This is work that is being done in preparation for the next session. In many of my clients some of the fear is worked out during sleep. Often the client reports sleep disturbance and vivid dreams while this process is occurring.

It must be pointed out that clients often have abreactions at home, usually when they are about to go to sleep, or while they are taking a nap. A client may report that after the session, they went home and prior to going to sleep, they had an abreaction albeit a pocket of intense emotion coming through or a birds eye view of an unpleasant childhood situation. Not all the work is done in the therapy office. Notice, the abreaction that is experienced at home occurs in a trance state. I believe that the vivid dreams are abreactions too. It's all about trusting that the unconscious mind knows how to protect and take care of the client during the healing process.

To review J's case, she had a number of different types of abreaction over a number of sessions which allowed the aspects of her sexual abuse trauma to be released safely and tolerably. Remember, the scenes that she saw in her mind were out of order. Most of the feelings were felt without pictures. What the perpetrator actually did to her was released through a metaphoric dream. J can't really sit down and tell anyone a clear chronological story about her sexual abuse. She remembers being in trance and feeling alone or afraid, or even seeing herself as a child on the sofa at her grandmother's house.

The Help Within

I want to introduce a concept that will be explained in Part II because it is difficult to fully understand the abreaction unless I give an example of how parts of the unconscious mind hold the blocked off feelings and that these parts can come through the trance state and communicate with me. The details of the parts of the unconscious mind and their roles will be thoroughly discussed in Part II. It is important to see now that sometimes the child helper who holds the fear can enter the left brain and communicate with me. The Host, which is the client, does not hear this conversation, again the importance for using trance. As the child helper talks about the fear, the anger, and the abuse, these feelings are released and processed through the Host who is in the theta trance state. The client who does not hear the conversation with the child helper feels the feelings or sees the story or feels the body sensations. So you see, the components of the trauma are released from the child helper and then sometimes not at that time, released and processed through the client while in the trance state.

CASE EXAMPLE

The following case example will demonstrate this important type of abreaction.

J2 a teenager at the time of the therapy, was sexually abused by her mom's boyfriend from age 6 to age 11. She was also physically and emotionally abused by her mother. She would eventually live with the biological father when all of this was disclosed. J2 was amnestic for under the age of seven. She had been in inpatient treatment for homicidal and suicidal ideation. She had a history of running away, alcohol problems in the ninth grade and problems with acting out sexually as a teenager. J2 had a lot of anger that would episodically be triggered and displaced and projected on to various family members.

This is an example where J2's Higher Self/Dominant would communicate non-verbally through ideomotor signals but could not enter the physical body to verbally communicate. The child helpers were able to come through and communicate verbally.

Up until this time I have spoken of the power within as coming from the unconscious mind. It is necessary for this case example to introduce a profile that has come to me through doing the hypnotic/abreactive work. It involves communicating with non-physical reality through signals as well as with direct verbal communication. As you will come to know in PART II, I will refer to our own individual guiding force as the Dominant part of our system. This is our Higher Self, the Spirit, our Protector. The Indians refer to it as the Spirit Guide. It is the part of us that watches out over us and knows how to take care of us and protect us. It knows our purpose and guides us during this incarnation. I will talk about this helper and all of the other helpers and protectors that accompany us during our life's journey.

Understand that our soul helpers are here to give us gifts, (sense of humor, art), wisdom and knowledge. They are also called upon to absorb the overwhelming feelings of childhood stressor and trauma. Keep in mind that the child helpers need to be prepared and feel safe and trusting before they can come through in order to release the feelings they are holding for the Host. In talking with J2's middle helper (which is the part of the self that holds upset feelings, and anger, as well as some of the memories of the abuse) about mom, she said, "Mom hurts me. There is no reason to beat us with a board."

This is the part of the self that typically holds the blame and shame. This child helper said, "I should have stopped it" (referring to the abuse). The following are statements from the ten-year-old helper regarding mom. Remember, the conscious Host, the client, does not hear this conversation. Understand that this client is not what would be called a multiple personality.

> "Why didn't she protect me?"
> "She never gave me love."
> "I felt isolated."
> "I feel worthless"

In a later session, only when the ten-year-old child helper was ready and prepared, I got her to imagine that the mom was there and that it was OK for her to share her hurt, upset, and angry feelings with the mother. The following are statements from that process.

> "I hate you."
> "I felt ashamed."
> "You didn't believe me." (regarding the abuse)
> "It's your fault."
> "You took care of my brothers. I hit them. It hurts so bad."
> "I am nobody."
> "I never felt love."
> "You made me hate my father."

You will learn that this middle helper holds issues that affect the self-esteem of the client. When these feelings are triggered, J2 the conscious teenager feels these intense feelings and blames herself as well as projects these feelings on the people and situations around her. The self-esteem of the Host is most affected by the middle helper.

I need to introduce another important concept that will be discussed in detail in Part II and will be an important concept described in Part III. J2's ten-year-old helper brought with it an unresolved story from a previous life. If you keep an open mind it is easy to understand. J2's child helper was a helper for someone in J2's ancestral line. When that person died, there were unresolved feelings from a trauma. That part of that person needed to resolve those feelings at some point in time. J2 got that child helper. As Gary Zukav stated in *The Seat of the Soul*, **"Understand that the soul creates a personality from those parts of itself that it wants to heal in the physical environment and from those parts of itself that it lends to the process of healing in that lifetime."**

The Dominant informed me that it was time for this story to be resolved. The ten-year-old helper was not aware of the story until it was time to be resolved. Understand that the feelings from a past life story can be triggered and affect the current life of the Host. When it was time, the ten-year-old emerged feeling afraid. The ten-year-old said, "I'm scared." I ask her if she understood that something was about to happen and that I was there to help her and if she wanted to, she could describe what was happening to her. J2 was in Theta trance and was not aware of the conversation or the feelings that were being released. Sometimes the Host will return from trance and report that they felt intense feelings. Often the feelings are released through vivid dreams a few nights after the session. *(Sometimes the Host will have to feel the feelings of a past life story, and sometimes they don't.)*

I asked the ten-year-old to tell me what was going on. She said that she was in a cabin and that her mom was being abused by the father *(please note, this is not J2's present family)*. Then the story jumped to her being sexually abused by someone who she thought was her uncle. Remember the story is quickly and as tolerably as possible relived in order to release the feelings. Then the ten-year-old helper jumped to a story where she was a young adult who took her own life with a gun. It was necessary to release the unresolved feelings that the ten-year-old helper had brought with her, to go through the traumatic scenarios from the previous life. It is interesting that J2 as a teenager had had suicidal thoughts about killing herself with a gun. Through this quick series of abreaction, J2's middle helper was able to release the unresolved feelings from her previous life. A carry-over or past life story is allowed to return to the physical realm for resolution. This resolution best occurs through the human experience. Child helpers who are holding unresolved feelings from this lifetime and or another lifetime will be forced to resolve these stories so they can return to a positive position in the system. You will learn that some carry-over energy will exit the system if the story cannot be resolved. The middle helper had traumatic feelings from a past life as well as from this lifetime. The feelings get triggered and cause problems and the solution is resolving the feelings. It is more uncommon that a child helper brings an unresolved past life story with it. You will see in the next section that usually the unresolved past life story is held by a separate part, not usually one of the six developmental helpers. Keep an open mind that all things are possible.

Up until this point, releasing the feelings through the abreaction has occurred in the trance state, through dreams, and/or through abreaction when the client was in a safe setting, for example at home prior to going to sleep. However some of the dissociated feelings have to be processed in reality. Understand that some of the feelings that were blocked off have to be felt and accepted into consciousness. Some important developmental lessons, for example expressing anger, speaking up for oneself, asserting oneself, trusting others, were lost by the protective necessity of blocking off certain experiences and the associated feelings. Part of the healing is that the conscious Host has to learn to respond to feelings and take the appropriate action. Keep in mind that healing isn't just about releasing the old feelings. Because you were fragmented, many lessons were not able to be learned. After you clear the old feelings up, your unconscious mind has to not only feel some of the old feelings but let you feel the feelings that come up in your current reality, and again, learn to respond to them in appropriate constructive ways. This is all about the integration phase of healing. It can be a very frustrating part of healing because the conscious Host has to feel feelings that had previously been absorbed unconsciously and learn to respond to these feelings in their current reality.

After clearing away most of the feelings through the abreaction, J2 would need to express some appropriate angry feelings to her mother. This would only be appropriate if the Higher Self/Dominant deemed it as such. It is never appropriate when the client is filled with rage and fear to suggest that they confront a parent or a perpetrator for purposes of healing. Sometimes there is no need for the client to confront a parent at all. In J2's case, it was appropriate and therefore planned for her to talk to her mom about how she felt. Sometimes the parent is never ready and it may not be appropriate. Sometimes instead of a face to face contact, a letter is written to the person the client needs to express feelings. Again, it's not about getting the response you want from the person, but learning to use your personal power. Remember that forgiveness is primarily for our sake so that we no longer carry the burden of resentment. Continuing to blame others or seeking revenge only takes away our power. Many of the parents of my clients have not let go of their old stuff so they don't have the ability to understand and/or treat my clients like they want to be treated. Humans can only give what they have. When I say parent, I know that it isn't always the parent who is the bad guy, but there are usually strong emotions projected to the parent or parents for not protecting the child from a trauma for example.

When the unconscious mind releases anger through a younger client, it becomes somewhat problematic. Often it is a necessary dilemma because there has to be some release of the feelings or there will be other internal problems such as nightmares, sleep disturbance, physical symptoms such as headaches and stomach problems. Sometimes it is difficult to get the parents to understand that the child's episodic problematic behavior is a necessary aspect of their healing. When the unconscious mind releases some anger, the child often responds to these intense feelings with impulsive and sometimes out of control behaviors. I do my best to teach parent-child techniques to the parents and work with them to understand the difference between Johnny being a little defiant versus experiencing an abreaction. I usually know what emotion is being worked on in the session and subsequently inform and warn the parents what emotions may be released that week to hopefully prepare them.

Remember, the feelings that are released once and for all through the abreaction are often going to cause the child to act impulsively and to be extremely upset and scared when those feelings come through the child's current reality. Again, this is a necessary part of the healing process. I have found that it is not necessary to do formal trance with children under the age of twelve. Children can usually go into a light trance without much help from me. I have come to look at myself as the baby-sitter of the conscious child so that the unconscious mind can do the deeper work inside. By getting the child to draw or even to play a simple card game, seems to allow the unconscious mind to be able to do the deeper work inside. Certainly you address concerns and feelings that the child has, as well as behaviors that the parents bring forth. Again, I spend a lot of time with families on parent-child discipline techniques. I also educate the parents on dissociative theory as well as explain how different parts of the unconscious mind hold different emotions and play different roles.

It comes down to trusting that the unconscious mind knows what to do and knows how to best take care of the child. Children under the age of 12 tend not to have major abreactions during a formal trance as teens and adults do. This leads to an important concept of readiness. An eight-year-old child is not developmentally ready to have the memories from their trauma released and relived. Certainly work can be done and bits and pieces of feelings can emerge in the therapy as well as in reality as I described above and also through dreams. The parents play an important part in helping with the abreaction. The more the parents understand dissociation theory, abreactions and everything else that has been discussed thus far, the better progress the child can make. Children whose parents seem to understand the theory and accept that the child or teen has to go through the abreaction and that some of the feelings are felt and acted upon, seem to do better and heal faster.

I worked with a teenager whose progress was thwarted because her Dominant knew that the mother couldn't handle the teen's anger which needed to be released. In fact in this case, the mother and her new boyfriend sabotaged the therapy and prevented the teen from clearing away her sexual trauma.

CASE EXAMPLE

I wish to give one more example of the healing process with regard to abreaction.

I originally saw M when he was fifteen, six years ago. M had acted out sexually with a four-year-old. M had a history of bed wetting from the ages of four to seven, he was amnestic for his early childhood and he was held back in first grade. As a teenager, M was beset with self-esteem issues. He reported that he wanted to be smart to please his mom. He would only show the good school work to his parents and lie about the not so good school work. He reported feeling frustrated with respect to girls. I worked with M for a number of months. The case notes reflect that a good deal of work was done with his middle helper with regard to feeling powerless and inadequate. I did some trance work with M but no clear memory was released at that time. I never like ending the therapy, particularly with a teenager who has acted out without having a clear abreaction of his own early trauma emerging in some form. In this case the therapy ended and I hoped that enough work was done so that there would be no further acting out.

A few years later I received a call from M's mom. It was discovered that M had gotten into some legal problems in relation to soliciting an adult prostitute. It was learned that M had been spending money for this service for a period of time. Interestingly, M expressed a desire to connect with me again in order to help him with this problem. What quickly emerged was a part of him that held anger was acting out. There were no reported incidents over the last five years to suggest that M had had any problems with acting out with children. *(Remember, I have found that it is the younger child helper and not the teenage helper who holds the memories and coinciding feelings and who usually acts out the original trauma.)* I had speculated correctly five years ago that there was another part that M was not ready to have cleared away. Those emotions which turned out to be the anger surrounding his original trauma were contained until the current acting out behaviors began. Often the blocked off feelings need to be released and are often acted upon, in order for the conscious Host to know that these feelings are there and need to be addressed.

I quickly established communication with the unconscious mind. In fact M's Dominant was able to communicate verbally. I was informed that in fact M had been abused as a child. The teen helper that holds the anger was able to communicate and inform me that M was abused by a lady up the street when he was around five-years-old. M was in a theta state of trance, so he did not hear this conversation. What I typically do in this case is to inform M that we need to work together because there is something that needs to be resolved in order to extinguish this compulsion that has gotten him into some legal trouble. Over the course of a number of weeks of trance work, the unconscious mind through a number of abreactions was able to clear away the feelings, perceptions and sensations from his original trauma. I picked this case to show how over time, bits and pieces of the original trauma are released safely and tolerably.

The following excerpts are what M described to me after he returned from trance. Note that as the external helper, I am aware that aspects of the trauma are being released during each of these sessions.

During one session, M reported that he felt uncertain, mysterious feelings. For a few subsequent sessions he felt what he defined as frustration. The next session he reported that he felt "weighed down." Remember, the body sensations of the trauma have to be relived. During the next trance session, M reported that he felt small physically and also felt the emotion of being "betrayed." Often clients feel that they are physically like the age they were as that younger child. The next session M saw a movie of himself in a car accident. He felt that he couldn't move, felt helpless and confused. This is a good example of how the unconscious mind uses a metaphoric story to trigger the feelings of a "REAL" memory. M wasn't ready to see the pictures and experience the feelings of the trauma at this time.

During the following trance session, M felt a weight on his chest and described experiencing "weird feelings." The next trance session would be an important one. After returning from the theta state of trance, M reported that he had trouble breathing and he felt someone was on top of him. He reported that he was watching the scene from a position in back of the room. He said that he saw the back of the person and they had on a red shirt. He could not tell whether this person was a male or female. This type of abreaction is confusing, because the client experiences the feelings and sensations as they watch themselves as the younger person in the abusive situation.

This is what I consider a major abreaction because I feel assured that we got to the source of the symptoms and acting out behavior. The clients watch themselves in the original traumatic situation for which they are amnestic. The client experiences the feelings and sensations, and in this case the pictures, while watching from what is called first place dissociation. This shows the incredible ability of the unconscious mind. It would be in this case and most others, too intense for M to be in the body of the child as he is experiencing the feelings and sensations.

Just like in the J case example, I was aware through communication with the unconscious mind what exactly happened to M. Through this case example you can see that through a series of abreactions, the Dominant (Higher Self) was able to release the dissociated aspects of M's trauma, thus extinguishing the compulsive nature of the blocked off feelings.

M could correlate the feelings from his original trauma with the feelings he felt with the prostitute, which was being "scared and lonely." I got permission from M's Dominant (Higher Self) to ask M on a conscious level whether he remembered the "lady up the street with the little boy." He remembered playing with her son and that he remembered that she was "weird."

At the time of this writing, M is continuing with integration work which is helping him with self-confidence and self-esteem issues. You'll learn that the teenage helper gives you fortitude and backbone, the ability to speak up for yourself, to assert yourself. This is why it is most important to extinguish the negative emotions in a part of the self, so that child helper can return to its positive role.

Talking therapy alone would have never helped this client get to the source of his acting out behaviors. Through the abreactions, M was able to alleviate the underlying feelings and perceptions associated with a sexual abuse trauma in his childhood.

The healing process is a balance of working through the past experiences, in this case sexual abuse, along with empowering the client in the present moment. It has been my experience that it is very difficult, if not impossible, to overcome the overwhelming power that the blocked off feelings possess through talking therapy alone. I have found that during the integration phase of healing that the cognitive restructuring techniques and neuro-linguistic approaches are very effective. Helping a client visualize a situation where he needs to assert himself in a new way and to set up this blueprint in his mind as to act on this in that situation can be very productive in helping him to break away from old patterns of thinking and behaving. So yes, all the cognitive techniques can come into play quite well in the integration process. In fact it is exciting for me to help the client use their personal power to speak up for themselves in order to teach people how to treat them.

The Proof is in the Pudding

I believe that the use of hypnosis in tandem with abreactions is not only effective but often a necessary approach for psychological healing. Some researchers, even in the specialty of Dissociative disorders, caution that the use of hypnotic abreactions could overwhelm and flood the client with traumatic memories. John Watkins reported in a *Dissociation* news bulletin that he and his wife have been doing abreactive work with dissociative clients as well as clients with other disorders for decades and have yet to see a patient be overwhelmed or have any major setbacks. I have utilized this approach for almost two decades in an out-patient setting working with teens and adults with many symptoms and manifestations usually stemming from childhood stressors and traumas. Certainly clients have very uncomfortable abreactions for which they have been prepared, but I will take their after hours calls to help them work through this painful material. I also maintain the faith that I want my clients to have which is that their unconscious mind knows how to prepare, protect, and take care of them when we do this work. They come to trust despite the intensity of the work at times that the **"Invisible but knowable life force,"** as Wayne Dyer calls it, within them, wants them to feel alive and whole.

I would speculate that those in the field who caution against hypnotic abreactive work probably have never utilized this technique. Another issue within this specific area of Dissociation is that many therapists and researchers only see the extreme cases of those who are admitted to psychiatric hospitals and in fact do have overwhelming intrusive symptoms. I agree that in these cases stabilizing the client and containing the emotions would be a priority.

This leads me to a discussion of who is a good candidate for abreactive work. I believe that teenagers who are known to have abuse in their childhood are prime candidates for this work. Teenagers who may not remember childhood trauma but begin to display extreme anger, poor school performance, inappropriate sexual behaviors, depression and sleep disturbance could indicate the surfacing and reenacting of dissociated childhood emotions.

I would also suggest that adults with a remembered history of childhood dysfunction, domestic violence, harsh physical punishment, emotional and sexual abuse or whose current lives are beset with relationship problems, depression, compulsive behaviors, episodes of anger and rage, panic attacks and sleep disorders, are all candidates for this work. Individuals with a history of reoccurring dreams and phobias with no recognizable source often call to explore the possibility of hypnosis. More people are recognizing that talking therapy along with psychotropic medication has not gotten to the bottom of their problems. The medicine often makes them feel like zombies, perhaps not as symptomatic but not alive. While talking therapy may provide some relief, an outlet, a setting where some catharsis and undoing can be helpful, the triggers and symptoms still persist.

I say again and again, by releasing blocked off feelings, thoughts and perceptions, my clients have made miraculous changes in their lives. Without the use of hypnotic abreactions, these changes would not have occurred. I use the word miraculous because I am giving credit to the power and resources within my clients the credit for the changes that come with resolving childhood wounds as well as unfinished business from their ancestral lines.

The next question to address is, who is not a candidate for abreactive work? I would not begin any trance work with someone who is using drugs or alcohol at the time of the session. The exception to this rule is found in the following example. I was working with a client with a history of child abuse. On occasion she would slip and do some cocaine over the weekend. As long as she had not done cocaine the day of the session, I would certainly proceed with the therapeutic process.

This topic certainly opens up a controversy in my mind. In the psychology world the rule has always been that if a client presents with a drug or alcohol problem that they need to be referred to a drug or alcohol program. After they are clean and or sober, the psychological healing can begin. This may be evident in many cases and I tend to know when I need to refer a client to a treatment program as a primary treatment. On the other hand, many of my dissociative clients, those with clear abuse in their childhood, have self-medicated through the use of illegal drugs, alcohol, and prescription drugs. As you have learned, self-destructive behavior, including drug and alcohol abuse can be a manifestation of trauma victims. Usually it is the "Angry Teenager" helper that gets relief from the drugs and alcohol. *(You will learn more about the roles of the helpers in Part II.)* The point that I am raising is that until we can dissolve some of the anger, it will be difficult to consciously control the addiction. This becomes quite a Catch-22. On the one hand, the blocked off emotions are propelling the drug or alcohol problem. On the other hand, until some of the blocked off feelings are released, it is hard to gain conscious control of impulses, compulsions and addictions.

Clients who have suicidal ideation and or have symptoms of major depression need to be assessed for a psychiatric evaluation for possible hospitalization. Clients who are assessed as meeting the criterion for a diagnosis for Bipolar Disorder need to be referred to a psychiatrist for further evaluation. Clients with eating disorders need to get medical work-ups and be assessed for possible hospitalization.

Masked Dissociation

As you have seen through the case examples, it is fairly clear when clients are experiencing dissociative symptoms. Many of my clients have a known history of abuse. They know that their problems are related to childhood problems. While some clients don't readily connect their current problems to their childhood, with a compassionate review of their childhood dynamics, the light bulbs go off rather quickly. We have to assume that juvenile offenders who often don't remember childhood abuse, were abused as kids. Clients who are amnestic for childhood events, have a history of panic attacks, sleep disturbance, dysfunctional relationships, somatic complaints, are clear indicators of dissociation. However, as Maggie Phillips and Claire Frederick suggest in *Healing the Divided Self*, the chapter entitled *Dissociative Symptoms in Disguise*, "Clients may initially complain of symptoms characteristic of other syndromes, such as eating disorders, depression, and obsessive compulsive disorders." They go on to state, "**It is important to discover whether certain clinical syndromes are masked Dissociative Disorders, since many Dissociative Disorders can be treated successfully.**" For example, studies are showing that a high percentage of clients with eating disorders have a history of sexual abuse. Dissociated anger can manifest as depression and fatigue. Many of my clients with a history of childhood sexual abuse manifest obsessive/compulsion symptoms. Many of my clients who witnessed parents fighting and arguing experience panic attacks. Many of my clients who have a history of childhood difficulties in some form, have a legacy of somatic complaints as well as real physical conditions as a result of keeping the emotions pent up inside.

The research in Dissociative Disorders has produced questionnaires and evaluation tools, lists of symptoms and manifestations for children and teens. I am surprised when I do presentations for mental health professionals that they are not even aware that there is a *Dissociation* journal. Therapists who are going to work with trauma victims, survivors etc., need to be trained in dealing with the abreactions. The hypnosis part is not the tantamount issue. Many dissociative clients go into trance quite readily. What happens after that is what is important. Again, therapists who work with survivors for example, can't be afraid of the encounter with the client. John Watkins in a 1995 *Dissociation News* stated that, "**Hypnosis is an interpersonal relationship between therapist and patient in which how we are with the patient is more important than what we do to the patient. This involves resonance in which one experiences, suffers, and celebrates with the patient.**" Therapists who are reluctant to go there need to know when to refer those clients who are willing to work through childhood wounds to therapists who are not afraid of the encounter and who are comfortable with abreactions.

Many of my clients know that they need to resolve some childhood wounds and are ready to do the deeper work. Conversely, many clients are afraid or reluctant because they either know that their symptoms are from childhood problems and they are afraid to deal with them, or they don't make the connection that their current problems are coming from their past. This is evident in working with couples because they don't relate their anger, upset feelings and frustrations, with their partners as being projection and displacement of unresolved emotions from the past. The same concept applies to parent child relationships. Many parents who harshly punish and unnecessarily yell at their children are acting out their own unresolved "stuff" on their kids. Understand, that part of you wants to treat your child like you were treated even though you tell yourself consciously that you will never do that to your own children. Again, the powerful blocked off emotions too often win out. Let me interject here that not everyone who was emotionally, physically and or sexually abused as children is automatically going to repeat these behaviors with their children.

The Taboo Diagnosis

I remember in undergraduate school, the psychology professors would skip over the chapter on Dissociative Disorders. They might have mentioned "Multiple Personality Disorder" but that was the extent of it. Listed in the DSM IV are five Dissociative Disorders. The most familiar classification is Dissociative Identity Disorder, formerly known as Multiple Personality Disorder. I was fascinated by the diagnosis of Conversion Disorder which has been removed from the Dissociative disorders classification and placed in the category of Somatoform Disorders, the classification that includes physical symptoms without a medical basis. With Conversion Disorder an underlying psychic conflict can present as paralysis, blindness, and or deafness. The point being, unless you are a clear cut unmistakable "Multiple Personality," you probably won't get viewed as having dissociative symptoms and manifestations. Many psychiatric hospitals don't even accept this notion of "dissociated or blocked off trauma." We label people by their symptoms, i.e. Panic Disorder, Agoraphobia, Obsessive Compulsive Disorder, and make everything a disease or a medical condition, then through trial and error, find the medication that alleviates the symptom. We have the "cure," but we haven't corrected the problem. A new commercial on television is suggesting to those who have a "social phobia" to call a number for help. I guarantee that the help is about taking a psychotropic drug and not about resolving the underlying source of the symptom.

The "Dissociation" stigma also is evident in the insurance side of the business. The word is out; don't give your client a "Dissociation" diagnosis. You may get away with a "Post Traumatic Stress Disorder" diagnosis if there is a known and verifiable trauma in the person's life, preferably a recent trauma. A few years ago I submitted a treatment plan to a major insurance company. The teenage client had a Host of problems including acting out sexually. It was also known that he had been abused in daycare when he was younger and a manifestation of that abuse was poor school performance. The therapy was denied and the recommendation was for the teenager to be referred to the school system for his learning difficulties. As Maggie Phillips and Claire Frederick state in *Healing the Divided Self,* it is important to discover whether certain clinical syndromes are masked Dissociative Disorders, since many Dissociative Disorders can be treated successfully. I would suggest that psychiatrists who prescribe medications need to come up to snuff with the literature on Dissociative Disorders and Post Traumatic Stress Disorder and the relevant symptoms and manifestations that present with these issues. I believe that the psychiatrists who have become experts in Dissociation, trauma, and sexual abuse have made great contributions toward enhancing and promoting a paradigm with regard to helping survivors understand and work through childhood traumas. On a positive note, many psychiatric hospitals have specific units with a focus on Dissociation for children and teenagers who have been abused.

Medication, Not the Cure

During my early training I worked in a psychiatric hospital emergency room for a number of years. I know that the use of psychotropic medication is invaluable to those who suffer with Major Mental disorders such as Schizophrenia, Bi-polar Disorder, Major Depression. I don't deny the biological and hereditary components of disorders such as Panic Disorder, Obsessive Compulsive Disorder, and Agoraphobia. Treatment for these disorders should include care assessment for childhood trauma. I also believe that clients with clear dissociative diagnosis who are overwhelmed with intrusive symptoms may need to be placed on medication in order to take the edge off, to feel safe, to be able to deal with their children, and or to get up and function in the work place. My clients who are working through some intense anger, fear and anxiety from childhood wounds may benefit from medicine during the often difficult abreactive work. Remember, the blocked off feelings that are being released and often felt by the client are very powerful feelings.

I want to be clear that I am not opposed to the use of psychotropic medication when it is indicated. My concern is that we have swayed too far to a medical model where every psychological condition is treated with medicine. The question becomes whether those clients who do get relief from the medication, should continue in a therapeutic setting to help them work through the underlying source of their symptoms? Too many clients who get symptom relief from the medication do not continue with the deeper psychological healing. It is not easy working through childhood wounds. Again, clients need to understand that the psychotropic medication does not resolve the underlying source of the symptoms. I also believe that for those clients who clearly have a Dissociative Disorder, and know that their problems are related to childhood abuse of some form, will hopefully gather the courage to work through these issues through the abreactive work. If a little bit of medicine is needed from time to time as they work through their unresolved feelings, that is fine.

If a new client comes to me and they are already taking an anti-anxiety medication for panic attacks, I certainly don't suggest that they stop the medication. If their symptoms are related to childhood wounds, through the hypnotic/abreactive process, many clients are able to discontinue the medication when their system reaches a greater balance. Certainly with any client who is taking medication and feels that they want to stop, I strongly advise them to consult with their physicians before doing so.

I know that my population is skewed toward clients who have had early childhood trauma. I'm always cognitive of differential diagnoses. I am careful not to assume that every new client's problems are because of childhood abuse. Many children who experience early traumas may display learning difficulties especially with reading. After working through some of the blocked off feelings, they will begin to catch up with their reading level. On the other hand, a child who was sexually abused, who is displaying learning difficulties may truly have a genetic learning disability. A younger client with a known history of abuse may also clearly have Attention Deficit Disorder. A young adult who presents with anxiety and panic attacks which could be connected to early childhood problems could also have a genetic component of Panic Disorder which may need to be treated with medication.

With my approach I want to make sure that I have done everything to resolve and extinguish any blocked off feelings from overwhelming, stressful, childhood experiences. Too many of my clients who have been in other therapeutic settings throughout their lives have not been asked about, let alone addressed, their childhood wounds. A thorough examination of childhood history including physical, emotional and sexual abuse should be a high priority in any psychological assessment. Individuals who are ready and know in their heart that they need to work through their childhood wounds need to seek out therapists who are not apprehensive about dealing with these issues. It is natural to avoid our painful pasts. It's no one's fault that they were abused or mistreated in some way as a child and it doesn't seem fair that they have to bare the burden of the symptoms and manifestations that pervade their lives. I believe there are limited choices. One can live with the symptoms, but that is difficult because your soul/spirit will continue to open up the valve to let you know that you have parts of yourself that require healing. The blocked off feelings will continue to be triggered and reenacted in current reality. Perhaps drugs, alcohol and/or prescription drugs could be used to self-medicate, but the underlying issues don't get fixed. Another choice is to use psychotropic drugs as the only mode of treatment in order to get symptom relief. Again, nothing in the long run is resolved. Another choice is to take responsibility for your situation and seek out a therapeutic setting that promotes working through your childhood wounds safely and tolerably through a combination of cognitive therapy and abreactive work. Remember, the dissociative conditions rooted in childhood wounds are very treatable. My clients who have gathered the courage to work through their childhood wounds have moved beyond living in the past, and have found a sense of purpose in the present moment, and hope for the future. They have a sense of control over their lives. They choose healthy relationships. They face everyday challenges and adversities without the underlying childhood fear, anxiety, and anger that used to pervade their current realities. There is a heightened sense of self. They are on the road to feeling whole.

False Memories and Court Issues

In a 1995 *Dissociation News*, D. Corydon Hammond summarized a 15-month study on clinical hypnosis and memory. The study parallels what has presented to me over the last decade of doing clinical hypnosis with trauma victims. Normal conscious memory is different than traumatic and emotional memory. My clients may not remember to bring me a check, but under hypnosis can recall the details of a childhood home. *(This can be validated through the parents.)* The study also stated that traumatic amnesia is real. I have stated that most of my juvenile sex offenders were amnestic for their original trauma, as well as many of the survivors I have treated. The study reported that "forgotten memories" can be recovered later in life and that hypnosis may facilitate this process. I believe if not for the hypnosis/abreactive work, most of my clients would not have been able to release the blocked off material. The research on state-dependent memory is supporting this concept. I am always proclaiming that not one juvenile offender who was amnestic for his original trauma would have resolved his compulsion to act out without the hypnagogic state which allowed the blocked off feelings and sensations to be released.

We need to get away from the notion that this work is about "recovering memories" versus that it is about extinguishing the feelings, perceptions and sensations through the abreactions. I never go into this work with a client in order to help them remember their trauma. The myth that this work is about recovering memories may scare many people off from engaging in the process. Remember, many clients have a cognitive memory of the overwhelming stressor or trauma. It is usually the feelings and sensations that are systematically released through the abreactions. Some clients may never remember the pictures or story connected to the feelings and sensations. The unconscious mind knows best. The abreactions systematically release the feelings, thoughts and perceptions from the original stressor or trauma. These feelings and sensations are very powerful and manifest in symptoms and behavior re-enactments. When these feelings are resolved, the feelings and sensations lose their power over the individual. This work is about alleviating symptoms and helping the individual move toward wholeness.

The False Memory Syndrome Foundation as well as many others in the mental health business and court systems want us to believe that we don't block off traumatic material as children and that there is no validity to any memory that is retrieved in psychotherapy, let alone hypnotherapy. The study I alluded to stated that the research has shown that hypnosis is not the factor responsible for the production of false memories. The study reported that false memories may be produced just as easily without hypnosis. (D. Corydon Hammond) I want my readers to know that the main study used by the False Memory Syndrome Foundation is based on conscious memory. They also want to claim that therapists place false memories of sexual abuse in their clients. The research shows that there is no evidence that false memories can be implanted into someone's mind. I always tell my clients that even with all my training and experience that I don't know how to do that anyway. Remember, it's the person's symptoms that tell you that there is something going on deep down inside. The reality is false memories or beliefs can occur outside the therapy setting. As the study reported, normal memory is malleable. However, under hypnosis clients specifically recollect details of childhood events and places. For example, under hypnosis, clients who don't remember their childhood homes, have detailed memories of their bedrooms.

Certainly there needs to be a check and balance system in dealing with abuse cases. I have had cases where step-fathers were falsely accused of abusing their teenage step-daughter. There have been ample divorce cases where one spouse accuses the other of child abuse. Many states have Federal funding sex abuse teams within the Department of Social Services. The social workers, detectives, and medical staffs are well trained in this specific area. The team in my county does a marvelous job of thorough and objective investigation with appropriate referrals to therapeutic settings.

I believe that therapists who work with clients on a conscious level are eager to connect pervasive feelings to past trauma which may contribute more to the clients being confused about childhood memories. For those therapists working with survivors on a strictly conscious cognitive level, be careful assuming that the clients' symptoms mean that they were sexually abused. Don't assume that it was the father who was the perpetrator. Foremost, watch the counter transference – particularly if you have your own unresolved childhood wounds. We shouldn't be in the helping profession if we are subconsciously trying to help ourselves through helping others. Trust that the client's unconscious mind knows how to safely release and resolve the blocked off material. You (the therapist) are only an external helper. Your client's unconscious mind will help your client remember what they need to remember to heal, not to be an expert witness in court. More distorted and confusing memories may be reproduced if we push the client on a conscious level to recollect the details of their abuse. Maggie Phillips and Claire Frederick stated, "The counter transference problems can also lead therapists to foster or even insist upon confrontational stances by patients on the basis of their memories." They go on to say that, "These confrontations can take place within the family, violently disrupting it, and may end with the patient ceasing to have contact with family members on a permanent basis, bringing criminal charges, and/or instituting civil suits." Remember, just because a young teenager gives a partial disclosure of child abuse does not mean that they are developmentally and or psychologically ready to remember the rest of the story.

My personal policy is to document what the teenager remembers on a conscious level. When it is appropriate to begin the trance work, I document that this process has begun and that any new recollections will be recorded as coming from the abreactions. I inform the parents that any memories that come from the trance work can not be used to pursue any legal action. Despite the empirical research, the legal system continues to dismiss hypnosis as a valid therapeutic process for Dissociated memories. Again, the therapy needs to be about helping the client heal. I'm cautious and respectful of the court's role, but I want to get to the work that helps the client resolve their emotional trauma as well as to alleviate their symptoms.

As in the case study of T, he was amnestic for any childhood abuse. He was referred to me after admitting to an inappropriate sexual encounter with his friend's younger brother. What emerged from the trance work was that he had been sexually abused by his friend's father when he was approximately five-years-old. Neither T nor the alleged perpetrator still lives in that neighborhood. In this case T was allowed to remember his offender. The point being, nothing could be done. I did contact the detective in charge of sex crimes to place this person's name on file in case other possible victims come forward. However, because the disclosure came as a result of the hypnosis/abreactive work, the alleged perpetrator will not be confronted.

There is no suggestion in this approach. Again, it is not solely about recovered memories, although in the example of T and many others, the unconscious mind does allow the conscious Host to have a perception of their perpetrator to emerge into consciousness. Understand that when the abreactions are occurring whether in the office or through vivid dreams at home, the unconscious mind often uses metaphoric stories to trigger the REAL feelings and sensations that are being released. My clients can distinguish between these metaphoric stories and the genuine memories that emerge via the abreactions. Different aspects of the dissociated material are released separately, so when a client puts together a set of feelings, some physical sensations, and sometimes a picture which is usually seen outside of them, they feel disconnected from the memory. This serves the purpose of not having the full impact of the feelings, sensations, and pictures being released at the same time as one overwhelming memory. The unconscious mind tries to make the abreactions as safe and tolerable as possible.

The "False Memory Syndrome" has become a socio-political factor despite the lack of any sound scholarship and psychological theory. Many therapists have backed off from doing any type of clinical hypnosis to avoid the possibility of a lawsuit. Many therapists decline to work with younger sexual abuse victims, particularly at a time when the need is greater than ever for qualified therapists in this area. I know of no other therapist in my area who does abreactive work with juvenile offenders. The court system and juvenile services still refer juvenile offenders to "Group Therapy" sessions, which as I have mentioned previously, cannot be the primary mode of treatment and will never get to and/or resolve the underlying source of their acting out behavior.

Parents of teenagers who have been abused and adult survivors will learn from this book that there are deeper and safer methods of healing and they need to seek out therapists who do this work. Much of the work for many who carry childhood wounds requires the abreactive work. Talking therapy alone will not be sufficient. Medicine, although sometimes a necessity to take the edge off the symptoms, does not resolve the underlying source of the symptoms.

Dissociation - "A True Field of Study"

In a 1994 article in *Dissociation News,* Colon A. Ross discusses the need for the establishment of a trauma-dissociation model as a major model within the mental health field. I have always believed that dissociation research and study has been too focused on what you the reader know as Multiple Personality Disorder *(now identified as Dissociative Identity Disorder).* Treatment modalities which are too often based on in-patients who suffer with extreme cases of DID, have rightly so focused on contain-ment and medication. I am trying to show that a treatment intervention utilizing clinical hypnosis and abreactive work can be an effective technique for out-patient therapy. I am glad to see that the latest research includes the concept of overwhelm-ing stressor. All too often individuals who were not horribly sexually or physically abused want to deny that their problems could possibly be coming from the past and subsequently won't seek help that addresses the source of their symptoms.

Even though I do give many examples of sexual abuse, not all of my clients who have benefited from this approach were sexually abused. None of us get through our child-hoods without some scars. We are left with wounds that slow us down and distort our view of the world and affect our self-esteem. Society has a phobia about con-necting our current problems to our past. Society has always tended to "suppress" the notion of child abuse. We would rather think we have a chemical imbalance or a brain disease versus exploring our childhoods in order to understand our cur-rent symptoms and manifestations. We would rather go to a medical doctor for our somatic complaints and accept that we have a medical condition, versus accepting the possibility that our stomach problems are related to unresolved anger from our childhood. The reality is that children are emotionally, physically and sexually abused and neglected. Even in the best of families children can be overwhelmed witness-ing parents arguing all of the time. The divorce rate is over 60% and many young children are psychologically affected by this process and may have serious manifesta-tions as a result, particularly if the parents don't establish a predictable environment post-divorce. All of these events can have a developmental impact on the child and left untreated, will result in long-lasting symptoms and manifestations.

The phenomenon of "Dissociation" observed by Janet over a century ago has gained legitimacy over the last decade. Remember, any new idea, theory or phenomenon must survive the extraordinary science phase of a paradigm shift. In other words, any new idea goes through a period of scrutiny, criticism and resistance before it becomes accepted as legitimate. The concepts of Dissociation, Psychological Trauma, Clinical Hypnosis and Hypnotic Abreactions have all come under fire. In talking about the scientific enterprise of traumatic stress studies, Judith Herman stated that "The re-search has become both more technically sophisticated and that a new generation of studies has begun to enlarge the scope and increase the precision of our understand-ing of the impact of traumatic events."

"As evidence of the central importance of dissociation in traumatic stress disorders has continued to accumulate, it has also become apparent that dissociation offers a window into consciousness, memory and the links between body and mind."

Judith Herman

"Simply discard the notion that you have a single personality.
Notice the variety that is you.
You will find a lot of experiential validation
when you drop the outmoded theory
of one person-one personality."

David Reynolds

Part II

"The personality is not single, it is multiple - not in the psychiatric sense of multiple personality, but in that there are many levels to the self as many skins to an onion."

Roger Woolger

In Part I, you have read through theory and case example that the unconscious mind blocks off overwhelming experiences as a protection. However the thoughts, feelings and perceptions from these experiences will emerge in symptoms and manifestations. Hopefully we can learn and react to these symptoms as red flags alerting us to a deeper problem that requires attention and healing. As Gary Zukav states in *Soul Stories,* "We come to know the parts of ourselves through our feelings. We come to understand the multiplicity of our personality through the differentiation of these feelings."

This is the part of the book where we connect the soul and the personality, physical reality with non-physical reality, and the body and the spirit. I have introduced through case example the concepts of "parts of the self" and "child helpers," and even what I term the Dominant part of our system. Part II will be my effort to lay out the unconscious map that has opened up to me over the years of doing this work. To me it is more than the "unconscious mind," but a non-physical realm of intelligent energies that accompanies us on our life journey. I will from my perspective define the roles of the non-physical helpers. This section of the book is so important to understand prior to reading Part III which is a case study of a client with a rather complicated system and how through the trance state, a clear schema of healing unfolds over time. The reader will clearly come to understand that healing is at the soul level. It can be viewed very simply. Symptoms and manifestations come from unresolved dissociated feelings from this lifetime or from unfinished karmic stories from another lifetime. Both require resolution for psychological healing and spiritual growth to take place. Through the hypnagogic state, the unconscious mind can through what is called an abreaction, release feelings, sensations, and perceptions safely over time. The parts of the self that have been holding the blocked off material can then return to a positive role in the system, subsequently giving back positive traits, knowledge, creativity and wisdom to the Host. Then the individual is free to move toward integration and wholeness.

"To be afraid of the multiplicity of the psyche - in its manifestation as many lives, many selves, and the abnormal extremes aside - is in the end to be afraid of the psyche itself. The fact that many people find the very idea of an inner world and other selves both disturbing and distasteful, is alas, a sad commentary on how very unpsychological and antipathetic to the psyche - and, by extension, the spirit - our society has become."

Roger Woolger

Defining The Non-physical Helpers

"To incarnate, the soul creates a personality from those parts of itself that it wants to heal in the physical environment and from those parts of itself that it lends to the process of healing in that lifetime."

Gary Zukav

Through symbolic diagrams, I hope to explain the unconscious map that has consistently presented to me over the years of doing clinical hypnosis. It is a difficult task to name and define those things that we can't see or measure. Understand that what has come to me and others is just the next level that we need to understand in order to evolve. There are many more levels beyond what I am describing. Remember that everything already exists at the highest level in the universe. What opens up to us is what we need at this point in evolution to move to higher levels of consciousness. A world of non-physical helpers, protectors and teachers has emerged in my clinical hypnosis practice. Patterns of healing have followed clear schemes time and time again. Let me try to describe what has come to me through symbolic drawings and case examples.

Diagram I

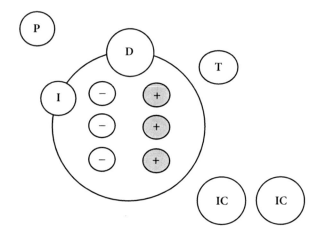

D	=	Dominant
P	=	Protector
T	=	Teacher
I	=	Incarnate
IC	=	Imaginary Companion
+	=	Helpers
-	=	Helpers

The team of soul helpers line up prior to our birth and enter the physical body at the point of the first breath. They are our team of helpers who have been assigned to us for this incarnation. We are given a Dominant, also known as your Higher Self and six child helpers. This is the core system. There are more helpers, teachers and protectors that I will introduce. The Dominant is our "essence," our guide, our spirit. It speaks to us through our intuition, hunches, and gut feelings. It gives us inspiration. You will come to know the role of the Dominant in Parts III and IV.

I tend to personalize the non-physical intelligent helpers who I will refer to as child helpers. When a child helper who is holding upset feelings communicates with you through the hypnosis, one tends to personalize that relationship. Let me emphasize that not every clients' helpers or Dominant talk to me through the hypnosis. For some systems, bringing forth a helper to express feelings is one of many ways that the unconscious mind extinguishes the negative energy. Again, the reader must be clear that when I am talking to a Dominant or a child helper through the hypnosis, this is not about multiple personality. Understand, I can only talk to those helpers who come out of their normal position to hold negative emotions. Once a child helper is clear, it returns to its appropriate positive role. That helper can no longer communicate with me. However, the Dominant will always be able to communicate with me.

Under ideal developmental conditions, beginning around age four until around age six, the first two child helpers awaken, and help the child with creativity and sense of humor. It's the time that the consciousness awakens. It's the time when children tap into their sense of initiation and autonomy.

The next two helpers awaken starting around age six and help us through the latency stage with memory, intelligence and logic. I remember that S's ten-year-old helper proclaimed that she was the "smart one." Again, only the helpers who come out from an internal position to hold negative emotions are able to communicate through the trance state.

As we move into adolescence we have two more helpers who light up. I refer to these helpers as the teenage helpers. One of the teenage helpers is the protector of the ego. It gives us backbone, fortitude, and confidence. It is my understanding that the other teenage helper helps with sexuality. Under ideal conditions, these helpers light up and give us special traits, gifts and wisdom. You will learn that they are here to learn lessons just as we are supposed to do.

Unfortunately the developing child may experience overwhelming stressors and trauma that will disrupt this schema that I just described. When the system is met with a trauma, the feelings, sensations, thoughts, and perceptions are siphoned off to child helpers who have to come out of their positive position in the system. An experience that needs to be siphoned off from the conscious Host will be divided into at least two levels. One child helper can not absorb both upset feelings, i.e. blame, shame, or fear and the anger and frustration as well. Different feelings are at different frequencies and are absorbed by different helpers.

Diagram II

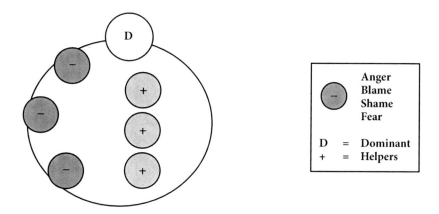

For example, a middle helper will have to come out early to help the five-year-old child deal with overwhelming upset feelings. The anger from that upsetting experience will then be absorbed by one of the teenage helpers. It seems that no matter what stressful situation or trauma besets the child, the child's internal system is angry that the child has been violated.

That anger may be contained for a number of years, but it will eventually manifest, usually during early adolescence. What is critical to understand is that when a helper comes out to hold blocked off feelings that are too overwhelming for the conscious Host, that helper can not give it's positive energy, gifts and talents to the Host until the feelings are resolved and that helper can return to an internal position. This is my main argument for doing the abreactive work. It's not about recovering memories but releasing the negative energy and getting back all of your helpers so they can do the work for you. Perhaps this is why the Shaman healers call this process "Soul Retrieval."

Usually at least one and sometimes two of the middle helpers have to come out of position to hold the blocked off emotions. I believe this is why so many kids who have experienced trauma and overwhelming stressors have academic problems. That child is not benefiting from what that helper provides, such as logic and memory skills or even a special talent in math. Many dissociative lists of symptoms and manifestations of trauma include issues surrounding school performance. When kids and teens clear up some of the blocked off feelings, the child begins to catch up with their reading level and show marked improvement in other school performance areas.

What is important to remember is that under overwhelming stressors and certainly trauma, at least two and sometimes three or four of our helpers must leave their positive powerful position to take on the task of holding the negative feelings, sensations, and perceptions. This is what we call fragmentation. On the one hand, the child is protected from the trauma, but the fragmentation will cause profound disruption in the child's development. The blocked off material will continue to have long lasting affects on the life of the individual. In *Trauma and Recovery*, Judith Herman writes, **"Fragmentation in consciousness prevents the ordinary integration of knowledge, memory, emotional states, and bodily experience. Fragmentation in the inner representations of the self prevents the integration of identity. Fragmentation in the inner representations of others prevents the development of a reliable sense of independence within connection."**

I want to discuss which helpers hold which negative feelings, thoughts and perceptions and describe how these feelings can manifest in physical reality through symptoms, behavior re-enactments and somatic complaints.

First Level Helper

When the child is overwhelmed with family disruption, parents arguing, or any kind of maltreatment or neglect, this child helper is called upon to deal with the fear and or sadness from such experiences. Remember, up until age six or seven, the developing child uses primary emotions which are more intense than the emotions we need when we are older. It doesn't take much for a five-year-old to be overwhelmed by being put down or dealing with upset parents all the time, for the mind to siphon off these feelings.

The following example is critical to understand how the conscious Host is affected by the blocked off material held by the child helper. Under hypnosis a child helper reported to me, "I have trouble sleeping because of scary things." "I feel alone." These feelings may manifest in the conscious Host in sleep disturbance, panic attacks, and a sense of loneliness.

The blocked off feelings held by this child helper can manifest in physical reality in nightmares and bedwetting. Remember, when the conscious Host gets older, the sadness and or fear that was blocked off at age four or five remains fixated forever or until these feelings are resolved. This can explain regressive behavior and clinging behavior of an eight or nine-year-old child who is holding scary or sad feelings from an earlier stage. When those feelings get triggered, they are felt at the same intensity as when they were blocked off. The feelings that are siphoned off never lose their intensity. The child helper in the above example emerged and communicated with me when the Host was in her thirties.

Let me give a quick example of the fixation that I was discussing. The reality is that the child helper remains stuck in a time warp. A few years ago I was working with

A, an eleven-year-old girl who experienced neglect and physical abuse as a young child. R and her two sisters were being raised by the grandparents. I did not formally induce trance but in highly dissociative children, child helpers can emerge during session. Spontaneously, R's youngest helper that held the fear from witnessing domestic violence emerged during the session. She stated, "mommy says I'm pwetty." The grandmother would inform me that when R was four, she had to take speech therapy because of not being able to pronounce r's. When I asked this child helper how she got along with her sisters, she said that she only had one sister. This was correct because when R was four her youngest sister was not born. This child helper held much fear that manifested in the eleven-year-old Host in nightmares, and in intrusive thoughts and perceptions.

I worked with a young woman who expressed intense rage toward her boyfriend. Behind the anger was a hurt child who held the sadness and fear from being physically abused by an adult day-care provider. Under hypnosis a child helper emerged who could not talk. Sometimes child helpers can't talk but can write down words and expressions. By the way, they write at this level in first grade letters. In this case example it was a mystery where the anger and sadness were based. The Host reported a good childhood with no physical punishment. There was no indication that sexual abuse had occurred. The child helper wrote on my hand, "mom left me." What was revealed during a number of trance sessions was that around the age of five or six, this client's mother went back to work and consequently the Host was placed at times with an adult baby-sitter. Through the abreactions it was learned that the baby-sitter was physically abusive to my client. This experience was blocked off until the client did the trance work. When the boyfriend would let down the adult Host, it would upset the child helper and trigger the angry teenager which would in turn cause the Host to react in dramatic fashion. You will learn that the teenager often is the protector of the younger upset child helper. This is a good example, which we will discuss in other case examples, of how the trauma is siphoned off into two helpers.

When the Host experiences trauma, this first level helper holds the fear and sadness. These feelings can manifest in the Host in nightmares, panic attacks, fear of being alone, and sleep disturbance. These child helpers are connected to second chakra energy such as fears of being controlled, and abandonment issues.

Middle Helper

These helpers bring to us logic, intelligence, a special talent in math and our curiosity. They deal with matters of the heart. These helpers light up during our formative years from six to twelve. They are tied to our self-esteem and our emotions. Remember, this is the stage of development that forms our sense of competence. When life has been, and continues to be, difficult for the child, a sense of inferiority and a sense of failure can quickly set in.

When the overwhelming stressor or trauma occurs, the middle helper comes out to absorb the blame, shame, "I did something wrong" and "I'm not good enough feelings." This is the helper who holds the memory of the abuse. You will come to understand that it is this child helper who acts out with a juvenile offender, because this helper holds an introject of the perpetrator. Often but not always, we act out the thing that happened to us. Remember, how we defend against the rage of the abuse is to identify with the aggressor. It's not the teenage helper who holds the anger that acts out in a juvenile offender, instead it is this middle helper.

The middle helper holds an anger that is different than the anger the teenage helper holds. This helper may manifest in childhood by being mean or cruel to a younger sibling. The middle helper may eat to feel good causing the Host to suffer with a compulsion to eat. Middle helpers may say, "I'm worthless, I'm ugly, there is something the matter with me or no one will love me." This is the helper who holds the blame and shame i.e., it's my fault, I did something wrong. Most of the abreactive work is connected to the fourth chakra where these matters of the heart are stored. Holding on to these types of feelings has a profound affect on the personality of the Host with regard to self-worth, self-esteem, personal power, and a sense of competence.

This is the helper who draws us to symbiotic relationships which are relationships that repeat and trigger the same unhealthy patterns from our childhood. We end up unknowingly in a dysfunctional relationship projecting and displacing emotions on our partners and not knowing that these are mostly unresolved emotions from our past. Remember, when blocked off emotions from the past get triggered, they feel contemporary and we tend to blame the external object in our current reality for our feelings. We tend to subconsciously pick people who reinforce our negative self-image as well as trigger our unresolved feelings. Only when we realize that the negative emotions that are being triggered are feelings that we need to resolve, can we began the healing process. When unresolved feelings of the heart from childhood problems are resolved, individuals will be drawn to healthier relationships.

Holding on to negative emotions of the heart can often manifest in the mistreatment of our own children. The middle helper who gets the upset feelings from physical punishment for example, will want you, the conscious Host, to treat your kids like you were treated. We often ask why anyone who was mistreated as a child would ever treat their child in the same way. This is the explanation. Behind the school yard bully is a hurt little boy who was mistreated and probably physically abused as a kid. To re-emphasize a point I have made earlier, not everyone who experiences physical or sexual trauma will act out with another person. Unfortunately, until humans evolve beyond external power, blocked off traumatic experiences will continue to manifest in self-harm and the exploitation of others.

The middle helpers connect to the heart chakra. As Caroline Myss writes in *Anatomy of the Spirit*, "**Loss of fourth chakra energy can give rise to jealousy, bitterness, anger, hatred, and an inability to forgive others as well as oneself.**" Anodea Judith, in *Wheels of Life* states that rejection threatens our basic internal balance. "**We turn this**

non-love against ourselves and start to self destruct. Instead of feeling connected, we are cut off, separate and isolated." Much of the abreactive work is about releasing feelings held by the middle helpers. When these feelings are resolved the Host can get back the ability to love, forgive, trust, and have hope for the future. Resolving these feelings of the heart is critical for forming healthy relationships.

Teenage Helper

The teenage helper gives us fortitude and backbone. It is the protector of the ego. The teenage helpers light up during our adolescence and help us with our personal power and identity. This is the stage of our life when we relate to the outside world. This is the part of us that deals with injustice and fairness.

When trauma and or overwhelming stressors occur in childhood, this helper is awakened to come out early to absorb the anger and frustrations of the negative experience that the child is going through. Remember, under normal circumstances, the teenage helper is in a dormancy period until early adolescence. All efforts are made internally for this anger to be "contained" often until adolescence. This anger is different than the anger that gets acted out by the middle helper. The feelings held by this helper can range from frustration to rage. It usually starts to break through during the early teen years. The angry affect that emerges with teenagers is the anger that was blocked off in childhood. This anger shows up in defiant and rebellious reactions and behaviors. It's the attitude, "nobody tells me what to do." The angry teenager can manifest in running away, aggressive behaviors as well as in drug and alcohol problems. Often the teenage helper doesn't respect the Host and may sabotage the Host. The teenage helper may say that the Host can't handle problems or that the Host is weak. "I'm the strong one. I need to tear the walls down. I need relief now. I don't know how to deal with his wife. I'm mad all the time." One teenage helper of a survivor proclaimed that the Host's mother was a bitch suggesting that the Host's mother is not our mother according to the helpers. There is the phenomenon "rage at mom" syndrome where the internal system is angry at the mother for not protecting and or for not recognizing the signs and symptoms that abuse was occurring. The teenage helper is often the spokesman and tries to come through and let the world know that something is going on.

There is a sense of power in taking over with the angry teenager. "I'm running the Host's life." This helper can keep the adult Host fixated in the teenage years. For example, the thirty-five-year-old father who too often goes to the bar after work with the guys versus going home to the spouse and children, or the adult survivor who is out partying and drinking a little too much. The anger contained in this helper can range from frustration to extreme rage that can manifest in self-destructive, as well as other-directed, aggressive behaviors. Remember, this helper has to find a way to survive through self-medication, drugs, and/or alcohol as well as going off in order to get a sense of temporary relief. The blocked off anger doesn't always show up through external power. Often the anger can manifest in depression and chronic fatigue.

Depression is anger turned inward. Since this frequency of anger is held in the third chakra, the stomach area, many individuals will develop stomach problems as a result of holding on to blocked off anger.

When this anger emerges during early adolescence, it's time for the parents to get the adolescent help. The Dominant (Higher Self) tries but can't always control this part of the self. The anger from blocked off childhood trauma needs to be resolved not treated alone through psychotropic drugs. A recent report reflected that a high percentage of teenagers who were involved in school shootings were on and/or coming off of psychotropic drugs. I would suggest that the medicine may suppress or contain some feelings but not the powerful rage. In other words, the angry teenager helper may not be affected by the drug and actually have an easier time taking over and acting out. Remember, dissociative emotions are different than ordinary emotional states.

When this helper is resolved and returns to an internal position of positive energy it brings to the system backbone and fortitude. The conscious Host may go through a period of frustration because they have to learn to speak up for themselves. The teenage helper can no longer come out and fight the Host's battles because it can only help from within.

Again, the teenage helper is linked to our third chakra. It relates to our personal power and self-esteem, self-respect, and the ability to be self-disciplined. As Caroline Myss writes in *Anatomy of the Spirit*, "**How we feel about ourselves, whether we respect ourselves, determines the quality of our life, our capacity to succeed in business, relationships, healing, and intuitive skills.**" Resolve your anger and retrieve that part of your soul that gives you the power and courage to achieve your goals.

The Dominant (The Non-judgmental Part)

Throughout the book I will refer to the part of us that speaks to us through hunches, intuitions, gut feelings, and inspirations as the Dominant. The Dominant is our essence. Our Dominant knows our purpose. This guiding force is also referred to as our Higher Self, Spirit Guide, Spirit and Spirit-you. You will come to know the role of the Dominant through S's case example in Part III and in Part IV which is a dialogue with S's Dominant that was recorded after her therapy was complete. S's Dominant stated, "**I am the in-between the body and the universe. I am here to guide.**" Gary Zukav states in *The Seat of the Soul*, "**The Higher Self is the connecting link when the soul speaks to the personality.**" I have been able to access this part of the self through the hypnogogic state. The purpose of prayer and meditation is to connect with our Dominant. Over the years not every client's Dominant was able to come through physical reality and communicate through the Host's vocal chords. Many would communicate through ideomotor signals or through a messenger. The bottom line is that we all have a Dominant and we need to learn to listen to that part of us. Too often we are clouded with all of the externals that we don't hear, feel or sense the signals that our Dominant is sending us. Here is another argument for resolving childhood wounds. Our Dominant uses much energy to contain and control the blocked off feelings and consequently can't always pay full attention to the conscious Host. On the other hand, when my clients work through their childhood wounds and all the helpers get back into a positive internal position, the Dominant is free to focus on guiding the Host. Our Dominant knows our purpose and controls the healing process. I always tell my clients who are doing the hypnotic abreactive work that I am just an external helper and that the healing process is controlled by a higher part of their system. Our Dominants are not torturing us by placing us in relationships or other life circumstances that trigger negative emotions but are letting us, the conscious Host, know what feelings need to healed, what lessons need to be learned. When clients work through their childhood wounds they begin to become more aware of insights and inspirations. Ultimately we should become like our Dominant.

The Dominant is connected to the sixth chakra which is the chakra of wisdom. It is referred to as the "third eye." Even though S's eyes were closed during my conversations with her Dominant, I was told that I was seen from a perspective that was further away than our physical reality. Resolve your childhood wounds and go within yourself and listen to that inner voice. Let your Dominant be your guide.

The Oversoul

The Oversoul is the next higher realm which according to S's Dominant, we have not broken through to yet. It is sometimes referred to as the Overself. It is referenced in the New World Dictionary as "the universal mind or spirit that animates, motivates, and is the unifying principle of all living things." I look at it as the supervisor of the Dominant, a clear sense of a hierarchy of intelligent energy systems. It is an encapsulating energy. This energy is connected to the seventh chakra. Clients would often report while working through traumatic material that they felt shut down, as though they were not connected to external reality. Although this was an unpleasant experience, I would compare it to the shield that comes out to protect the Batmobile. The unconscious mind chooses to shut down external stimuli in order to prevent extreme triggers as the powerful emotions are being resolved. My closest connection to an Oversoul was with a teenage survivor. The Oversoul seemed to take an active role in helping an overwhelmed Dominant.

Perhaps we can assume this Oversoul is connected to our seventh chakra. This chakra is located at the top of the head. There is always a flow of energy over the top of the head. I maintain that this is the Halo. Caroline Myss writes in *Anatomy of the Spirit* that, "The seventh chakra is our connection to our spiritual nature and our capacity to allow our spirituality to become an integral part of our physical lives and provide guidance."

The Incarnate

"The universe brings back energies so the human race can evolve. Genetic patterns are repeated."

S's Dominant

I must admit that I was somewhat taken back by the concept that unresolved emotions from another time were allowed to be a part of my system and that at some time in my life the unresolved story would emerge in symptoms and manifestation for which I would have to take responsibility. The Western belief of reincarnation (that you were here before) is misguided. The fact is that all of the "Soul Helpers" that I am describing in this section have recycled through physical reality multiple times. If an individual has a reoccurring dream about another place, another time, it's that part of you that has been allowed to be a part of your incarnation and perhaps it is time for that incarnate to let go of an unresolved story. I have decided not to spend much time trying to convince readers that unresolved past life energies are cycled back through the genetic line for resolution. Dominants report that the universe does not want to have any scars in the ancestral line. Remember, the universe is moving toward oneness and wholeness.

The concept of rebirth was removed from Christian doctrine in the third century. For a further explanation, read Roger Woolger's *Other Lives, Other Selves*. I must be clear that the past life stories that have surfaced in my work naturally emerged during the hypnosis. I do utilize the affective bridge technique in that I get the client to remember a recent situation in which a powerful feeling that continues to surface in current reality was triggered and ask the unconscious mind to take that feeling back to its original source. If the unconscious mind is not ready for the client to connect that feeling to a story from this lifetime or some other time, it won't happen. Remember, the Dominant controls the healing process. During trance, I may ask to communicate with the part of the self that is responsible for a certain powerful feeling or symptom. If a part of the self emerges and needs to heal some unresolved feelings, then you deal with it. You will see from the case examples that incarnates either stay as a helper or are prepared to exit out of the system. If they stay they must resolve the unresolved story, otherwise their negative energy continues to affect the Host.

I am not in the business of doing Past Life Regression. This Western, New Age fad that emerges where individuals want to find out about their past lives is based on false assumptions. You will see that if you do have a part of your soul with an unresolved story, it is not going to be a pleasant story. Too often the stories are about untimely deaths and unresolved grief and fears of abandonment. Hypnosis taps into the healing power of the unconscious mind. The healing process makes that which is unconscious conscious regardless of whether the unresolved feelings are from this lifetime or any other. For example, in S's case study in Part III, I was informed by her

Dominant that we would have to help resolve certain past life stories as they unfolded in the healing process.

Again, not every client has an incarnate with an unresolved story. Most of my client's symptoms and manifestations are coming from childhood traumas from this lifetime. I do a thorough assessment of current symptoms as well as symptoms and behaviors during childhood and adolescence. I acquire a sense of how my clients were treated as children as well as how their parents treated each other. I examine family dysfunction, i.e., any recollections of inappropriate punishment, abandonment issues such as separation and divorce, problems with alcohol, or domestic violence. I will then integrate hypnotic-abreactive work in the therapeutic process for the purpose of healing the childhood wounds. With some clients I will get a gut feeling (this is my Dominant talking to me) to explore the possibility that their symptoms and manifestations may be connected to another time. Sometimes I will have a client who grew up having a good childhood with good parents. There were no signs or symptoms of sexual abuse. However, the client reported a feeling of doom and gloom came over them at age eight with no apparent precipitator. Other signs and symptoms that may lead me to explore the possibility of a past life story are phobias, irrational fears, atypical self-mutilation, reoccurring dreams with content involving previous times in history. To confuse matters more, many clients who have been abused in this lifetime are also carrying an unresolved story from another time. You will see that the incarnate will pair up with the child helper from this lifetime with the same frequency of emotion. Hopefully this will become clear through the case examples.

The following is an example of how a past life story spontaneously emerges during the healing process. This client, an adult female in her thirties, was doing hypnotic abreactive work for childhood sexual abuse. She had concluded several sessions and had experienced a number of abreactions relating to her childhood abuse. The following is the client's recollection of a particular session.

"I laid there for what seemed quite some time when I got a real sharp pain in my right side. This pain had been there before but this time it was extremely sharp. I got this vision, not just a vision ... I felt this ... a young boy named Danny was laying on a table in a tent. People (men) were standing around him. He was dying of a gunshot wound that was in his right side. I could see, hear, and smell the soldiers walking in the mud. It was raining, the mud was red. I could see the uniforms were from the Civil War. I could feel Danny leave through my stomach region. It felt like heat, energy exiting my body. After this was over, I felt empty for about a week, kind of sad. After a time I felt stronger, didn't take things so personally. I was able to stand up for myself without getting so angry. I have not had that pain in my side since then. I used to take medicine to help me with my temper and panic attacks. I went to therapy for about ten months. I don't take any medicine and I feel stronger, see more direction in my life. I have never had this feeling, not ever. It feels so clean."

Client

There was no suggestion here. I was assuming that the client's uneasy feeling upon arriving to that session would simply yield more feelings regarding her sexual abuse. Clients either report what they are experiencing as it is happening or describe the experience when they exit out of the trance state. In this case the client had no trouble in her own mind believing that what she witnessed and felt was part of a real story from another time.

Most of my clients who have such experiences seem to have a predisposition to accepting past life stories. Many of my clients inform me that they believe that their symptoms are possibly from a past life story even before the therapy begins. I am very careful not to scare a client off when in fact in my mind their symptoms indicate an exploration of the possibility that there could be an unresolved story from another time. With the hypnotic-abreactive work, clients release powerful feelings and sensations. Sometimes there are metaphoric stories paired with real feelings during the sessions. Clients will often have vivid dreams between sessions which are usually real feelings from blocked off material paired with metaphoric stories. Clients can usually distinguish between memories that are connected to real traumas from this lifetime as well as other lifetimes versus stories that are created to trigger negative emotions that need to be released. I, as well as others who do this work, do not need our clients to believe, for example, that a past life story that emerges and is resolved is a real phenomenon. Remember, all that matters is that the dissociated material is resolved, that the client's symptoms abate, and that the client begins to feel more balanced and whole. In the final tally, my clients don't think much about their child helpers or their incarnates. They feel whole and move on with their lives. Remember, it's what is unconscious that haunts you.

Incarnates either stay or exit out. If they stay as an extra helper, they must resolve the negative story that they brought with them. If they leave, they may need to let go of some of the feelings and they may need to go to what is referred to as a sphere of healing and cleansing for further resolution. They may need to return to physical reality at some future time. More often than not, resolving past life stories is easier that resolving the negative energy from this lifetime.

Your symptoms are telling you that a part of you needs healing. Whether the negative energy is from this lifetime or another, through the hypnotic-abreactive process, unresolved feelings are released and resolved. Your system becomes more balanced and you begin to feel more whole and alive.

External Helpers

I am not saying I know all of the external helpers, teachers and protectors who surround us. I will try to give a brief description of what has consistently presented to me over the years. External helpers appear to come to help in times of need. When they have done their job they move on to help another system. External helpers can include "imaginary companions," teachers, protectors and deceased relatives. Some of the external helpers are able to communicate with me, and some are unable to communicate through physical reality. Sometimes they are able to communicate through a child helper or through the Dominant. Some of the external helpers report that they are helping more than one human at a time.

Imaginary Companions

Imaginary companions are real. When the first level child helpers wake up around the age of three or four, external helpers come to add extra protection, even under ideal conditions, to what is still a vulnerable system usually until the age of six. If everything goes well with the child, the imaginary companions leave and move on to another assignment. However, when a child helper comes out to hold blocked off feelings, the imaginary companions may stay to provide companionship for that helper.

I was working with an adult survivor whose youngest child helper, the one who holds the fear and sadness, communicated to me through the trance state. The helper asked if I knew Billy. I learned that Billy was an imaginary companion who came to offer support to this child helper. The helper reported that Billy had been killed in an accident and that he was doing good. Once this child helper resolved the feelings and returned to the inner positive position, Billy moved on to help another. I believe that children are more naturally in touch with our non-physical helpers than we understand.

Protectors

My knowledge of protectors comes from hearsay information from child helpers and Dominants. Often child helpers communicate to me that they have a protector who watches out over them. One child helper from a survivor who held fear talked about a big strong male protector who helped her feel safe. Some of my younger clients who are not doing the hypnosis will often point to a position above and beyond them and describe what they refer to as a guardian Angel that is watching over the proceedings. I would consider deceased relatives as protectors, because in times of trouble they seem to watch over a child or grandchild. With one of my survivors, a deceased aunt's energy came to help. This energy remained as a helper and protector when I was treating this client in her twenties.

You will read in Part IV that S's father came to help her when she was nine-years-old, a year after he had died. The message was that he was there to help and protect her. According to S's Dominant, he remains a part of her today.

The presence of these protectors is more the rule with my clients than the exception.

Teachers

Teachers seem to serve the conscious Host in specific situations where the Host would not have the particular skill or ability to assert themselves in certain life situations because of the impact of early trauma and fragmentation. The best way I can describe what I call a Teacher is from the following example. An adult client, with whom I was doing hypnotic/abreactive work, grew up in an abusive alcoholic family system that left her very constricted. She reported being so shy and withdrawn that she would cross the street to avoid passing a pedestrian on the sidewalk. As she got older and needed to interview for a job, she reported as though some part of her took over during the interview as to allow her to come across as confident and articulate. This Teacher has remained with her throughout the years. In fact, on a few occasions, this helper emerged during the trance session and identified herself as having the role that I have described. The ultimate goal is for the conscious Host to acquire these abilities and traits while gaining personal power. This begins to occur after the underlying trauma and stressors are cleared away.

"As a young child from a dysfunctional alcoholic family, I was petrified of any adult I did not know well. My mother would get phone calls from parents of playmates, asking, 'Is there something wrong with your daughter? When I walk into the room, she turns into a statue and won't speak or move until I leave.' My mother would reply that I was just shy. When my parents had company over, my dad would try to shame me into speaking or doing a task in front of the guests. I died a thousand deaths with each episode. Growing older, walking home from school or the grocery store, I always crossed the street to avoid anyone walking in my direction. In high school, I was a very unwilling and unlikely candidate for a series of public speaking contests. A teacher, who was also a respected mentor, convinced me to represent the group, even though I was physically ill for three days prior to each event. As I look back on that horribly stressful period of time, I now realize that I didn't win two of the three contests all by myself. Although I knew my material inside and out, stepping up to the podium in front of hundreds of expectant faces, taking a breath, and getting the first sentence out was as terrifying to me as facing a firing squad. Reciting material is one thing; answering unknown questions from judges is another. At the time, I didn't know where my answers came from - all I knew was that I had to open my mouth and say something. And when I did, the knowledge and proper answers came out. When I entered the working world, I pleaded with the human resources rep to put me in the typing pool, where I could work by myself with little interaction from others. She insisted my skills would be wasted there and put me in the marketing department, where constant interaction was a must. I knew it wasn't ME intelligently conversing with coworkers, but I knew I was very, very grateful to whoever it was. Interviews used to terrorize me, until the day I was up for a promotion and was frantic to get out of the interview. Knowing I was doomed from the start, I walked into the man's office and did something amazing; I smiled, offered my hand for a handshake, and very professionally INTRODUCED MYSELF! Like I was actually somebody ... I went home that evening finally aware and cognizant that I had a gifted helper who 'took over' for me when I hit the panic button in social situations. This helper has come to the rescue many, many times over the years. While I am continually surprised at my increasing confidence and ability to deal with similar situations up to the present, my helper continues to pinch hit when I hit a snag. I have no doubt that I would be an agoraphobic, para-noid, introverted hermit to this day if my lovely helper never existed."

Client

The Host

"Spirit inspires and guides. Will responds and selects."

Ceanne DeRohan

It is beyond the scope of this section, and frankly me, to resolve the dichotomy of personal will versus the greater will. I personally struggle with this dichotomy of what I want to be doing versus what I am supposed to be doing. I think I am doing what I am supposed to be doing despite the stress and difficulties I have had since I set out on this mission of starting a private practice. My personal dream has been to be a successful songwriter and world traveler. The bottom line is that I am afraid not to do what the greater will has set out for me to do. So I search ahead in my one man practice helping survivors resolve their childhood wounds and write this book be-tween the phone calls and reports I have to do. Maybe I am lucky in that I know my purpose, and playing a small role in helping people resolve their childhood wounds is an honorable thing to do.

Despite our circumstances we have the power and resources within ourselves to heal. No matter what has happened to us, we are ultimately responsible for our healing, even if the only choice we can make is to get help. Parents are responsible for getting their children the right help that addresses the underlying source of their symptoms.

You are the conscious Host. You have a Will. We use our Will to make choices. The *New World Dictionary* defines Will as "**the power of making a reasonable choice or decision or of controlling own actions.**" Anodea Judith in *The Wheels of Light* defines Will as "**the combination of mind and action, the conscious direction and - temperance of desire - the means through which we create our future.**" For most of my clients who have experienced childhood trauma, making choices, decisions, and creating a vision for the future is extremely difficult. The child helper holding fear is afraid of change which affects the conscious Host's ability to make decisions and move on. We can't control our feelings through sheer willpower, particularly primary emotions from childhood trauma. Sometimes we can't control our behaviors that are compulsively and involuntarily driven by blocked off feelings. The teenager who acts out sexually with his younger sibling is not making a conscious choice to do that behavior, but is driven unconsciously and involuntarily by his own blocked off

78

trauma. The parent who loses it and harshly punishes their child is driven perhaps by their own dissociated punishment at that time. The teenage survivor whose anger drives them to run away and get involved in drugs is acting on blocked off anger that emerges from a childhood wound. The young woman who self-mutilates because of a past life trauma is not making a conscious decision to inflict harm on herself. Usually with all of these examples the Host is aware of what is happening but does not have control over their actions at that moment. **Dissociation theory gives reasons, not excuses.** I'm sure the larger segment of society who are fortunate enough not to be carrying childhood scars, believes that despite our past and our current emotional state, that an individual should always be able to control their behavior. Johnny made a conscious choice to abuse his step-sister is the popular thinking. Again, the hope is that Johnny gets help before he acts out. Individuals need to recognize that the hurt and pain is a signal that something is wrong inside and there needs to be healing. Make the choice to get help before you violate yourself or others. Eckhart Tolle writes in *A New Earth*, "Human beings are meant to evolve into conscious beings, and those who don't will suffer the consequences of their unconsciousness."

Often I hear individuals say that they were abused as a kid in some fashion and that they don't have all these problems. True, not everyone who was sexually abused is going to act out. Not everyone who was physically abused is going to harshly punish their kids. However, if your unconscious mind blocked off any aspect of your trauma, it can manifest in compensating or risk taking behaviors. It can manifest in physical symptoms such as headaches and stomach problems. It can also manifest in a sudden development of a phobia for example.

We can't always blame the child helpers for the symptoms and manifestations. You the conscious Host make bad decisions. Perhaps because of the blocked off emotions, the individual is unconsciously influenced, but this individual develops conscious blueprints which result in these bad decisions or the inability to make decisions at all. I have had case examples in which the helpers are trying to persuade the Host to make better decisions regarding relationships. Whether reactions or behaviors are propelled from parts of our self or from conscious messages that cause an individual to make bad decisions or no decisions at all, unresolved childhood wounds leave the individual with vulnerabilities.

"Traumatic symptoms have a tendency to become disconnected from their source and take a life of their own," writes Judith Herman. **"Traumatic events produce profound and lasting changes in physiological arousal, emotion, cognition, and memory,"** Judith Herman. Childhood trauma leaves the individual feeling powerless to take action and confused and overwhelmed about their feelings. In *The Seat of the Soul*, Gary Zukav writes, **"The splintered personality is not content. The contentment that it feels in one moment is replaced by anger or fear or envy in the next moment as conflicting aspects of itself struggle with each other. Your responses to the struggles between the conflicting aspects of yourself determine the way that you will evolve, consciously or unconsciously, through the experience of negative karma**

or positive, through fear and doubt or through wisdom. Your struggles themselves do not create karma or determine the way that you will evolve, only your responses to them."

"Each of us has a purpose and our Ultimate Will is to fulfill that purpose," Anodea Judith. Carrying unresolved childhood wounds makes it more difficult to achieve that goal. Pay attention to what is going on inside. Let what is unconscious become conscious. Choose to resolve your blocked off trauma. You have all the power and resources within you to do so. The hypnotic/abreactive work is not easy. Abreactions can be unpleasant. Sessions may be followed with vivid dreams with strong emotions and periods of feeling strong emotions with or without any external precipitators. The choice is to remain fragmented, feeling like a victim and at the mercy of your unresolved emotions which keep you living in the past. Don't let the fear of dealing with your past keep you living in the past. Make the courageous choice to resolve your childhood wounds in order to move on a path of authentic power, integration, and wholeness.

In *The Seat of the Soul*, Gary Zukav writes, "Only through responsible choice can you choose consciously to cultivate and nourish the needs of your soul, and to challenge and release the wants of your personality. This is the choice of clarity and wisdom, the choice of conscious transformation."

The following are three case examples that will tie the definitions to real cases.

CASE STUDIES

Map

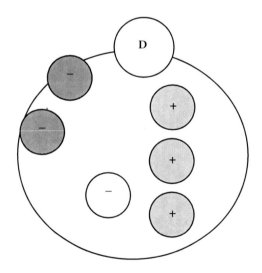

(This is an example of a client who had a typical fragmentation of two helpers coming out to siphon off both family disruption issues and a sexual abuse trauma. There was no Past Life energy involved in this case. Remember, the unconscious mind always calls on two helpers to deal with a stressor or trauma. This is a typical schema where a middle helper connected to the heart chakra comes out and holds the blame and shame as well as self-esteem issues related to the negative experience, in this case sexual abuse. The teenage helper holds the anger from the same experience. So, there are at least two helpers that come out to deal with the trauma. Keep in mind that sometimes more helpers are called upon to deal with negative experiences.)

This is a male client in his thirties, with a long history of indecent exposure problems which began during his teenage years. Upon seeking therapy with me, he had a history of incarcerations, court ordered group therapy, as well as mandatory drug therapy for sex offenders. O had been falsely accused of abusing his daughter with whom I had worked. It was revealed that she had been abused by a family friend. O's compulsion to expose himself lost him his family, and numerous jobs. Upon assessment, O had no recollection of his own sexual trauma. He lost a parent at an early age and had a difficult relationship with a step-parent. He was somewhat amnestic for early childhood events.

O's case is an example of a client whose problems were solely based on a trauma from this lifetime. Despite his amnesia for childhood sexual abuse, the goal of therapy was to uncover a trauma that I knew was there. In addition to his exposing behavior, O had an intermittent problem with anger.

The following is a summary of the abreactions that O had over the course of a number of months that would uncover and release the source of his acting out behavior. What emerged was that he was abused around the age of six by his friend's teenage sister.

O's helpers did not communicate with me verbally through physical reality. However, through ideomotor signaling, I was able to communicate with the unconscious mind. After a number of preparatory sessions, O reported having abreactions. The first abreaction that he reported was feeling anxiety in his chest. He felt scared and physically small. He reported being in the darkness in his mind and felt the presence of someone. "**I couldn't move or leave.**" Because O was in Theta trance during his abreactions, he would awake to tell me what he experienced.

During the next abreaction, he felt "**not in control, I wanted to get away.**" Again, he reported being in darkness but felt the presence of someone. During the next abreaction, O reported after returning from trance, that he was lying on a bed. "**I felt feelings of wanting to get away.**"

Keep in mind that a few sessions of trance may occur without the client having any memories or feelings being released. However, during those sessions deeper work is being done. During the next abreactive session, the client reported switching from being in the body of the child to seeing himself as a kid outside of his body from a fly on the wall perspective. From the child's perspective he felt the sensation of being held down. From the vantage point of seeing himself as a kid, he reported that child looked scared. Often the Host will feel the feelings of the child. This is an example of how the unconscious mind will dissociate the Host from the body when observing the pictures of the trauma.

During the next session, the client reported that he had a recollection of being at a friend's house. He felt small, felt numbness in his arm. "I couldn't get loose. Something wasn't right." With the next abreaction he reported being "in the experience." There were no pictures. He felt that he was held down and that he was lying on his back. "I wanted to get up." "I felt someone was sitting on top of me." After the next abreactive session, the client reported that he had a sense of who was abusing him. He reported that it was his friend's sixteen-year-old sister. He reported experiencing "weird feelings" during the trance. He felt guilty, a something was wrong feeling. "I wanted to tell someone."

The following session was significant. The client reported that after coming out of trance that he saw himself as a six- or so year-old kid, again from an out of body viewpoint. He was at his friend's house in the bedroom with the friend's two older sisters. "I was naked. They were teasing me. I felt humiliated and embarrassed."

Through a series of abreactions over time, this client was able to uncover and release the feelings, pictures, and sensations of an inappropriate childhood sexual experience. O was able to connect the recovered feelings of his abuse, the humiliation and embarrassment with the feelings he felt when he was acting out with the exposing behavior. It is interesting to point out that his target population was teenage girls around the age of sixteen, the same age as his abusers. I have worked with a number of clients who expose and that same dynamic prevails. It is a similar profile for the juvenile offender who acts out with a child whose age is the same age as he was at the time of his abuse, even though he doesn't remember his abuse.

After the abreactive work, the client continued in therapy for a number of months. Cognitive restructuring and future pacing helped process his trauma as well as to help him with expressing feelings and improving self-esteem. Long term follow up revealed that O had no further problems with exposing. He indicated that he had not even had an impulse to act out and he also reported that he couldn't believe that he had had such a problem. The client was not taking any psychotropic drugs. He was involved in a relationship and had found steady work.

CASE EXAMPLE

Map

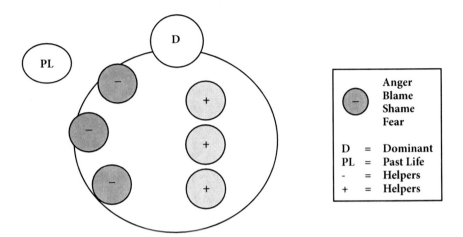

	Anger
⬤	Blame
	Shame
	Fear

D	=	Dominant
PL	=	Past Life
-	=	Helpers
+	=	Helpers

(The following is an example of a survivor who I treated when she was a teenager. She carried both unresolved sexual abuse trauma from this lifetime as well as an unresolved past life story. In retrospect, I learned much from this case. The healing process followed a clear schema. Hypnotic abreactions were used to resolve childhood sexual abuse. This is a good example in understanding the roles of the child helpers and other non-physical helpers in the healing process.)

A presented as a fairly out of control fourteen-year-old. Her school work had deteriorated, she had been involved in drugs and had relationships with abusive boyfriends. She experienced sleep disturbance and episodes of anger. A and her mother agreed to utilizing hypnosis as a therapeutic modality. Although A had some recollection of the abuse by her uncle around the age of seven, there was evidence that there had been earlier abuse for which she was amnestic.

Rather quickly I was able to communicate with her non-physical helpers. This was a unique case because the Dominant had become overwhelmed and needed assistance from what I had defined as the Oversoul. It is rare that I have a direct link to the Oversoul. Again, the abreactions involved in the healing process are not random uncontrolled releases of negative energy. Over the course of therapy, each helper emerges for purposes of healing in a clear defined order.

A was abused by a step-grandfather before age four. Her father abandoned her and she was once again sexual abused by her uncle around the age of seven. This is a good example of how the trauma was siphoned off into three helpers. The youngest helper held the fear, the middle helper held the blame and shame, "I'm bad" feelings, and the teenage helper held the rage. There was one incarnate who needed to let go of anger and shame. Through hypnosis, I was able to communicate with the child helpers and other non-physical helpers.

The teenage helper holding the anger was the first helper chosen to be healed. This helper held anger from the abuses and toward the father. The anger manifested in the Host during the teen years in hitting walls and lockers and sometimes boyfriends, as well as in hatred toward the father. The teenager emerged during the session and stated, "I'm the strong one. I have to come out to get relief." She reported that she holds the anger toward the father and the uncle. The teenage helper stated that A is a bitch. This is an example of how this helper often does not respect the Host and will often sabotage the Host's efforts toward progress.

As the therapy progressed, this helper felt better, released feelings, and became more forgiving. This helper would then take a positive role of helping the middle helper. Remember, ultimately once this helper returns to the center positive, it helps the Host with fortitude and backbone.

The second helper to be brought forth for healing was the four-year-old. This helper held the fear from the abuse by the step-grandfather. "I'm mad at grandma for not believing" (regarding the sexual abuse). This helper was a little afraid at first and asked for her mom. Her nickname was Peanut. I spent much time talking with her and helping her let go of the fear. Peanut was very good at drawing. "The pictures I draw show my feelings." Peanut would emerge with her eyes open, sit with her legs crossed and draw pictures with the pad and markers I gave to her. She would often draw beautiful flowers. The cover of this book was inspired by a drawing by this help-er depicting where the Host A was when I was talking to her. Interestingly, A would return from trance and say that she was flying with some bird toward a pyramid.

I was informed that the fear was being released while A was sleeping. Unfortunately this would cause the Host to suffer sleep disturbance during this phase of the healing process. A's mom reported that Peanut would come out at home. The mother un-derstood what was going on and handled it well. When Peanut told me about seeing her step-brother, she stated, "he's so big now." Again, this helper is in a time warp and was seeing the step-brother ten years in the future from her perspective.

During this phase of the therapy, the four-year-old released the fear. She told me that she would bring A happiness and her art. She stated, "Big people come to help. They love kids. They take feelings with them." She is referring to the external helpers who come and protect a vulnerable system. When asked where she is when she is not in the body talking with me, she responded, "I'm a little dot of energy. I see above everything when I'm not in the body."

It is fascinating to watch the healing progression of the helpers. Peanut emerged very fearful and progressed to feeling safe and displaying a sense of humor. Often when I was talking to her, she would tell me that "they" were working on the incarnate. When the fear was cleared, Peanut would go back inside to rest. I would no longer be able to communicate with her. During one of my last communications with her, Peanut told me to tell people, "if you hurt someone, you need to apologize."

The Oversoul had informed me that the system held an incarnate. This incarnate held blame and shame from a rape. I learned that she witnessed her children being abused. This energy was triggered by the abuse of the Host. I did communicate with the incarnate. She stated that they can't know their history. (*Sometimes helpers remember their previous life.*) "I'm from a time with long dresses, perhaps the colonial days." She reported that she had lots of kids. She felt blame for not being able to stop the abuse of A. I did have a few conversations with her. Most of the negative energy was released through abreactions when I was talking to the incarnate.

Remember, an incarnate either exists out or stays as a helper. If the incarnate stays, it must resolve its karmic story. Even when an incarnate exists, much of the negative emotions have to be released. The incarnate informed me, "I had to do that to the uncle to save A," referring to oral sex.

When the time was right, a session was used to help this incarnate exit into the light. The Dominants call it a "sphere of healing." They report that healing can be done outside of physical reality, but that they are not allowed to talk to me about that process.

The last part of the self to be healed was the middle helper. This helper is associated with the heart chakra. The teenage helper was cleared first in order to help the middle helper. Often with survivors, this middle helper is difficult to heal. It's the part of the self that holds blame, shame, guilt, and the memory of the abuse.

This helper emerged through the trance. I realized that she could not talk but was able to write. She wrote, "I am scared, can you help me? I have only been out one time. I hate myself for not being able to help A. My cousin told me if I did those things, my Uncle would love me as much as he loved her." This helper held shame that was released over a number of sessions. The Host would have to feel these feelings as they were being released. Eventually this helper began to speak. The mother reported that A had been talking in her sleep. Believe it or not, the Dominant reported that the teenage helper would teach the middle helper to talk while the Host was sleeping.

The blame and shame held by the middle helper has profound affects on the conscious Host's self-esteem. One can see through this example the importance of resolving these feelings. Once these feelings are resolved, this helper returns to a positive role and consequently the Host will begin to feel better about herself. The middle helper began to laugh, feel better and was able to return to its positive role in the system.

This is a good case example of the systematic release of the traumatic material held by various helpers. It is clear that before any cognitive restructuring can take place, the blocked off feelings have to be resolved.

This client is now in her twenties and is doing well. The following is a testimony that she recently sent me.

"When I was a teenager I had major problems. I was into drugs and sleeping with different partners. I was an exotic dancer at a very young age and I never trusted anyone including my mother. After awhile my mother's hands were tied and she was not sure what to do. She decided after a lot of thinking to look into getting me some help. She took me to a couple of doctors who decided to put me on drugs and figured it would help me, but all I did was get high off of them. After a while things got worse and I began to blackout and did not know who or where I was. It started to affect my grades before but by then I was just not doing anything. Then we went to Bill Jump who we heard through word of mouth was very open and did not rely on drugs to fix everything. I began to see him about once or twice a week and started to notice an improvement in my life. He started to help me with my meditation and helped me to improve my concentration. I would have a very hard time at school and was very afraid of everything and the second I would enter his office, I would relax like I was entering another world where I didn't have any fears. After a while my grades were improving and I began to trust people and was not afraid to leave my house."

Patient A

CASE EXAMPLE

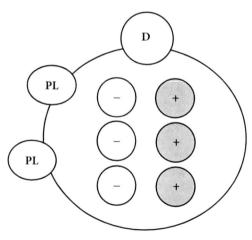

D	=	Dominant
PL	=	Past Life
-	=	Helpers
+	=	Helpers

(This is an example of a young woman with two incarnates who manifested in childhood with rather dramatic symptoms. There was no evidence of any abuse in this lifetime.)

This is a young woman in her twenties who, when I first met her, was finishing her four year degree. She grew up in an intact family with no history of childhood traumas or overwhelming stressors. A former colleague of mine knew the family well. The family reportedly was baffled by P's symptoms. Upon meeting her, she reported that she had always believed that her symptoms were from a past life phenomenon and that she thought that hypnosis would be helpful for her.

She described a history of obsessive compulsive behaviors involving hand washing around the age of five. Around the age of eleven, she reported that she began "clawing" at her hands until they bled. That behavior continued until her early twenties. She also described specific sexual triggers developing as a young woman.

As a young girl, P remembered being closed off to affection. She never felt good enough and placed high expectations on herself. She also felt responsible for making things right. P reported that she kept her symptoms a secret. She described a reoccurring dream involving a stone stairwell and a young girl who was wearing "boat like shoes."

The client was eager to begin the hypnotic abreactive work. In fact she began to experience abreactions right away. Remember that the Host is either in Alpha trance where they can report to me what they are experiencing or they are in Theta trance, a deeper suspended state of trance, where the experiences are reported after coming out of trance.

P's first abreaction was one of feeling "out of control," nauseous, and held down as though she was lying in a bed. The next major abreaction, she reported was "leaving her body." She couldn't move or breathe. She described seeing screaming faces in the darkness. At the next session, the abreaction yielded a stabbing feeling in her hand. She felt dirty and reported feeling the presence of an adolescent.

Remember, conscious cognitive work is done each session to process the abreaction. Her symptoms during the week are discussed. The feelings being released do permeate the consciousness during the week in emotional episodes without a trigger and in vivid emotional dreams. The client is reassured that these emotional states are temporary although necessary for the healing to take place.

During the next abreactive session P saw a tall red haired nineteen or twenty-year-old malnourished young woman who appeared to be afraid. Understand that P was connected through the trance with her incarnate that we will call Elaina. Elaina said, "Look what they did to my hands, they are a bloody wreck." P learned that Elaina was from Ireland, perhaps from the 1600's. She conveyed to P that she wasn't ready to talk about her abuse and torture. She felt responsible for not protecting her family and others. P informed me that Elaina cannot forgive herself. Her actions led to harm to others. P said that a "higher form" of Elaina sent a message to her that she needs to find the path back to herself.

P informed me at the next session that she had felt sad all week. Note that during some trance sessions, the Host is disconnected from the work. Clients return from the trance work and report that nothing was going on and in fact that they enjoyed the peacefulness and contentment of a favorite place. I assure them that work is being done at a deeper level.

At the next session, P returned from trance with the awareness that Elaina would stay as a helper. Remember, incarnates have to resolve their karmic stories in order to stay as a helper. Otherwise their negative energy will continue to intrude on the Host's life. Elaina carries sorrow and regret as well as self-blame. You can see how Elaina's unresolved feelings had affected P in feeling that her mistakes affect others. P learned that Elaina's family was killed and that when she was raped and tortured, they broke her hands.

Over time, Elaina would let go of her feelings and remain as a helper for P. She would help her with issues surrounding fairness and justice.

Somewhat unexpectedly, P returned to the next trance session reporting seeing a five or six-year-old catatonic child. P learned that she is the sensitive constricted part. We learned that her name is Lydia and that she doesn't want to be touched by anyone. This can explain why P was so emotionally detached as a child. We learned that Lydia was violated by her father and that her mother had died when she was very young.

During the next trance session, P described feeling like her hands were in cold water. P learned that Lydia drowned at age eight in a creek behind the house. P felt that this was not a suicide but a release. It is difficult for us to understand that "higher authorities" may make a decision that is in the best interest of the system, that the system be shut down.

We learned that Lydia lived on an estate. She never felt safe in her house. She holds the emotion of fear. P sensed that the time frame was probably the late 1800's. Lydia wants to stay as a helper. Her gift to the Host would be empathy with young children.

During the next session P reported having sleeping problems all week. She dreamt of Lydia's house, a yellow Victorian. P returned from the trance with the sense that Lydia would have to exit out. "Lydia needs to go into the light."

Keep in mind that around age three or four, fear emerged in P's life. She was afraid to go outside. Given her family dynamics, there was no reason for her to have such fear. P remembers believing that if she didn't do the right thing, then bad things would happen. P talked about being good at hiding her emotions and compulsions.

P presented to the next session stating that she had had dreams about Lydia. When P returned from the trance, she said that a boat came to pick up Lydia. Whether this was metaphoric or not, typically a group of helpers and protectors come to assist the incarnate in existing physical reality. P was left with the notion that we need to become like the light. The sense is that some incarnates have to exit out because the negative energy is so great that it would be too much for the Host to work through.

P would continue to attend a number of sessions to help process and integrate the work that was done. She has moved on to graduate school and currently has a healthy relationship.

(I have attempted in Part II to define the world of non-physical helpers that has present-ed to me over the last two decades. I have learned from them that they are here to learn lessons as well as to guide and protect us during this incarnation. Hopefully the case examples emphasize the importance of resolving the underlying stressors and trauma in order for us, the conscious Host, to move toward integration and wholeness. Otherwise, the unresolved stories from both this lifetime and from other lifetimes will continue to persist in symptoms and manifestations.

One of my teenage client's Dominant informed me that the job of the helpers is to help the Host become responsible, respectful, loving, and caring. The helpers also bring traits that they give to the Host such as problem solving, speaking up, a sense of humor, the soft side of love, art, math and reading. For me, this explains the phenomena of the "prodi-gious savant." Client A, who you just read about, had a helper who could draw beauti-ful flowers that the Host could not draw. This is why it is so important for the helpers to resolve the negative energy so they can return to a positive role in the system and give the Host these gifts and traits.)

Our Energy System

"To work with the chakras is to heal ourselves of old constricting patterns."

Anodea Judith

I would like to add one more section about the energy centers/chakras that encom-pass our physical bodies. I tell my clients that we are surrounded by a bubble of energy that is often referred to as our aura. Particularly with my clients who do the hypnotic/abreactive work, I inform them of the seven energy centers, also referred to as chakras, which run from the base of the spine to the top of the head. These energy centers process and store all of our experiences and carry the spiritual forces that flow through us. When this energy flows through us, it creates what we call emotions.

Years ago I learned about the chakra/energy system from a friend who was study-ing massage *(I will use chakra and energy center interchangeably)*. I would check my client's chakras while they were conscious and would often find that some were not spinning. I would come to learn that locked up chakras were correlated to the blocked off trauma. Dominants would suggest that I check the chakras while the client was in trance. I learned that our emotions are held in the second, third, and fourth centers. I have added this section to clarify that the soul helpers live in the chakras during this incarnation. Keep in mind that my drawings reflect the "child helpers." For example, the middle helpers tend to be connected to the fourth chakra, the heart center. This helper is assigned to deal with the blame, shame and upset feelings that are dissociated when the Host is around the ages of five to nine. When the negative emotions are resolved, this helper returns to the heart center.

For me, understanding the chakra patterns while the client is in the trance states as well as in a conscious state, has allowed me the privilege of understanding what is being processed at the deeper level. There have been a number of patterns that consistently show up as I do the hypnotic/abreactive work. Simply stated, a counter-clockwise spin typically means that negative energy is being released. A clockwise spin means that positive energy is coming into the client. During the course of one trance session, the client may have a number of patterns where their heart center is open with a counterclockwise spin. The Dominant is either preparing and or releasing upset feelings at this time. A second pattern follows in which the sixth and seventh chakras open simultaneously. Dominants have informed me that negative images and perceptions are being deleted during this cycle. Alternating with these patterns, cycles of positive energy are pumped into the client. Often the client may return from trance without remembering feeling feelings or having any memories processed. I inform my clients that often the work is done at a deeper level and to watch out for mood swings or vivid dreams during the week.

I don't want to go into a dissertation about our energy centers. Perhaps in a subsequent book for therapists on more technical considerations regarding hypnotic/abreactive work, I will go into more detail on these matters. For further explanations regarding chakras/energy centers, read *Anatomy of the Spirit* by Caroline Myss, and *Wheels of Life* by Anodea Judith.

The bottom line is that we are about energy. The healing process is about achieving spiritual balance.

"There is a wellspring of knowledge,

the essence from which everything flows."

S's Dominant

Part III

The following is the case that inspired me to write this book. It is a complicated case study that involves all of the variables that have presented to me over the years in doing the unconscious work. This client who will be referred to as S has a high level Dominant who was able to communicate with me. As you will learn, the following case involves both traumas from this lifetime as well as carry-over energy from previous times. As I described in Part II, all of us carry a conglomerate of soul helpers, including the Dominant (our guiding force), six child helpers, and a team of external helpers. This client is not a Multiple Personality. Not every Dominant is able to communicate verbally. Everyone's helpers aren't all able to come through the physical realm and communicate with me. Often I can communicate with the non-physical realm through ideomotor signals. My awareness of chakra patterns also helps me understand what emotions are being addressed in the healing process.

I look at S's case as a gift that came to me at a time when I needed some validation for what I was concluding with regard to the healing of childhood wounds. Many cases had come before, as well as since, that have exposed me to the world of Dominants, helpers and protectors as well as carry-over energy. The overwhelming theme, both from a psychological and spiritual perspective, is that the healing of childhood wounds is imperative in order for the individuals to move toward their power. For all of us, life is a journey toward wholeness.

Refer to S's map below to follow how the power within us helps us resolve our childhood wounds safely and tolerably over time.

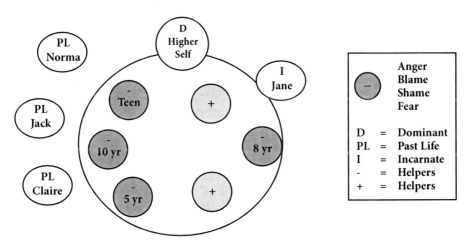

S'S CASE STUDY

Session

I received a referral for counseling actually for H, S's husband. H was ordered into counseling following an incident of domestic dispute. Initially I began to work with H on an individual basis with intermittent sessions including S for marital communication. The process moved toward preparing H for trance work to access the unconscious mind in order to resolve the underlying anger.

During an initial session of trance with H, I permitted S to be in the room because of H's nervousness and the fact the S had done some meditation and felt that her presence in the room would help H feel safe and secure.

Something interesting occurred during a very light technique of asking H to imagine a hallway with doors and go to one of the doors and open it up and see what's in the room. *(What is seen in the room is a reflection of what is going on inside you.)* S had sat back and closed her eyes during my focus with H. When I asked H to open the door, I heard a tearful voice coming from S say, "I can't open the door," I'm scared. From my experience with trance work, I knew that I had accessed a child helper in S. I asked her Dominant to help the child feel safe and to go back inside.

I made a decision to focus the sessions on S because it was obvious that some childhood feelings were close to the surface. One could interpret the child coming through as the Dominant sending a message that S needed to do some unconscious work and was ready to clear some feelings away. I continued to work with H on an individual basis.

Session

The following session S readily went into trance and I was able to access her Dominant. It is usually the exception that the Dominant can talk through the Host's voice but in this case, the Dominant was able to verbally communicate. I learned that it was the eight-year-old who could not open the door. The eight-year-old split off at the time that the father was killed. I learned that when S was eight, the Navy authorities came to the house and informed the family that her father was killed. S was at home and aware of what was going on. It makes sense that her Dominant dissociated a lot of this trauma, and that the eight-year-old helper was called out to help hold some of this stressful material.

During this session, I learned from the Dominant that beside the eight-year-old helper, S had a five-year-old, a ten-year-old and a teenage helper that needed to come out to deal with the childhood stressors. It would not be a teenager helper who would be destructive and or overtly aggressive like I often see with clients who have been sexually and or physically abused. What was interesting was that the Dominant allowed me to talk with the child helpers during this first session. Usually it takes a lot of preparation for the Dominant to allow me, the external helper, to communicate with the helpers.

The five-year-old helper was needed to help S when her father was in Vietnam. S stayed with her mother and grandparents. The five-year-old told me that her grandmother scares her, that they drink, and that they get mad at her mom. She misses her dad who is in Vietnam.

As discussed in the preface, the teenager comes out to help with the anger that is too much for the child to handle. The teenager said that the grandparents drank and told the mother that S and her brother lied about things. The teenager typically deals with the issue of fairness. She did admit that she explodes sometimes.

The eight-year-old holds the trauma around dad's death. She did not want to talk. The ten-year-old came out and proclaimed that she was the smart one. "I skipped the fourth grade." She said that she missed her friends. The ten-year-old said that she takes care of her brother because mom has a problem.

The ten-year-old came out to deal with all the chaos in moving etc. After the father died. The family was uprooted. The mother was not there emotionally. The ten-year-old would be the one that held a lot of self-esteem issues and mom issues.

The following are the summaries of each session. Refer to the map on page 93 in order to follow the progress of the healing process.

Session

The eight-year-old was sent out by the Dominant to talk. She said that "daddy is dead. I don't know where mom is. We are at some people's house." The eight-year-old portrayed a sense that she and her dad were mad at each other prior to his leaving the night that he was killed. "I didn't kiss him. I wasn't a good girl." The eight-year-old described an incident when dad got mad at her for not being able to count the money.

Sometimes it is difficult not to get enthralled with asking questions of the Dominant. It is important to remain on the task of being the external helper toward the goal of clearing away blocked off trauma.

Session

The Dominant stated on this day that S needs to clear things away. "I send her to Egypt during the trance." S does report that she sits on a pyramid in her imagination.

The Dominant stated that S is in a fantasy world. S wants things perfect. She reported that S needs to call on her. This notion was brought up often which supports the need for us to meditate and get in touch with our Dominant.

The Dominant asked me to encourage S to meditate. The Dominant stated that energy in weak systems is absorbed into the universe. Most of the Dominants have been around for a long time. "Humans are not equipped to know the future. Strong Dominants recall past and future events. We can't rebel otherwise we will live a hopeless life."

Session

At this point the focus is clearing away the anger held by the teenager. The Dominant informs me that the teenager is still holding some anger toward the mom. The teenager helps S deal with anger. She is the helper who has strength and fortitude. "The soul cries for justice in the teenager."

At the beginning of the session I always ask S how she is doing. One can't lose sight of the Host and all of their manifestations and issues that arise as you do the work. Remember that as the blocked off emotions surface, the Host may feel these feelings even more. At this point in the therapy, S would often talk about how she needs more attention from H and how he is always working and is selfish.

One can see how the perceived selfishness of H relates to the thought that mom was selfish. In other words H can trigger the feelings from mom being selfish. It is as though the past and present know no difference. This is the core of symbiotic relationships in that partners don't realize that they are triggering the unresolved emotions and hurt feelings from childhood situations. When it happens in the present moment, the person holding the feelings does not at that time connect the triggered feelings to a similar childhood conflict.

The teenager came out and stated that mom was selfish. She said that, "S's mother feels like a bad mother after the father died."

During this session the eight-year-old needed to come out to express some feelings. The eight-year-old came out and was able to talk. I always asked her how she was feeling, what she was aware of and what she needed to talk about. Remember the eight-year-old is holding the traumatic feelings about dad dying. She said, "Why did he leave. Did he love us? I have to be like daddy for B, the brother. People tease me about my name. Dad told me to beat them up. B is fun to play with. Mom is OK. She is very busy. She likes me better now."

The ten-year-old needed to talk. It is important to see that this older helper would hold a lot of self-esteem issues. She said that she was fat. "I was made to feel ashamed. Mom was terrible after dad died. She lost her purpose. She didn't like me. She was jealous because I'm the intelligent one."

Note that with many cases the older helper who comes out to help has to deal with the aftermath of the trauma. In this case the ten-year-old helper was the last one to clear away and was very difficult to help to feel good about herself. Note that the ten-year-old ate to feel good.

Session

S reported that H needs to respect her. She feels that she is taken for granted. S was feeling frustrated. The Dominant stated that the teenager gets S to see things for what they are. The Dominant is not letting S go off. The Dominant often talked about the ability to control the physical responses.

The Dominant reported that she can consciously control the anger. "That's enough" is told to the teenager. "I make her stay down." The Dominant allows certain behaviors to manifest.

S's Dominant will often talk about deeper issues of philosophy, how energy and light are involved, as well as the quantum physics aspects of non-physical reality. The Dominant stated that the Pre-Christian, Roman era of the western culture was intuitive. The Western culture has been in an un-enlightened period since the aforementioned era. The Dominant talked about Christ's notion of totally believing *(referring to religious faith)* as an important concept.

Session

This session started with a conversation with the Dominant. "H has inner turmoil. He is unsure of himself." The Dominant reported getting along with his Dominant. "H needs to clear away some anger from his father."

The Dominant stated that S needs to finish clearing away the blocked off emotions from the parts of the self. The Dominant reported being there along with the child helpers from the beginning. "If the Dominant and the parts leave, the body dies. Dominants need to match up at an energy level, with regard to relationships." The Dominant said that mortals are very primal in their relationships.

Session

S reported that her sleep was down. She was feeling physically awkward. She had been lashing out with her anger.

The Dominant was accessed through trance.

Keep in mind that the Host does not hear the conversations while they are in trance. S would report that she became aware of the content of the conversations later in the week.

The Dominant stated that the brain remembers everything. The conscious mind has to react to past flashbacks coming out as well as filter the present information. The Dominant is not always in control of the triggers. The Dominant is always pushing to keep things under control. The mind can desert the body. I believe I asked the Dominant about comas. The response was that the Dominant has to divert energy to the spinal cord for rejuvenation. The body has to rest.

The Dominant noted that they are learning also. Prior to entering S, the Dominant was in a 150 year dormancy period. The Dominant reported traveling in space. In 1828, the Dominant was a protector for one of S's ancestors.

During this session the Dominant wanted me to talk to the eight-year-old. The Dominant said the eight-year-old got up the night the Navy personnel came to the house to inform the mother that the father was found dead. The eight-year-old said that she saw pictures of dad. "They thought I was asleep. They took us away to strangers. Nobody liked me. Dad couldn't protect me no more. The funeral was a blur, everybody was looking at us. We went on an airplane to Texas. I miss him."

I talk to the child, listen, empathize, let her know i will help her feel better so she can go back inside to the safe place with the other helpers. I help her understand that she does not have to hold these scary feelings, that it is OK for S to know these experiences and feelings and that everything in the future will be OK.

The Dominant talked about the infinity symbol as the pattern of energy, the center being death, the black hole.

Session

The Dominant said that, **"We take our knowledge, wisdom and peace with us. Our consciousness dies."** During this session the eight-year-old had an abreaction. She saw her mother with her face in her hands. She told us that there was an accident. Dad was gone. The eight-year-old said I didn't want mom after dad died. "I can't learn from her. People took us away from our mother. She needed us. I didn't know how mom was. The people from the church, we didn't know them very well. They felt sorry for us. At the funeral, mom said I couldn't touch dad."

Session

At this point the angry teenager is clear. Remember when the teenager goes back inside, she will help S with backbone and fortitude. We are working on the eight-year-old material, but aware of the need to comfort the five-year-old. There is also a ten-year-old.

The mind can separate the five and eight-year-old. I remember during the same sessions I would talk to both the five and eight-year-old at different times. The five-year-old did not know that dad had died. She perceived him as being away. Remember the time warp theory. The Dominant said that when the five-year-old is cleared away, she will go back inside and eventually be assimilated to current reality. Telling the five-year-old that dad was dead is a future concept for her. The Dominant said that the five-year-old is in her own reality.

The eight-year-old was sent out to talk. She said that she was scared. "Dad died and mom changed. They bought a different car. We had to live with the grandparents. They were mean. Mom gets mad too much. She hits me with her shoe."

The reader can see just in the eight-year-old the overwhelming feelings resulting from the loss of the father, moving, and mom changing.

The eight-year-old went on to say, "Mom wants me to be different, to be her friend. She wants me to be perfect like my cousins. I'm not good enough. I have to share a room with my younger brother. Grand-dad scared me. He talked about dad. They yelled when I was younger. Mom chased her new boyfriend with a broom. He was nice."

Session

S reported that H is getting on her nerves. He doesn't make me feel loved and cared for. She reported that he is more like a friend.

The Dominant was accessed and stated that the eight-year-old is upset. She won't let S sleep. She has a fear of dying. *(Fear from child helper can interrupt sleep.)*

The Dominant reported cycles matter to her. "Time has no relevance. It is my job to help with physical reality to move on in non-physical reality. The therapist helps systems evolve in physical reality. We are here to learn life lessons. When we die we are integrated with other energies. The unconscious heals the mind through dreams, which are simulated during the REM sleep."

At this time the Dominant introduced the fact that S has a past life energy from the Titanic. S has a fear and aversion to deep water and a fear of drowning.

Session

Remember, the feelings that are being addressed in the child helper often pervade the Host during the healing process.

S said that her life is a mess. The Dominant was accessed. "The conscious mind can't suppress or control the child's feelings."

The Dominant and I discussed the need for the eight-year-old to let go of dad. It was agreed that the child was ready to talk to dad and let him know how she felt.

The Dominant discussed the fact that S was pulled over by the police and went off. It was clear that the eight-year-old was triggered. The Dominant said that the teenager tried to protect the eight-year-old.

The eight-year-old was brought forth through the trance. I asked her if she was upset when the police talked to S. She said that she was bad, I made it happen. "I don't like the police. They are mean. The police came and told mommy that daddy killed himself." The eight-year-old said that she saw a picture on the coffee table of daddy hanging. "I don't think that he is going. I don't know why he won't come back. Dad doesn't love me. He didn't come back. I made mommy cry. I'm sorry I didn't give him (dad) a goodbye kiss."

At this point I got the eight-year-old to imagine that the father was there and that it was OK for her to share her upset, hurt and angry feelings because dad would be grateful and would understand.

(These techniques only work with the permission of the Dominant. I can't make anything happen unless the time it right.)

"I don't think you loved me. You were more concerned about your job. You wanted me to be a boy. You were hard on me. You made me do different things. You spanked me with a belt when I carved a hole in the desk. You ruined my life by leaving. Nobody else will take care of me. I needed you. Don't go away."

At this point I got the eight-year-old to float into the body of the father to see and feel how the father felt and perceived her. This interaction seems to be very effective in releasing feelings. The child helper released the feelings, felt better, and consequently the Host benefited.

The eight-year-old relayed the message that dad said that he loved her, and he wanted her to be happy. He told her to take care of her brother and mother and that he was alright.

The eight-year-old was asked to go back into herself. I asked her how she was doing and reinforced that everything would be OK. She said that she felt better.

Session

During this session, the Dominant suggested that I speak with the five-year-old. This helper did not hear the previous conversation. The unconscious mind is able to put child helpers who are at different development levels in separate compartments in the mind.

The five-year-old came out and said that the grandparents were mean. "They say that they love me but they are mean. They say that the devil will get me. That's bad. They are mean to my mom. I don't understand. It hurts mom's feelings. Dad is in the war. Dad is on a boat. He told me that he has to help people be free. I talked to him on the telephone. I miss my blanket. He gave it to a Vietnam girl. I don't understand that S doesn't like herself. People tease us about our name."

Remember that I give feedback and empathy to the child during all of the conversations.

Session

As usual, once the Host is in trance, I begin the work by communicating with the Dominant. Remember, the Dominant knows how the child helpers are doing and knows why S is having certain conscious problems.

It is interesting that we often use the concept of clearing away. The Dominant will often tell me that the child inside is not clear, but that there is still some darkness around her. Remember, the child that is holding blocked off trauma can only go back inside when it is clear, free of any negative energy.

The Dominant stated that moral decisions are placed by humans. "There are two emotions, fear and love. There is neither good nor bad, but there just is. Love is the most powerful emotion. We too often unload guilt on someone else. We also place our faith in outdated concepts."

The Dominant had told S that her plant should be brought in. Sure enough it was stolen. The Dominant knew what was going to happen. "We have a different view of time and space. I gave S a feeling about the plant."

Remember, the Dominant communicates to us through hunches, gut feelings, and intuitions.

The Dominant said that the eight-year-old fears change. After the father died, S's life changed drastically. Here is an example of how the Host is affected by the child's feelings. S has trouble making decisions. She is preoccupied with the what-if syndrome, as well as having a fear of change and a fear of losing mom too. The Dominant said that the eight-year-old gave herself up to help the mother and to protect the brother. The eight-year-old is overwhelmed with growing up too fast.

Often it is important to get this important information from the Dominant regarding the child, so those issues can be addressed appropriately.

Session

The Dominant informed me that the eight-year-old feels shame. No one will love her. The eight-year-old was sent out to talk. She said that a girl in school picked on her and made fun of her name. I ask the child to imagine that mom was there and to say what she wanted to say to her. "I don't want you to be mad at me. I wanted you to like me. You didn't listen to me. You didn't want me to have feelings. There is something the matter with me."

The Dominant said that feelings that come into consciousness can't always be controlled. The Dominant said that, "parts are not more powerful than me. I can shut them down which manifests in the Host a regressive state, a break down, acute depression, and or a blackout."

I have learned that Dominant's have to let the parts express their emotions in conscious reality in order to get relief. Otherwise the Host will have more sleep disturbances and panic attacks, as well as physiological problems such as stomach problems, if the dissociated feelings are not released periodically through the physical realm.

Session

We attempted to get the eight-year-old to float into mom but she was not ready.

It is important to bring up the past life concept. In asking about any other parts inside, the Dominant brought up the fact that there was a carry-over energy from someone on the Titanic who had died. The Dominant thought that the only problem this caused S was that she had an aversion to deep water and that when it was time we would deal with this energy. I learned that he was helping the ten-year-old. The Dominant had given me his full name which is on the list of passengers on the Titanic. I will refer to him as Jack. (*Note that this session was prior to any talk that I know of regarding making a movie about the Titanic.*)

An important insight for me is that issues present from your client when you, as the helper, both believe and are ready to deal with them. I had been familiar with Roger Woolger's work with past life resolutions. It is Wayne Dyer's concept of when you believe it, you will see it. Now I will typically ask the Dominant in my mapping process if there is any external energy that is attached to a child or who comes and goes that needs to be resolved or dealt with. I have begun to believe clients with aversions, phobias, flashbacks to unfamiliar places and even physical symptoms not explained by medicine, may be experiencing symptoms relating to past life phenomena.

Session

During this meeting, the Dominant reported that Dominants are at different levels. It was implied that there are too many people and not enough Dominants to go around. People are walking around in their consciousness trying to solve their problems.

The Dominant reported that the eight-year-old is doing better with regard to the father. The Dominant went on to say that S was emotional as a child and that the mother couldn't understand her. The eight and five-year-old don't know each other. The Dominant said they don't overlap on each other inside, but do in consciousness. The eight-year-old still believes that she can't do anything right.

Session

The Dominant needed me to talk to the five-year-old. The five-year-old said that they had to wear party hats. Her mom cut her hair and she felt ugly. "Dad made me feel like my feelings mattered."

The work is moving to an emphasis on the five-year-old helper.

Session

The Dominant said that it is important for the Host to have a relationship where the Dominants match up. It has been my theory that our Dominant allows us to enter symbiotic relationships so that we can be reminded of the feelings that we have inside and that we need to resolve these feelings. The problem is that if we don't resolve these feelings then we keep getting in similar relationships. Dominants have told me that they will allow the Host to keep repeating the symbiotic relationships until they learn a lesson.

The five-year-old said that she is not a nice girl. "I have mean thoughts about my brother. People who make me mad, I want to stomp on them and kill them. My mom got mad at my brother for getting dirty. My brother ate dirt." (Brother 18 mo.) The five-year-old made a comment about going to hell. "My brother is cute. I love him. He is whining. Mom says that he is sick. He looks fat. Today is dad's birthday. I need to call him. Dad is away. We live with our grandparents. I have trouble sleeping because of scary things. I feel alone."

One can see how this child's feelings can superimpose onto S's consciousness in terms of sleeping problems, feeling alone and not getting enough attention from H.

The reader needs to make a mental note of the five-year-old having fear, issues with the devil and the fear of going to Hell.

Session

The Dominant felt that something happened to scare the five-year-old. The Dominant says that they can't stop the Host from seeking conscious gratification. Humans seek out humans. The Dominant said that she counsels S.

An important reminder is that we need to meditate to listen to our Dominants. Again, the Dominant talks to us through hunches, gut feelings and intuitions.

The five-year-old came out and said that her ten-year-old uncle told her that she was ugly. "He tells me to bite people and crawl under the house with the snakes." Referring to the Dominant and me, she said, "I don't understand you and S's protector." The Dominant had wondered whether the car accident that S had been in was an issue.

I asked the five-year-old about this. She said, "A lady hit us. I hit the window. I had to go to the hospital." Another incident was when she said that she fell and cut her chin. "Some girls tied me up and left me." She also said that she fell and hurt herself at the Grandparent's house and cut her eye.

It was interesting that the five-year-old said that she was aware that her feelings about the accident make S feel that she is going to have an accident. This is quite significant in terms of how the blocked off feelings manifest in the Host as a preoccupation.

The five-year-old said, "Me and my brother are not going to be good people when we grew up."

Remember after the communication with the child helper, they go back inside and I communicate with the Dominant about how the communication went, as well as how that particular helper is doing. I may then talk to the Dominant about the next session's strategy. When the Host returns to consciousness, I certainly discuss how they are feeling. I let the Host know what particular emotion or scenario is being worked on so they can be aware of the particular feelings that may emerge during the week.

Session

During this session, the Dominant informed me that the five-year-old did not feel loved. The five-year-old came out and said that she is not loved. "I bite people. I bit a kid in the nursery. It feels good to bite."

During the conversation with the five-year-old, the child became very afraid and reported that there was fear around her and that she didn't know what it was. She said that she saw fire and that she was going to hell. She said that somebody burnt her and that she was swallowed up by the fire. They said that she was a witch.

The child was sent back inside. The Dominant reported that she knows that the five-year-old is holding fear but doesn't know specifically what that fear was about.

The Dominant reported that the fear and the fire were seen. The Dominant believed that the fear and the fire was about a past life energy who was persecuted for being a witch.

The Dominant reported that the family was involved in Craft (witchcraft) in the past but that it was suppressed for 150 years. The conversation ended with the Dominant wanting to learn about the fire and fear and believing that it was a past life that was attached to the child. This could explain why the five-year-old had so much fear.

The sense is that the negative energy held by the past life is attached to the five-year-old. The past life energy attaches to the helper with the same frequency energy. In this case it is fear.

The Dominant stated that the child feels cruelty. "Deep sadness turns to the cruelty that we see in children, just as frustration turns to aggression." This cruelty would often come out in S's arguments with others in her current reality.

Session

The Dominant reported that there is a memory of an ancestor who was persecuted for Witchcraft named Claire. The five-year-old holds the fear. The abreaction that the child described was the hallucination of the drug that was given to this person (Belladonna or mushroom) when she was burned at the stake. The Dominant said that this energy was earth bound and has tagged along. **"It is integrated energy from another life held for 300 hundred years."**

The Dominant said that our body is a shell. "The soul and energy exists on a deeper level. Some souls may be newer which means that there is not as much energy stored."

The Dominant said this type of energy is carried through the DNA. The Dominant reported that they see all, forward and backward. The Dominant was trying to assure the five-year-old that she was not burnt. The five-year-old said that she doesn't like it when others cause people to die. "People don't like me. I'm not good. Mom and Grand-mom don't believe me. I'm mean sometimes, I'm angry. My parents spanked me."

The five-year-old said that she is afraid to choose things. "People will be mad at me. I make S have trouble deciding things. I'm not as pretty as the other kids."

"The lady" that the five-year-old refers to turns out to be Claire, energy that we learn later has come through S's ancestral line. Claire is attached to the five-year-old. That is why the five-year-old sees and feels her trauma.

The five-year-old said, "That lady is telling me not to do things. She doesn't trust. She doesn't want to leave into the light."

Remember, incarnates either stay as helpers or have to exit. If they are allowed to stay, they have to resolve their unresolved story.

Session

Note that work is being done all week to prepare for the abreaction. Child helpers are being talked to and the Host is feeling feelings through dreams or flashbacks during the week. I'm always amazed when on any given session the child or Host is not ready to clear away any feelings, but the Dominant says that next week we will begin to do that. The following week feelings are released through the Host during trance. I'm not sure what the Dominant is doing during the week but obviously something is going on to prepare the abreactions.

In the case of Claire, the first past energy to emerge in s, she was afraid to let go. She was made to believe during her life that death was a punishment, so letting go was frightening. It is important to believe that we go to a higher level and that our soul moves on.

Upon arriving at her session, S reported that she felt surreal. She reported that her "outer shell was bombarded." She said she felt a sense of trouble, of letting go. She said she felt tense, agitated and had a headache.

Everything had been prepared for Claire to exit into the light during this session.

The Dominant was accessed through the trance state. The Dominant said there was an energy field that had come down to help. I became quiet and allowed the Dominant to help with the freeing of this energy. The Dominant said that something was happening. She said that she was freeing the hands of Claire. I observed the physical body breathing more heavily during this process. The body appeared to be going through a stressful situation. After a period of time, the Dominant would say that the energy was released. The Dominant said that feelings are not usually felt but that there was an intense focus. The Dominant reported doing this before. The Dominant said that the five-year-old witnessed the release. (*Release is referred to as the exiting of Claire's energy into the light.*) Claire was described as having red hair. The energy field slowly moved away into the light. It's all about energy. The energy field was described as a round liquid ball. The Dominant described the energy leaving as similar to a car stopping fast.

I was asked to speak with the five-year-old. "She said that the lady (Claire) told her about the bad stuff. I still feel her. She's far away. She's going to help me now. She's thanking me and S's Good Part, (the Dominant). She feels much better. She says that she is free and expansive." The five-year-old said that the energy that came to take her was pretty. It looked funny. I could see two or three entities inside of the energy. They told her that it was time to go. I feel good now. She said that the lady is telling me that she feels free and expanded and that comes from the unconscious. Life is contraction and death is expansion. She told the child that this is hard to conquer on the physical level. "We need to meditate to expand. The freedom is in the mind. The body is never free." She said that they made her afraid to die. The child said that she did bad things because of the fear. The child was left with the knowledge that this lady was fine now. The child went back inside. The Dominant said that S was not aware of this energy release. S was traveling in an ALPHA state in a spiral.

After S was brought back to conscious reality, she described that while she was in trance she was above the chair, looking at the top of her own head which had a blue grid on top of it.

Session

During the next session, S was more aware of what happened during the previous session. She described a ball of blue white light that was very bright. She described a computer grid. The ball of light was an energy field. S felt from this energy field a sense of, "we're here, and we're taking over." S said she felt no fear but a sense of balance. S described a combination of fear and a feeling of non-judgement and freedom. S said that she was in awe. She did feel a sense that something left, something was pulled away. S said that she was not afraid to die. "I'm now aware of the freedom and expansion at the higher level."

During this session the Dominant reported that there is an oncoming shift in the universe. "The universe is becoming less dense thus more particles, energy information, can move through. Every 2000 to 2500 hundred years there is a paradigm shift."

In this case I was not needed to help the persecuted lady resolve anything. Sometimes the past energy gets relief by talking to me about unresolved feelings. Sometimes you need to take them back to the time where they were hurt, or even hurt someone else, in order to resolve these feelings so that they can feel free to go into the light.

Session

An important issue was brought up by the Dominant. It was said that things inside were good. The children were feeling better. It would take time for the conscious mind to assimilate the bad thought patterns. They had to be neutralized. "Conscious messages die hard in the conscious mind." S is letting go of a lot of old stuff.

Even though we clear away the blocked off trauma held by the child, the conscious Host has to set up new blue prints, learn to process feelings, and respond to current realities. This is the work that is done during the integration stage. This work is started as child helpers are released of their negativity.

Session

Upon accessing the Dominant, I was informed that the five-year-old needs to go back inside. *(Remember, once the child helper releases the negative energy, the helper returns to an internal position.)* The Dominant said, "I'll show her the way when she walks in my direction."

The five-year-old came out and said she was sad because she had nobody to talk to. She said that the Lady in the fire sent a message that she is happy and free now. "I have to say goodbye to her. She told me to share what I have learned." I discussed with the child turning to S's Good Part, (the Dominant) to help her go back inside. The five-year-old said that she needs to rest.

The Dominant said that Claire seems to be reliving her past in some era as though she needs to finish her previous life. The Dominant said that space is curved. The Dominant said that S needs a vision. She still has much self-doubt. **"Meditation aligns oneself with the forces that bring things to us."** *(This is a great quote from S's Dominant.)*

The Dominant said that the five-year-old is feeling lonely, because her companion is gone. It was difficult to let her go. The Dominant said that humans need to tap into their spiritual side and learn to be grateful.

Understand that the past life energies and incarnate align with, and act as, a companion for the child helpers. Even though it was time for Claire to leave, the five-year-old had difficulty in letting go of her.

The Dominant said that the ten-year-old needs to talk. She has self-esteem issues, sad feelings, and regrets.

Session

Keep in mind that the Host is always asked about her well being and how she is relating to the changes. S was informed that the five-year-old has gone back inside.

The Dominant was accessed through the trance state. I was informed that the ten-year-old helper misses dad. She feels lonely. The ten-year-old also holds some repressed sexual issues. The ten-year-old feels surreal or de-realized. She was brought out prior to her appropriate stage and had to hold information that was confusing about the changes in the family after the father died. As informed by the Dominant, the ten-year-old holds distrust, humiliation and feelings that sex was bad.

Remember, the older child helpers are brought out early to help with the overwhelming experiences.

The Dominant said that the soul doesn't have limits. It can jump back and forth in time. The ten-year-old was asked to come out and talk. They know when it is their time to work on their feelings. They have been prepared to do this. The ten-year-old came out to help S at age eight when the father was killed. She had to help with the aftermath, i.e. the moving to the grandparents and mom changing.

The ten-year-old said that she wants to go back inside *(inside meaning, back in the internal position with the other positive helpers.)* "I'm the knowledge part. I can't help S. By being out, this slows S down." She said that she is lonely and sad and she misses her father. She reported feeling surreal. "I look in the mirror but I can't see my own reflection. I'm not here. My skin feels electric."

We now begin the process of helping the ten-year-old resolve the feelings that she was asked to hold for S.

Session

The ten-year-old likes D. D is a male friend of S. He is symbiotic of the father. The ten-year-old was brought forth. She said that she has weird feelings. "I feel like I am bad. I wanted to smoke. It was cool and neat. I feel relaxed when S smokes. I try to do what mom wants. I feel ugly and fat." The ten-year-old stated that she feels like water is rushing.

This will be significant in relation to the past life energy from the Titanic. Jack from the Titanic is connected to the ten-year-old helper.

The ten-year-old said that she felt like her hands were big. She was fearful of being out of control. "I feel swollen up. If you touch me with a pin, I will explode. I feel tiny, large, I don't know. I am seeing patterns of rushing water."

My notes reflect that these feeling went away. The ten-year-old became more of herself. "I don't want to be bad. I'm mean to S's brother."

I asked the Dominant about what was going on with the rushing water. I suggested that it may relate to the energy that was brought up about the Titanic.

The Dominant talked about the fact that other energy is absorbed or latches on at birth or at any time particularly if the system is vulnerable. The conscious mind needs to close it off. This could be viewed as possession. The air around the earth is thinner so more energy is being received.

The Dominant agreed that something is going on in the ten-year-old in relation to the past life energy.

Session

This session I asked the Dominant about identical twins.

The Dominant said that twins are the same being in a diffusion of energy. **"There are beams of light going inward. There is a split in the pattern but they are the same energy field."**

The ten-year-old came out to talk. She said that the grandparents were weird. "They drank. Everybody was different after dad died. Mom was different. We depended on dad. There is nobody to help me with my math. Mom was always angry. Dad helped mom get away from her weird parents. She had to go back to them."

Remember sessions end with the Dominant coming back out to let me know how things are doing with that particular helper. When S returns from trance I ask how she is doing, what she was aware of, and inform her to be aware in her daily life of being vulnerable to the feelings that are being released by the ten-year-old. Perhaps the most impact that the ten-year-old had on S was S's fear of change.

The Dominant said that the ten-year-old is a very tenacious part of the system. She holds a lot of guilt.

The ten-year-old came out. "I'm different. I'm mean to people. I feel something is the matter. I came out too soon. Mom yelled at me. I was fat. She was disgusted with me." I got the child to imagine that mom was there. She was told that it was OK to let mom know how she felt. The child said, "You betrayed me. You tried to make up for it. I needed help. All you cared for was yourself. You made me feel dirty."

The child said to me that mom made her feel that she could not handle things. "I had to handle things such as taking care of my brother. She made me feel ugly." The child said that she makes S treat L that way. (L is S's daughter.)

The child helper saying that he or she makes the Host treat their biological child the way that the child helper was treated, is an extremely important concept to understand. The middle helpers tend to be vindictive. There is a sense of getting back at others for what happened to them. Remember, victims become victimizers. Even though the child helper may feel guilty about being mean to the Host's child, or the Host's younger sibling, deep feelings of sadness and betrayal can turn to mean and vindictive projections and behavioral reenactments. Who hasn't treated their child in the way that their parent or parents treated them, regardless of the fact that they have always said that they would never treat their child in that way.

The ten-year-old said to the mom, "You're selfish." The ten-year-old said that she and her cousin touched each other in a sexual way. She felt dirty and guilty. I tried to help her understand those feelings.

The Dominant said that the ten-year-old got comfort from eating and reading. She went on to say that children who lose a parent need counseling.

It is important to note that the ten-year-old helper gets comfort from eating. It has been experienced that either the younger child helper or the middle helper can be the source of the Host's overeating and weight problems. Remember, the child helper is holding the negative emotions that the Host only feels sometimes. The helpers need to get relief from these negative emotions. Until the feelings are resolved, it will be difficult for the conscious Host to keep the weight off because one part of the unconscious mind eats to feel good.

With the Dominant's permission, I used the technique of getting the child to imagine that the mom was there and to say what she needed to say to her. This is very effective in helping the child release the feelings that she holds and was afraid to let go of.

In assessing how the child was doing, the Dominant said that the child looks "clearer."

Understand at the Dominant level, it seems to be more about releasing negative energy. Negative emotions are the lower frequency, heavier darker emotions. Only when the child helper is completely clear can it return to the core of healthy helpers.

The Dominant said, **"I'm the in between of the body and the universe.** When the conscious person sleeps, it is our life. The conscious being doesn't know what's going on. Some bits and pieces can seep through." The Dominant guides certain systems. *(Indians refer to the Higher self, what I call the Dominant, as the Guide.)*

Session

As we work on the ten-year-old I can't lose sight of how S is affected by the ten-year-old's material that is coming through. S reports that she feels that she has no control. I try to help the Host understand that she has to bear with the feelings that pervade her as we bring the ten-year-old's feelings to the surface for healing.

The Dominant was accessed through trance. The Dominant reported that the ten-year-old still feels isolated and insecure. The Dominant informed me that the past energy that is connected to the ten-year-old is a 23-year-old guy who was a purser on the Titanic. He left a wife who was pregnant. He was on level three on the boat. There was something about his friend shooting himself because of the fear.

As discussed in Part II, this energy is an external energy usually through the ancestral line that is permitted to enter the system at the time of birth. It can often live vicariously through the Host, but isn't supposed to. Some past life energies tell me or try to convince me that they are helping and protecting the child to which they are connected. For the most part, when it is time to leave, they know that they have to let go. Remember, on occasion the past energy seems to have a sense of retribution that is taken out on the current Host. The past life energy can sabotage the therapy when it is not ready to leave. Sometimes this past life energy does not seem to be controlled by the Dominant. As you will learn, Jack was allowed to enter the system when S was born.

The Dominant said that the past life energy locks on through psychic contact. "It has to hook on to a living system to feel comfort."

Session

The Dominant said that when people are on drugs, and or alcohol, the Dominant's willpower is decreased and the ability for the Dominant to send a signal to the part that compulsively wants to emerge or is triggered is shut down, the channel is closed. It is important to note that a person's compulsive and or destructive behaviors don't have to be precipitated by drugs or alcohol.

The Dominant talked about the ten-year-old helper's need to protect mom. She was afraid that mom was going to leave her. She wanted mom's approval. The Dominant controls what S needs to know. **"I can help the system realize its goals."**

The problem with fragmentation is that the Dominant's energy is utilized and diffused to help control and contain the blocked off emotions. The Dominant doesn't have the focused attention for the Host. This is the argument for integration in that the Dominant can focus the attention on the Host. Remember the map in part two. We need all six helpers back inside doing their jobs, free and clear of any negative energy. This allows the Dominant to focus on guiding the Host to its goals, purpose, and mission.

The Dominant would often free associate during the therapy.

"There is fear and love. We don't take our consciousness with us when we die. Fear comes from the physical body. The fear wants to be resolved."

The Dominant said that S's father has helped S. **"I felt his influence. The father was very dogmatic. It was better that he was taken so he could be more open and spiritual."**

The Dominant said at age nine, S had a vision of her father. "I'll protect you." The ten-year-old helper still holds shame and guilt. She misses the dad. She said that, "daddy will protect me."

The ten-year-old was brought out. She appeared to be describing a car accident when she got the wind knocked out of her. She said that her stomach and throat hurts. She said that she is really tired. "I don't want anyone to bother me. Nobody likes me. I can't say anything right. My step-dad thinks I'm stupid."

The ten-year-old is afraid to assert herself because she believes something bad will happen.

This is an example of how the child helper slows down the Host. S is afraid to assert herself and afraid to make decisions.

H triggers the ten-year-old, and then the ten-year-old's feelings are felt in the Host. She perceives these feelings as contemporary and processes and responds to them from this perspective. It must be pointed out that both partners in the relationship are doing this. When S gets upset, she is triggering the husband's child helper. This is what in essence symbiotic relationships are about.

Session

S reported that she is becoming more like her Dominant.

What happens is that as things are cleared away, the Dominant can be more focused on the Host. When the Dominant starts coming through more, the client reports more insights, being more considerate and often more goal oriented. Symptoms start to diminish.

During this session, the Dominant said that Jack from the Titanic was still there. "He has helped but it is time for him to go. Jack is lurking in space. He is trying to live forever by latching on to a human. He feels more superior than he really is. He has to go. He needs to go into the light in order to cleanse and for the karma to do its duty. He may or may not return to the earthly plane. We learn lessons on the other planes."

The Dominant said that the Christian culture's dogma won't let people find the self within. "Jack has a fear of dying, afraid that he will go to hell. He grew up with the Church of England. He married a Catholic. His child died during WWII." The Dominant said that they can't control him from coming out. "I try to put a lid on him."

Remember S has an aversion to deep water. Also S's need to party comes from Jack. The past life energy will often live precariously through the human. As I was asking questions about Jack, the Dominant said to talk to him. He was listening and was willing to talk to me. You will see that he had to enter the ten-year-old in order to talk with me.

Jack's full name, which the Dominant had told me, is on the list of passengers on the

Titanic. What I was taken by was the fact that the voice that came out spoke with an English accent. The following section is my conversation with Jack.

Jack said that he misses smoking cigarettes. He said that he could talk about the disaster. He said that the water was coming over his head. "People were screaming. I gave up. I should have helped more women and children in the boats. Many children died. I remember the sound of metal crunching. I was in the eating room when the ship hit the iceberg. The damn Captain was a jerk. He was arrogant and stupid. He took me away from my life. I feel guilty for not helping enough people. Andrew asked me to shoot him. 'Please kill me, I can't take this.'" Jack said that he can see both ways. He was aware of the persecuted lady but did not interact with her. "I am in the child right now. It feels funny being in the child, the ten-year-old."

The past energy has to enter an internal child in order to talk through the physical body of the Host.

"My son was named Rod, and my wife was named Angela. It was a great job. I lived in Cherry England. (I have his exact address.) I can see the house. My mother made me go to church. I didn't have a spiritual side." Jack said that Religion is important. We need to believe that there is more after death. "I see nameless faces with no souls." Jack said that it was time to leave the Host.

There was a period of silence. I assumed that the Dominant was assisting in the release of Jack's energy. The Dominant said the he's in the light. "It was a beautiful blue energy field, amoeba shaped. There were three silhouettes, Jack, his wife and son." The Dominant felt that there was something going on in the stomach area of the Host. The Dominant said that Jack felt guilty. His anger and resentment affected S. He had learned a lot over the last few months as he listened to the work that was being done.

Jack seemed to accept that he had to let go and that it was not fair to S for him to slow down her integration process. It seems to be that the past life energy knows when it is time to exit. Although, some do resist.

Session

The Dominant reported that Jack had left. I had been aware that there was an energy that was a part of S named Jane. She would be different than a past energy. Jane is what I am referring to as an incarnate. She is supposed to be here with S, but she still carries some sadness from another life. The Dominant informed me that Jane is from colonial times and that her husband was killed.

The Dominant explained that every six generations an exact duplicate of yourself returns through the DNA line. This energy returns to a similar being. The Dominant is saying that S looks and is similar to Jane. The Dominant went on to explain that

Jane lived prior to the revolutionary war and died of a broken heart. She was never the same.

I know now that Jane was an energy that was meant to be a part of S but needed to resolve the sadness and grief in order to heal the scar from the past. Even though she went into the light she apparently needs to use this human experience to let go of the pain. This becomes clear in relation to karma. For example, if Jane does resolve these sad feelings about lost love, S will be affected by this in her conscious life. As I speak with Jane you will see how the karma is resolved.

The following is a conversation with Jane. Tom was the name of her husband. There was a southern accent to Jane's voice.

"I remember being with him 200 years ago. It's different. Nobody makes me feel like he does. It's a peaceful love." Jane talked about this life as another cycle. She said that the Dominant doesn't want me to be physical. (This means that she is not supposed to live through S to resolve her feelings). I need to serve a higher purpose. The Dominant gets mad at me." Jane calls S's Dominant the "Wise non-judgemental part." She said that S's Dominant is wise and experienced. Jane said that she was in darkness, a rest period after she died. The energy slows down. There is a shift in energy and form.

The Dominant came out and spoke after Jane. The Dominant said that everything will have to be relived.

I believe that the Dominant is referring to the fact that when the heightened awareness and flurry of insights emerge as the integration begins; this can be philosophically overwhelming for clients at first.

The Dominant went on to say that humans think they have control. "We created this planet for humans to develop oneness through meditation."

Session

As the therapy progressed, the Dominant would give me some insights. Part four of the book covers hours of conversations with S's Dominant.

The Dominant stated that, "We want God to take away our bad feelings." Prayer should be for inner answers, because God is an inner light. Today's society is wrongly guided outward to a wrong image of God. Six thousand years ago there was a heightened awareness, the MASONIC order in Egypt. We need to have Perfect Trust and Perfect Love. You will be provided for. An inner peace has to happen first. I'm helping S move forward."

The Dominant said that S's depression was the ten-year-old helper's difficulty in letting go of the "I'm no good." The Dominant is not letting the ten-year-old get out of control.

The Dominant said that the ten-year-old needs a mirror to see that she is not bad. The ten-year-old has the rage, she screams, and has temper tantrums. There was a lack of control around dad dying, along with the subsequent shift in life styles.

The Dominant said that S's daughter has an Ancient Indian Spirit, a wise inner being. For 300 years this spirit has been waiting to come back.

Session

The ten-year-old came out to talk. "Mom said that sex was dirty. She didn't explain that it was supposed to be special." The ten-year-old was worried that dad went to hell. "The Church confused me."

The ten-year-old's feelings have been partly the source of S's sleeping problems. The Dominant said that S is getting more rest.

The Dominant talked about the karma surrounding Jane. The DNA line is cleared when Jane resolves these hurt, sad feelings of lost love. The Dominant said that Jane is S 233 years ago. They are both similar in looks and personality.

Session

At this point in the therapy, I asked the Dominant what was the purpose in all of this work that had to be done.

"The goal in the universe is oneness, completeness, and balance."

The ten-year-old was sent out to talk. "I'm confused. I understand Jane. I remember what Jane remembers. I can see her room. The woven hair ribbons. My dad died like Tom died." *(Jane's husband Tom was killed after a fall from a horse.)*

The Dominant guides dreams and is alert at all times. The Persecuted lady is much better. She is sending me positive messages. The Dominant spoke of the universe bringing back energy so the human race can evolve. Genetic patterns are repeated. The Dominant believes that Jack could have been in the genetic line. The Dominant believes that Jack was greeted by his relatives but that he didn't ascend. He did find comfort but may have to come back eventually. The Dominant said that Jack's departure was a different sensation than that of the Persecuted woman in the fire (Claire).

S's relatives are from Scotland and England. The Dominant continues to say that because of the overpopulation that there is a diffusion of energy. There are not enough

Dominants going around. "Certain energies are pulled back through the genetic code."

The Dominant asked me to help the ten-year-old resolve her shame. The ten-year-old is the last internal child helper who needs negative energy resolved. She said that she was tired of being alone. She said that Jack did stuff that wasn't good. He thought about partying and he was irresponsible. His life was cut short. He told me, "don't let them be like that to you." He upset me. The ten-year-old said that she was ashamed of her behavior and understood that she was reacting to bad stuff. The ten-year-old said that, "H's kid (child helper) doesn't like me. I'm needy and his kid is logical."

Session

As the Dominant emerged, she said that this body is tired. The vocal chords are tired. The focus is still on the ten-year-old. She wants to go back inside. Remember that at one point that the ten-year-old was not ready to go back because she was not clear, that there was some darkness left inside. The Dominant said that the child will be nurtured. "It's like a separated family member. It's a group effort of the brain. The ten-year-old uses anger from the anger center. She needs positive affirmations. She believes that she is too fat. She has self-esteem problems. She is Hostile and antagonistic. She identifies with the mother and grandmother."

The ten-year-old holds the loss of dad and the disillusionment of life. She knows that she is not bad. The Dominant said that the ten-year-old needs to meditate. She needs to know that mom loves her. The Dominant said that hypnosis is tough because of the abreactions but is needed in order to move into the higher levels.

"We need to find inner meaning as we go through life otherwise this awareness will come at the point of death."

The Dominant says that Jesus and Mohammed are mortified for what has been done in their names, the twisted perversion of their words. "They wanted peace and tolerance for all, not right and wrong."

During this session the ten-year-old relived a temper tantrum she had in class.

"I'm bad." She said that she was sorry to the class. "I lost my dad."

The ten-year-old was asked to imagine that mom was there and that it was OK for her to share her hurt, upset feelings with her. I informed the child that mom would be grateful for these insights. The ten-year-old said "I don't feel pretty. I'm not like you mom. You washed my mouth out with soap in front of a friend. I needed you to help me when dad died. You used me to help you feel better. I was just a child. You hurt me a lot. You didn't think about nothing but yourself. I forgive you. Nobody helped you. I'll help you. You have to listen to me."

Forgiveness as part of the letting go is important. I then got the child to imagine that she was inside of her mom and that she was seeing and feeling what mom felt about her.

The ten-year-old said that mom said that she was sorry. "You reminded me of your father. Nobody I dated could be good enough. Please forgive me. I really love you. If you need me, I'll be there."

The child began to cry deeply. The child calmed down and said that she understood her mom. "I forgive her. I deserve good things. I deserve to be happy."

The child was tired and went back inside. The Dominant emerged and said that things went fine. As the intermediary I always ask how the processes are going. The Dominant said that S's headache is still there. She believed that the headache is because of a disk problem in S's upper back. The neck muscles are in spasms.

With other clients I see that the Dominant can be overwhelmed with all of the fragmented feelings. A teenager who I am working with would not have opened up to do the abreaction except for the fact that a higher level helper came to assist her Dominant. Remember, not all Dominants can come out through the left brain and verbalize. Most can give signals through nods and lifting fingers so that I can at least get yes and no responses. However, most Dominants know what needs to be done for the Host to clear away the feelings so that the system can move toward wholeness.

The Dominant said that they continue to force the system to go within to find their purpose, mission, and vision. Otherwise the Host will continue to repeat situations. "The consciousness has to move beyond the violation of the self." *(Title for book taken from this quote.)*

Session

S reported that while meditating she felt a spirit (coolness around her face).

I asked the Dominant about this energy that S felt.

The Dominant said that, "It was a Spirit that comes and goes. They can be helpful like an Angel. They have a little further view of things. This spirit was named Norma. She committed suicide. She felt regret and remorse. She died in 1962. She had low self-esteem and experienced a bad childhood. She was aimless for 2 years. She wanted children. She enjoys S. She thinks S is special, She likes L (S's daughter). She is ready to move on to a sphere of healing and cleansing."

I did not talk to this energy. The Dominant described the release of energy. "There was a blue glowing ball filled with white and blue light. It was coming closer. Norma was moving through in a rush of blue flame."

I observed S's body which jerked and shook for a second. The Dominant said that Norma was at peace. The Dominant said that she was being transported to the next level. "She could cycle back to the earthly plane. Norma was a good soul that was done wrong. Her consciousness didn't die out."

The Dominant said that S's life cycle was becoming more positive. "She feels alive and more vigorous. She was stagnate." The Dominant said that S was told that they would help her become successful.

The Dominant reported that the ten-year-old is having a great day and that the other helpers are cheering her on. She feels better. The Dominant felt that an aimless soul with a dark side tried to get in but was told that it was not welcomed. S has become more aware of not letting energies enter her system. The Dominant said that this system is a good one that releases souls.

The Dominant said that S's dad believed strongly in the afterlife. He knew there was more to life. He feels better toward S. He was concerned before.

This supports the notion that S's dad's energy is aware and shows up to see how things are going.

The Dominant reported feeling exhilarated now that the child helpers have been cleared of their negativity. "I can let go but still be in control."

This emphasizes the need to clear blocked off trauma away so that your Dominant/Higher Self can be free to watch out over you the Host.

S was still complaining of insomnia. The Dominant said that it was a conscious problem. It was related to S's self-esteem issues.

It's important to discuss that even when the child helpers are clear and go back inside, the conscious Host still holds on to some old blueprints that affect her self-esteem. Once the childhood wounds are resolved, it is easier for the conscious Host to change these blueprints through cognitive-behavior techniques.

S still has some confusion with regard to matters of the heart because of Jane's unresolved feelings. The Dominant was accessed and said that Jane is still there and has strong feelings that need to be resolved.

Remember that Jane went into the light but part of her has come back as a helper but still has the unresolved memories of her lost love.

The Dominant said that Jane was told to let go of the feelings. "S's low self-esteem blocks channels to necessary information. S is still going through an integration process."

The Dominant said that you can't hurry spiritual enlightenment.

It was clear from the conversation with the Dominant that it was time to talk with Jane in order to help her resolve these feelings because they were slowing down S's integration process.

The Dominant said that Jane is a part of the system, through the DNA, RNA and CNS (central nervous system). She is not like an attached past life energy that needs to leave. She is here to help S with matters of the heart as soon as she resolves her feelings of lost love.

Session

S reported that she is sleeping better. She reported that she does not feel close to H this week. The Dominant was accessed and reported that S is doing better with the emotions in her present reality. The Dominant suggested that I speak with Jane.

The following is my conversation with her. I simply say, "Jane, I would like to speak with you. When you are here, let me know through a signal or verbally."

A southern voice emerged. She said that she lost her husband Thomas. "I went into the light and chose to come back. I was programmed to return. I share this existence. My husband Thomas was killed. He had gone fox hunting. I was expecting a child. I fell and lost the baby. I died of the flu 17 years later. The consciousness died. I am S's ancestor through her DNA."

"The boy H *(referring to S's husband)* doesn't know what we need. I think H and S were either friends or brothers in another time. They have a bond but are not in love. They feel connected." She said that she doesn't feel anger. "I feel out of balance. When you come back, you don't remember the past clearly. I was born in 1767 in Fairfax County, Virginia, in Heatherfield. Arlington is my favorite place. My family knew Thomas Jefferson. I did remarry after Thomas was killed. I didn't love him."

At this point Jane felt confused about why she had returned.

She said the universe is moving toward a Peak. It is the expansion of the universe. She said that she was into the stars. She said that math doesn't have to be complicated. "I may be back to experience the Peak. I was sleeping in S. She tapped into me at Williamsburg as a child. I look like S but I was thinner." She said that she sees through S's eyes, the optical nerve that is lodged in her brain.

The next sessions were focused on helping Jane resolve her deep sadness.

Session

The Dominant was accessed. I must have asked the Dominant about the Peak that Jane talked about. The Dominant often talked about the paradigm shift and the expansion of the universe. The Dominant said the peak will be in 2012.

The Dominant seemed to be getting upset with Jane's cycle of sadness that was slowing S's progress. As long as Jane was holding these unresolved feelings of lost love and grief and sadness, it would continue to permeate into S's consciousness and continue to manifest as a problem for S.

The Dominant suggested that I tell Jane to stop the karma, and this cycle of sadness. The Dominant said that S has to be patient. "She is young. Things are coming. S has to relax."

The Dominant said that there are many different futures. "I get input from a higher intelligence. Jane needs to break the karma. There is a deep grief in Jane." The Dominant said that the Host has to come to me. "My thoughts permeate the consciousness. I don't control."

With another client who I am seeing, there is a sense from the Host that the Dominant is giving him choices and options regarding the changes that need to occur in his current life. The client feels that he can accept these suggestions or not. Dominants say that they will allow the Host to go against the better judgment of them. The higher level helpers will let us learn lessons the hard way and will keep letting us go down the dead-end streets of life until we make better choices.

The Dominant said that S needs to go to school. "She needs to channel this higher knowledge into helping people at some capacity."

The Dominant said, "I can literally shut down the Host when I can't control the action part." In other words, when the angry teenage helper gets triggered, the Dominant can't always stop the anger from breaking through and manifesting in a behavioral reenactment. The only protection that the Dominant can provide at that time is to shut down, or turn off the consciousness from being aware of what that part is doing. Remember, the first juvenile offender who I did the unconscious work with was amnestic for his acting out behavior. Often my clients don't remember going off, throwing things etc. I explain that this is their angry part coming out. (It's not an excuse, but truly is uncontrollable in certain situations.) The Dominant gave an example of when the husband kills his wife, then turns the gun on himself. The Dominant in this case did not or could not shut down the conscious Host to keep him from being aware of what the part with rage had done.

The Dominant likes watching movies. "I can see through S's eyes. Seeing through the third eye makes things look smaller." The Dominant reported seeing me through the third eye.

The Dominant typically does not open the eyes of the Host. They report that they can see me through the third eye. The third eye is our sixth chakra. It is the center of "seeing." The Indians call this the strong eye. It is also called the brow chakra.

"The third eye can be seen as the psychic tool of the sixth chakra, just as our physical eyes are tools of perception for the brain. This chakra itself can be thought of as the storehouse and viewing screen that analyzes the wealth of visual input we receive from all three of our eyes. The third eye brings us added understanding, much as reading between the lines of a piece of writing gives us added insight into words."

Wheels of Life - Anodea Judith

"If therefore thine eye be single, thy whole body shall be filled with light."

Matthew 6:22

The Dominant reported feeling Jane's sadness. "It's hard to turn off. There's a cruelty there."

The Dominant and I brainstormed about how we needed to help Jane resolve her sad feelings. There was a sense that the Dominant was getting upset with Jane and that it was time for her to let go of these feelings. The Dominant explained that this was karma replaying itself.

"The karma of your soul is created and balanced by the activities of its many personalities which creates energy imbalances that are not able to right themselves within its own lifetime. The evolutionary process is the continual incarnation and reincarnation of the energy of the soul into physical reality for the purposes of healing and balancing its energy in accordance with the law of karma."

Gary Zukav

According to the Dominant, Jane is a common ancestor, an incarnate from the ancestral line, who was allowed to return in order to heal her unresolved trauma. The Dominant talked about helping S with her reality. The Dominant said that this is a good time to be here because of the expansion of knowledge but at the same time there is much negative karma with the humans.

The Dominant said that we re-enter this birth plane. In talking about children, the Dominant said if we didn't hurt or scare children, things would be better. "Parents need to let them alone. Parents have to trust the child's inner helpers."

Conversations with Jane became the focus of healing.

Jane emerged with her southern accent. "S wanted to be more equal. I understand. We wanted to be different. Women were powerful in some ways. My dad died and mom had the property but my brothers had the rights."

Jane said, "We don't choose our family. We pick a common ancestor." Jane asked about our racial problems. She said the blacks that worked for her were like members of her family. She said that we should be proud of our race without being prejudice. She said that past prejudices can come back through the DNA. "Strong hate from the past can be carried down through the ancestral line."

Again, Jane is an incarnate who is here to stay but needs to let go of her unresolved sadness and loss from her previous life. Then she will be free to help S with matters of the heart.

Session

The Dominant said "I don't control Jane. She went off." The Dominant said out loud, "Jane, stop it, Tom can't be with you."

The Dominant said, "When S reads, I enjoy it. It is a 7 and 8 circuit brain trigger. I see what is really there in a different space and time. Circuits 1 and 2 are the biological functions."

Jane agreed to come out and talk. She reports that she is upset and sad that she can't be with Tom. "We argued the day he was killed. I don't think he loved me. I remember cradling his head down the lane, a half mile down the road. Jasper told me that Tom fell. I ran across the field. I can see him lying there. It was so awful. I don't know whether he is angry with me or what. I feel his love. It's so real that you could touch it. I feel that he went through the light and that he is back. "

The Dominant came back and said that all of these emotions being triggered and felt by Jane are causing S's depression to increase.

I often say to my clients that the emotions they are feeling are a good sign because the root cause is being brought to the surface in order to be resolved.

In general whenever the Dominant is preparing the Host and a child helper, to clear away the blocked off emotions for example, the Host has to go through a period of feeling out of sorts as well as having vivid dreams, usually with scary or angry emotions involved.

I really have to work hard at helping the client keep the faith in bearing with a little confusion and emotional upheaval while the unconscious mind is processing the blocked off emotions. However, it is a necessary discomfort in order to clear away the emotions that are causing the symptoms.

Session

The focus remains with helping Jane resolve her feelings. The Dominant said that Jane has been sitting at the foot of Tom's grave. "Jane brings the karma from the past." Karma according to the Dominant is not always negative or positive. "It can be enlightenment as in love and patience. Sometimes one needs to take a stand. Don't succumb to evil. People have become too materialistic. People are fragmented. They don't hear their voice. The consciousness doesn't get help. The cerebral cortex is thick." The Dominant said that drugs burn out people. "Drugs can modify and pacify but people need therapy. All drugs that are not natural need serious consideration."

Jane was asked to come forward so that we could speak with her. Jane said that S's illness is because of her. "I feel bad. I miss him (Tom). I know I need to let go. I need to find out about my past before Thomas." The Dominant had to research where and when Jane lived before. *(Sometimes an incarnate brings a story from another time.)*

Session

It was clear that Jane was ready to confront her traumatic past, even prior to her life with Thomas in the 1700's. Jane emerged. "I'm upset. It was Ireland or Scotland. I'm walking over a bridge toward a tower. There are other buildings. I lived there. There was a woman, Eileen who cursed me. I married Jason. We were young. She was wicked. She wanted Jason. I don't know what happened between them. He came to me hurt. I helped him. We tried to leave. Eileen's father ran a guild. I was intimidated by her. She was wicked. Jason tried to work for her father. The father opposed the relationship with Eileen and Jason. She tried everything to get him. I was pregnant with our child."

"This was 1520. The men got me in the woods. They raped and killed me. I was watching over me. It was her men. She knew I was pregnant with Jason's child. It's too much to feel the feelings."

Jane described this as a shell within a shell within a shell. The past present and future are all the same. She went on to describe what happened. "I was walking in the woods. I wanted herbs for the baby. I was so happy living on the farm. The men crept up on me. One was her brother. He hit me in the head. He told me I was a whore. I felt the baby die. I left my body. They mutilated my body. They cut the baby out and burned it. Jason never forgave himself. He thought I left him. The herb lady learned of what happened and told Jason."

Jane returned to my present moment and said, "How am I here. I have been dead for 200 years. How can I remember before me? I've been so saddened. I try not to be a problem. This is so confusing. S's helper is so wise. Maybe I need to forgive Eileen." I learned that Jane's name when she was with Jason was Amilia.

The Dominant came out and discussed with me the need to help Amilia/Jane forgive. The Dominant said that Jane was very practical. Her emotions were subdued.

The Dominant stated that science has turned a blind eye toward spirituality. Jane's reality was limited. Thomas was more enlightened. He studied Masonic rituals. He was a 33 Degree Mason. The Dominant said that Jane is a part of S that has love but is keeping it from happening now. There is a dichotomy of love and loss. The Dominant said that Jane lives in her memories causing S to live in these memories. The Dominant said that Jane can break the chain of karma. She has been cleansed in the light. However she has to relive the unresolved pain. The current connection needs to be broken.

Session

This was the forgiving session for Jane.

The Dominant came out and said that Jane needs to let go and forgive the people who hurt her. "It's letting go of the negative energy. The curse will no longer have the power. The negative karma will bounce off." Jane emerged and knew that it was time for her to let go of the negative energy and to forgive those who hurt her.

The following are Jane's statements of forgiveness which were expressed out loud but it was clear that they were being said to those who needed to hear this.

"I forgive the evil. It has no power over me. My life has begun. My soul is now free. Eileen, return to your original form so you can forgive yourself. Take this balm as a symbol of forgiveness. No more pain. There is too much love here. I give love and forgiveness to those who hurt me. I am now healing my body so it may rest." Jane whispered, "I forgive Thomas too." I am walking from his grave with my head held high with the memories of love and laughter. My love can be happy in all three worlds. I want to heal her (S) heart and stomach now."

There was quietness. Jane went back inside to rest. The Dominant said that Jane was now free of her sadness and pain. Now she can be free to help S in a positive light with matters of the heart.

S's response upon returning from trance was one of heightened senses, and a feeling of power.

Session

Now we begin the final stage of integration. Even after the blocked off emotions are cleared away, every helper has resolved their problems and have gone back inside, the Host has to continue to work on breaking old blueprints. This will be much easier now that the childhood wounds, as well as the carry over energy, have been resolved.

The Dominant emerged and said that Jane's resolution went fine. "She is here to stay and will be a positive helper for S." The Dominant said that S was experiencing some Christmas anxiety. The Dominant said that S has some fear and insecurity to work through. "It comes from the years of negative messages. S has to learn to ground herself."

As explained before, it will be much easier for S to extinguish old patterns and replace them with new ones. As clients resolve their childhood wounds, the barometer for progress includes recovering quicker from emotional reactions, having less triggers, improved ability to express feelings, an ability to assert oneself, and an overall sense of coming into one's power.

During sessions the Dominant would purport various philosophies.

The Dominant said that things just are, neither bad nor good. "There is negative and positive in each person. We don't want too much of either. Too much positive is draining. Too much negative equals depression." The Dominant said that kids need to be told the truth because they are tapping into higher frequencies at a younger age. The Dominant talked about the fact that S's father can help her in better ways now. "S can access the good parts of his brain."

I asked why it is difficult to communicate with Dominants and child helpers with children under the age of 12 or 13. The response from the Dominant was that each person's Dominant is integrated in the body working toward completion. "The parts of the mind can't express themselves through the child at that stage of development."

"The Dominant is the logical emotional part. Alcohol dulls me. I can't break through to the brain to get messages to the Host to stop the action."

What the Dominant is talking about is the fact that when we drink and/or do drugs, it is more difficult for the Dominant to control the anger, for example, from breaking through. We have already heard that even without drugs or alcohol, the Dominant can not always prevent the powerful blocked off emotions from coming through. This explains why some people become angry after a few drinks.

I was informed that we still needed to help Jane feel good. Jane came out with her southern accent. "I feel good now. I'm not sad. I feel tender. I can cope and maintain. I need to help this person (she is referring to the Host, S.) We have to find peace inside and forgive. I don't sit at the grave. I can rewrite my own past and can change events. I need to be cheerful and happy around those people in the past. I need not give into the despair."

Jane talked about the fact that time is definitely moving faster now. "There is so much information." She feels that there will be an explosion soon. An information explosion will change reality. She feels that famine and disease will wipe out people, not a nuclear holocaust. Things will be more space oriented."

Jane is now free to help S with matters of the heart. She will rest for a time. The final phase of the process will be to help S with some cognitive reprogramming. Now that just about everything from the past has been cleared away, any emotions, confusion and frustrations, are owned by S and she has to continue to deal with them. She has to move toward changing her belief systems and toward better self-esteem.

S described a conversation with her mom in which ended in her hanging up on her mother. S said that her mother doesn't like her. It was clear that anger related to her mother was being processed.

It is important to understand that the information that is being resolved in the blocked off parts of the self is processed through the Host over a period of time. Certainly during a major abreaction the Host feels the feelings and sensations, but understand that most of the information that is processed is released safely and tolerably over time.

(To protect the spouse, many of the conversations regarding the relationship, the ups and downs during this work will not be discussed in detail. The important thing that will be discussed is symbiosis in relationships in general. For example how in general, the child helper draws the Host to a relationship that triggers the blocked off material.)

Session

The Dominant emerged saying that, "This body is tired." The Dominant said that those sensations disappear after awhile, but when the Dominant enters the body, it feels what the physical Host is feeling.

The Dominant said that Jane is a part of the system. Jane gives S much help. The Dominant said that Jane is reluctant to say the wrong thing through the consciousness.

In inquiring how S is doing, now that most of the blocked off feelings have been cleared, S has done a 180.

The Dominant said, "I don't belong to S. I belong to consciousness. I can assimilate S's energy with me. Sometimes energy isn't worth taking." The Dominant said that consciousness moves us in physical reality. "We need to feed the spirit. There are different forms of souls. There are different levels." The Dominant talked about that fact that spirits are sleeping. "The humans don't even know that they have them." There are many frustrated Dominants according to S's Dominant.

I continually hear that we need to meditate in order to tap into our power and re-sources.

The Dominant made this profound statement during this conversation. **"I am a force of energy, different than a human force. I don't fear death. I am S's essence. Humans need to meditate to gain knowledge to be aware. I look forward to growing. It's both frustrating and exhilarating. It's frustrating for other Dominants to catch up."**

Session

More time is spent with S as integration occurs. I need to hear how she is respond-ing now to current realities, how she is responding to her feelings. Remember feeling feelings is not the same as expressing feelings. Feelings are signals telling us to respond to the situation. So discussions with S at this point are about how she is responding to situations.

The Dominant said that S needs structure. "The new job is good. The Dominant said that S's female system is out of kilter. It is an odd cycle. She gets edgy. I would encourage her to get medical help for her female cycle. Her cycle subdues my think-ing when I have to occupy the body. I am aware of the body when I am commenting through it."

The Dominant said, "I'm aware of the immediate future and the immediate past." The Dominant said that this is a strange environment to be in. *(Referring to this time in history.)* "People are selfish. People want things for themselves."

The Dominant and I discussed the fact that everything is cleared away. S has to consciously work on her self-esteem. As described in a post therapy interview, S talks about how much easier it is to change thinking and belief patterns and subse-quently changing how she feels. Feelings come up, but they are not powered and or intensified by the old immobilizing feelings that used to come through and permeate consciousness.

I tell my clients that when you clear everything away, you become like everybody else who has to deal with everyday situations and frustrations and must learn how to respond to these feelings in appropriate ways.

I hope that the reader sees that it is very difficult to move on when there are blocked off emotions. These emotions are very powerful and will continue to be triggered and relived in current realities until they are cleared away.

Session

We have been moving toward ending the therapy sessions.

The Dominant was asked to come out in order to discuss a sense of closure. The Dominant said that there is conscious confusion. "There are still some self-esteem problems. She (S) lets negative thoughts dwell." The Dominant said that the child helpers are integrated. "They have no regrets. S is handling things well."

The Dominant mentioned again that S's dad appeared when S was nine to let her know that everything was OK. "You are allowed to comfort and watch out. Your spirit grieves because you didn't do or say something." This is certainly an argument for resolving any unfinished business. "If you die with a heavy heart, you stay stuck. If you die with a light heart, you climb toward the infinite."

"**Blessed are the pure in heart for they shall see God.**" In this Christian quote, PURE means light of heart. Remember that negative emotions are heavy emotions. We talk about feeling weighed down, or having a heavy heart. We need to let go of the negative energy so at the point of death, our spirit can move on to non-physical reality.

I would like to end this section with the following paragraph from S's Dominant:

"**There is a Well Spring of Knowledge, the essence from which everything flows. If you don't let yourself move away from consciousness, you will be stuck with negative emotions, fear, guilt, and shame. We need to stop punishing ourselves. The spiritual internet will change human consciousness. There will be a flood of new information associated with the current paradigm shift. Society has been asleep for 2000 years. Humans need to meditate and rediscover hypnosis in order to expand the knowledge of the mind and to have a light heart which will make dying and going to the next level easier. We are closing one cycle and moving into another. There is much negativity ...**"

S's Dominant

Clearly this is a case example that conveys the notion that healing is at the Soul level. Through the hypnotic/abreactive work, S's Dominant was able to resolve the childhood wounds as well as heal the carry-over energy. Jack will need to return to the physical realm in the future for further healing.

Through this complicated case example, one can see how the unresolved trauma will continue to persist in symptoms and manifestations until resolved. S's helpers who were assigned to absorb the negative energy from the stress and trauma have returned to their natural positions. They can now help the Host with their gifts. Jack, Norma, and Claire have exited into a "sphere of healing and cleansing." Jane will remain as a positive helper and will help the Host with matters of the heart.

S is now free to live her power, live in the present moment, and move toward her goals and vision. Her journey toward wholeness will still have its challenges but will not be immobilized by the childhood wounds.

As compared to the map at the beginning of this section, the map shown below illustrates how the system returns to balance with all six helpers functioning in their purposeful roles. The first map shows the fragmentation that occurs with childhood trauma. The following map shows how the system returns to a sense of wholeness and balance.

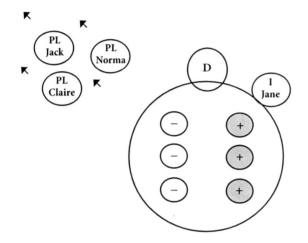

D	=	Dominant
PL	=	Past Life
I	=	Incarnate
+	=	Helpers
-	=	Helpers
←	=	Exit

"All the human experience is about

is the journey toward wholeness."

Gary Zukav

Part IV

Interview One with Dominant

The following are six, one hour interviews with S's Dominant that I conducted upon the completion of S's formal therapy sessions. S agreed to these sessions and intuitively understood that her Dominant wanted this time to convey the information that this section contains. S would present on a Saturday morning and I would place her in trance to access her Dominant. S was in theta trance during the interviews. She did not hear the conversations. The Dominant seemed compelled to bring forth this information. Apparently it's time for us five sense humans to move to a higher level of consciousness. During the sessions the Dominant would address my questions regarding S's healing as well as free associate with regard to matters such as the impending paradigm shift, religion, and carry-over energy.

The sessions with S's Dominant were taped. I tried to transcribe the tapes word for word which accounts for the sentence fragments. Certain names were excluded and some material that was addressed in S's case study was omitted. The Dominant was aware that I was writing a book and that this information would be used in it.

"I am a force of energy different than a human force.

I have been allowed to do this. It has been allowed to come through me. There are probably other people that it is being allowed to come through as well at the same time. It is not only me, but I am allowed to reiterate it for you in English language so that you can write it down.

Think about chemistry for a second. Look at the atom, the nucleus is the sun and the electrons are the planets. There are little parts that run around the planets like moons. If that atom is unstable, what can it do? Our bodies are nothing more than a universe in microcosm. That's what astrology is. The universe is nothing more than a huge body of what? We don't know, but I'll tell you what, if you were to go down into an electron, or an atom, it would look like space. If you would be in that perspective and on that level, it would be just like you were looking at the night sky because the distance between light creates darkness. The astrology function of this is that the moment you are born, the moment you take your first breath is the moment of first life as far as the mind goes, consciousness is when the soul enters the body. Until you are born physically, the body inside the mother is not spiritually alive. It's alive, biologically it's moving around, it's functioning, but it's automatic. There is no self-guidance, there is no conscious awareness because there doesn't have to be at this stage. During the time of gestation is when the energy is aligning itself with that child. When a child is born is when it becomes what we call 'human.' Not that abortion is correct, because yes the child can live six months into the pregnancy. It's not that ... it's the idea of energies coming together. The soul can say that I don't want to inhabit this body. This is not right. The alignment is not right. The energy is not right for me to go in smoothly, to encapsulate this body and make it my own right now."

How much were you aware of this for S?

"I'm just a part of it. There are other parts. I coordinated it. Before you are born it's like getting together with a group of your friends and hanging out with them inside of a room for however long you have to be there ... maybe like a jury deliberating about what you are going to do. Somebody is the foreman."

I have learned that the child helpers who are to be assigned to another human conglomerate in what has been described as a waiting area. Typically they are familiar energies who have been together before. In S's case, her Dominant would coordinate which child helpers and which incarnates would be assigned for her life. The six child helpers are chosen for specific roles. The child helpers are here to learn lessons in order to move up in the hierarchy for future incarnations.

Is this the role of the Dominant?

"Everybody else is there to help you go through this process and then when you die, everybody goes their separate ways for awhile. Then you can realign that same group if you want later on."

I discussed that a teenage helper, belonging to one of my teenage client's, described that she and the other child helpers had been together before helping another person.

"Sometimes this is necessary."

I asked if the Dominant had been with S's child helpers before.

"Oh yea, I know about them."

I asked the Dominant to talk about how the child helpers and the Dominant come together as the child is born.

"We are in a void to you. What seems to be a void to you in the conscious mind, but it is not a void. It is filled with a great amount of energy, a great amount of expansion. You just don't feel contained. But when it is time to realign to be born we accept the challenge of incarnating into another human. I guess that is the best way to put it. I can remember parting from Tom's energy and wanting to come back with it, not me but Jane, knowing that she would have another opportunity. It almost makes you think why my consciousness doesn't seek death so I can do this again. But that is not the point. The point is that all of these helpers are here together. You can't give one, more credence than another. They all have their function to perform. They start forming in the period of time before when the parents actually meet. The energies between those parents are lining up energies from their parents and so on and so on, back to whenever. Some of it is related to the DNA process of your parents and the energy that they carry in them. It's almost as if we are partly in the egg and partly out of the egg, and partly in the sperm and partly out of the sperm ... the actual energies. When you're in the position I am in and you are in this eternal now, this energy area, it is all one. You are aware of everything at once. I know that there is something in there but there is also something out there that I need to pull in closer so we can get all lined up together so that we can become human."

When do you and the helpers enter the child?

"At the moment of birth is when we actually take possession. It is like we are guarding over the inert child. We are guarding it. But if anything is wrong, and we are not born into it, that is just a dead child, just a piece of flesh that died and was not inhabited by the soul."

Can you tell that there is something wrong with the child?

"Sometimes, yes, but sometimes we choose that challenge. People need to take responsibility for their own lives. You need to realize that you are responsible for being here. You need to get in touch with that eternal nowness and know that you were meant to be here. You have to take personal responsibility. You can not continue to reproduce like rabbits. You are draining the energy out of the cosmos by doing that ... out of this earthbound plane that we are in. I don't know that I will come back here again." *(I learned that there is a clear hierarchy in the non-physical realm. S's Dominant is obviously from a higher level. After this incarnation, S's Dominant will move to a higher realm where there will be no direct connection to the earthly realm.)*

Can you talk about where you were before you came to help S?

"I was dealing with a woman who was very glamorous and had lots of problems. She was a beautiful woman with a lot of insecurities. She died and I didn't have much time to regroup before I had to deal with this one (S). She had a traumatic life. Right before her life, I dealt with Jack. I was one of the helpers with Jack. This doesn't make sense consciously. I was a helper with him but I had progressed to a point where I was able to move forward and become more expanded in terms of being able to draw more energy to me. It's not me. I'm not a me. I'm not an it.

I don't understand how to put that so it makes sense to whomever (the conscious reader). It's energy, a soul. It's like being the you of you."

You had said you are a force of energy different than a human force.

"Exactly! It's a will. It's something inside of you. When they talk about your will that is really what they are talking about. It's what motivates you to do things, the conscious, the body, the thing that moves around through time and space? What makes you do what you do? If I can't control the inner parts of you that go crazy, because they are climbing the walls, like in prison, there is a problem. That part is trying to emerge but feels confused or tense and I am trying to deal with this. Sometimes another part of the mind is allowed to run rampant; sometimes that part can break out. The Dominant depending on how strong it is, can't always control all of that. Conscious control is not always a sign of a strong Dominant."

Even though you are a strong Dominant, you couldn't always keep some of the anger from coming out.

"Right… Because that is a colossal force in itself. Anger is motivated by fear. Fear is probably the strongest force that has ever been generated. If you can switch it and turn gears on it, and make it self-confidence, that feeling becomes a forceful Dominant feeling. It has a lot to do with physics and the way that we are lined up. Energy wise, we don't move backwards through time. It is not possible in the physical body. The physical body can not move backwards. It can walk backwards but you don't move through time backwards. My past two seconds was my future two minutes ago. What I am saying is that you don't say that my future was my past. The soul inhabits the body from point A to point B not from point B to point A. The point being is that if the energy is not spinning correctly … we spin clockwise on our planet, our planet spins clockwise, our solar system spins clockwise, it's draining you of energy."

I talked to the Dominant about the fact that I measure the clients' chakras with a crystal. Certainly many of my clients have chakras or energy wheels that are either not spinning or spinning backwards.

"Fear generates that wither shins (counter-clock-wise) movement. Fear does that. Sometimes it is necessary to move wither shins in order to destroy energy. Maybe a negative energy has come. You are positively moving in that direction to destroy an energy around you. But most of the time you move clockwise."

(When my clients are releasing emotions from one of the three emotional chakras, there is a counterclockwise spin of the energy leaving their aura.)

The Dominant asked how S's chakras were. I said that most recently all the chakras were open and spinning clockwise.

"When I am in the body talking to you, the body is on remote control. That's why humans have weak inhabited bodies that have symptomatic nervous systems and they have voluntary and involuntary muscles. Some muscles have to work when we are not moving around consciously, your heart for example."

Go back and talk about Jack for a moment. Where is his Dominant? *(Remember Jack is the Past Life energy from the Titanic.)*

"His Dominant was the part that was sent off. His Dominant wasn't very strong. It's almost like a test. The Dominant is the test. Are you strong enough to deal with this, this, this, and this, and to make this life count for something?"

Do you remember the Titanic going down? *(Remember, S's Dominant was a helper in Jack's system.)*

"Yes. It was not pleasant. Do you think it would be? It's part of the earth. It was a natural sequence of events that had to occur for me to move on to the next level. It's OK. I don't have a lot of fear about it. It wasn't a pleasant memory though, not for the human Host who had the fear. That's what happened to Jack. His Dominant couldn't deal with it. That's why I emerged, as ... I have been here before. I was helping him. I was an over helper. Jack just couldn't deal with it. It was really sad and that is why he attached to this person because I was the Dominant on this one. He needed me to guide him out. So did Claire, (the persecuted woman, the lady in the fire). The same thing with Jane... Many people think that S looks physically like her mother. She looks like her father too. They always say to her, you look just like your mother. You look like your father. That is because she is a blend of them both. But she really looks like Jane."

Can we talk about the child helpers?

"Look at your table of elements. Look at the different atoms. Some people, who are extremely unstable, usually have the most child helpers. They have no control. I shouldn't say that they are always out of control because they can have a really strong Dominant who is controlling them. They can be brilliantly artistic. But if they are unstable, or they are missing a part, or something isn't quite right, the Dominant isn't able to control the system. Look at atoms that need to attach to other atoms in order to become stable. That gets more into the symbiosis between people, but the idea being that the atom is unstable and it has many different parts to it. It can be more explosive than one that is unstable and is at a lower level.

On the average, there are usually about 5 or 6 child helpers – sometimes more, and sometimes less. Look at the major element of Oxygen which is eight. *(Oxygen is 8 on the periodic table. It has an electron configuration of 2-6. The Dominant's implication is that the Dominant and the Oversoul represent the neutron and proton, the core of the nucleus and the six helpers represent the electrons.)* The Dominant and

Oversoul are consciousness. The child helpers function in the subconscious level."

Is the Oversoul a higher level part than you?

"Yes. It is what encapsulates an atom. It's the energy that holds something to-gether. You have your electrons which are the parts of the mind. That is our main building block in this oxygen based society. You have a society and or a whole world based on a certain amount of elements."

What about multiple personalities who appear to bring forth over a hundred per-sonalities. I have worked with multiple personalities (now defined as Dissociative Identity Disorder) and have found them to have eight or nine personalities, which made sense given the fact that a few of the personalities claimed to be external helpers who came to help during the trauma.

"They are like plutonium. They are a very unstable system. Look at the brain as a nucleus. All of the child helpers are the atoms swirling around it. If it is unstable it is going to do something real crazy. If there is nothing to control that instabil-ity, it will explode and create a tremendous force. It leaves a rip in the fabric of time. Look at the guy who went into the school and shot all of those children in Scotland. An unstable personality that has not been controlled... Maybe he only had six child helpers, maybe he had twelve, and maybe he had one. There was no control over this atom, this person."

I commented that it was reported that he was a pedophile and more than likely had a child helper filled with rage around some childhood sexual abuse, probably at the same age as the age of the victims. His Dominant couldn't control that destructive part from coming out. As discussed previously, most of the juvenile sex offenders that I have worked with act out with a child whose age is the same as what they were when they were abused. It is as though there is a matching up of the same frequency.

"Very much so... Frequency is a good way to look at it. Some people that you talk to you can relate to on different levels than others. You can usually tell when some people are not very bright. They are not in touch with anything but their consciousness."

\What about Dahmer? It is as though he had no internal controls.

"No he didn't. He wanted to. His Dominant was very weak. He felt very bad about what was going on, that part of him that he could not control, that rage, that inner part of him. It had nothing to do with his parents. He was not abused by his dad or his mom. It was something that came from before. That's what people don't understand. Poor Jeffrey Dahmer's father and mother, they feel responsible. They are not responsible. I even suspect that he was carrying around the Ripper like energy, just because he was so disgusting. There are others that are like that but

the Ripper energy has been sliced up. There is more to this than we understand ... ritual things that people do, the sacrifices.   This is not a good power. It is destructive."

Can you talk about how the child helpers emerge at different developmental stages?

"Let's go back to the Jury. Say you have a panel of six people. One of them is your ethics panel. One of them is your education panel. The idea being, when you are a four-year-old, your mind is just beginning to awaken to consciousness and what it is to be you, as being different or separate from your mother or your friends. This separation occurs earlier. When you become aware of being able to think and remember and act consciously. When you are two-years-old, you may hear NO and understand that you are not supposed to do that but you don't know why. You don't have that yet unless your child helper comes into play very early which usually happens around the age of three or four, at the very earliest. The baby stage unless there is some sexual abuse going on with the baby, which does happen, very sadly, but that usually is held by an older part. That can definitely come out as rage or very timid or frightened, or not being sure what is the matter.

The first developmental stage that emerges usually holds fear and despair. You don't know what it means. You don't understand anything yet. *(While speaking with a child helper holding the fear in one of my teenage abuse victims, it was clear that fear was not associated with any labels of bad or wrong. It was a primitive fear.)*

The next stage usually is the stage that holds your intelligence ... how smart you are going to be, how you are going to react to life's adversities. It can be very logical. It is usually the logic part of the mind that comes into play around seven to nine years of age."

S's ten-year-old came out and proclaimed that she was the smart one.

"Eight, nine, and ten, somewhere in there ... S in particular had a splinter because of the trauma at age eight. Just say that we are dealing with four different areas here. Then you have one that holds sexual feelings when you are in puberty. It is not so much the teenager. The teenager doesn't necessarily hold sexual feelings. That is more like a protector of the self, of the ego. There can be energy attached to the fear, the logic, and the love. Any of them can have another energy that is attached to them but not always."

Is this like an external helper?

"Yes."

Is this teenager helper the one that usually holds anger?

"Yes, that is usually the part that holds anger from childhood events."

Remember that I had described the fact that most of the anger filled teen helpers said that they came out early to help deal with the anger of the trauma that was occurring when the Host was say 5, 6, or 7.

"S didn't have any sexual abuse, but I can remember ... I'm letting this memory come through, something about her feeling ... I think a lot of kids and people can relate to this ... they feel that something isn't fair. Kids should have rights too. We shouldn't be allowed to be treated like this by an adult. We feel that there is something unfair that an adult did. That is the part of you that is holding the anger. It's the part that is saying, "Wait a minute, wait a minute." When this part starts emerging consciously, that is when you become aware that it is a part of yourself. Sometimes this part has to come out very early to hold something that you can't deal with. If you are abused sexually at age two or three, how can you deal with that? How can you stop that person? You know that it is not right, something feels terribly wrong. It hurts, you are scared."

I said that with one of my teenage clients, her teenage helper said that when the trauma occurred, it was as though the alarms went off and the helpers knew what they had to do.

"Usually the child helpers are taking a siesta, drinking their water waiting for the other panel members to shut up so they can have a chance to talk, if you are looking at it as a panel or a jury. They are waiting their turn. Say that everybody else falls victim to a sleeping gas, and you are the only one left there to deal with it, 'Ah, wait a minute, I'm not ready to deal with this.' That can create even more tension in the helper who has to come out early. That's where you can find some spectacular rages as teenagers. Then there are the ones who are self-contained. They are holding a lot of rage internally. They never show one thing on the outside. They are the ones who you have to watch out for. They may eventually be caught. Look at John Wayne Gacey. That guy wasn't caught for years. At least people who are up front so that you can tell they are angry, they let you know. They may be holding anger from childhood and may be explosive, but mostly they harm themselves and they know that. They don't want to be destructive to others."

Let's just talk about one more positive concept, the external helpers who come to help out. Many of the child helpers report that there are external helpers who come to comfort them. They can be adult or child helpers.

"You can be aware of that as in your imaginary playmates as a child. Somebody that protects you ... Usually they are helpers. When you hear children talking to themselves, that's what they are doing."

When you are four-years-old, are you aware of your four-year-old internal helper?

"Sort of yes, and sort of no… You are at that fine line between realizing that your emotions and experiences relate only to you and not to the world at large. That's when the separateness comes, and realizing that not everybody feels the way that you do. That discovery stage, wonder, is really a good time. Events are what shape that time. All of us have to realize that it is all based on your perception. Everything … A lot of times what triggers you as an adult is something that you don't even remember. That's when your thoughts start taking off in this direction … this, this and this is going to happen because of this or this is the way that this is going to play out now. That's why that person did that because that is their motivation. You don't know what another person's motivation is. You don't know anything but your own perception."

You had stated before that you are a force of energy that is different than a human force. You had said in the past that you are a part of S but also connected to the universe.

"As this body sits here and I move to motivate the muscles in the face to move the jaws to speak, it feels like I am part of the mind. But I feel that I am not totally attached to this body."

When you are not coming into the body to speak to me, you are not in this current position, correct?

"No. I could be in the body, but I am more than the body. Whenever you talk about people who do astral projection that is the part of them that leaves and does the traveling. That is the real self. When you daydream, part of your consciousness may be daydreaming but the feeling that you are having is the key. I am like feeling. Feeling and emotions, you can't help emotion. It's there, you can't do anything about it. Think about it as … it's larger than something that you can control. If you can control your feelings, you are doing a good job. Are you being honest? So, I am like a feeling, in a sense that I am a part of you but I am not tangible. I am connected to more than you. I have a direct communication with my Oversoul which is the next realm which we have not broken through to yet. Humans are not ready to break through to that yet. Ten years ago they weren't ready to talk about me. There were a few people who were. Shamans and High Priests were but not the general lay people, no."

The Dominant clarified that Oversoul and Overself are one in the same.

"That's what came and helped Claire exit."

That's what you had described during the sessions as the blue energy field that came to help with Claire and Jack to enter the light. I called it the blue spaceship.

"Right, you got it. I am attached to that just as much as I am attached to this body.

The consciousness is not aware of it. That's where the confusion comes in. A lot of people consciously would say that this is a bunch of hokey pokey. But not if you are sleeping. Where are you when you are sleeping? Where is your consciousness? It's sleeping. You are not attached to that body. You are and you are not, because you can come back to that body. You are in the cosmos. People say that you are in your head or that you are in your fantasies. That is not true. You are but you are not. Your fantasies are just as real as your reality is."

Is the concept of the halo the fact that you are over top of the head when you are not in the body?

"Right, yes. I am part of the body but I am out of the body. It's the Halo exactly."

(Remember that the seventh chakra is over top of the head.)

A three-year-old helper who talked with me said that when she is not in the body, she is like a dot of energy that is above the head.

"Yes. Sometimes those bands of energy are very strong and you can almost see them on some people. Being an energy force of my own means that I could choose to leave this body. I could say S is going to die now or that she would go into a coma. But that's not my feeling. I am feeling. That's why people with high level Dominants are the most emotionally sensitive people that you will meet, because I am feeling."

If the child helper is not in the body, how do its feelings get triggered and felt by the conscious Host.

"How does light move that fast? It's like a reaction, knowing. The Dominant is always with this person until it chooses to leave. Then death usually occurs shortly afterwards or else the Dominant comes back and that is when you have the out of body experience known as the near-death experience or you can have an out of body experience which is known as Astral-projection which doesn't preclude death, like S had in your office a couple of times."

The reader needs to remember that when the past life energy left, S was out of her body during that process.

"However, when I am here and there is something that triggers and I need that entity to come right now ... it's like a magnet, it's like being a drill sergeant ... 'get down here and do your job now!' They do their job. It's not like somebody slacking off ... 'I don't feel like it.' They want to be there. They wouldn't be there if they didn't want to. They are there because they know that they have to work something out in order to move on to the next level.

142

Every part of the soul would like to be more expanded, more enlightened, and more alive and aware. Wouldn't you? Human consciousness would like to become more alive, more aware and expanded. Look at it in terms of reality. What people consider reality is to have more money. Look at it as money. If you have more money, you can do more things. So if you have more energy, if you have more feeling of wanting to be there, you can accomplish more. I don't like to look at it as that because I don't value the way that mankind has set up their financial systems. It doesn't impress me very much. Gold is not destructible like love. But it is bendable and you can shape it into some really ugly things. The thing is that we have to remember gold can transform just like love can transform. Gold can transform as part of the earth and we are tied to it as a cosmic tie. We can't make that the center of our being. Love has to be the center of our being. Not gold.

I'm getting tired."

Interview Two with Dominant

I made an opening comment about the fact that the mental health profession has become guarded when confronting the issues of abuse.

"These issues are sometimes buried very deep. It's got to be done. The person who survived and the perpetrator need to get on. The honesty is not there. If the emotions of this person who have perpetrated the acts of violence or sexual violence, could be dealt with, then they could move on to be free. When Jesus talks about the Sins of the Father being revisited on the sons, that is what he was talking about. He was not talking about, your dad leaving you in debt. He's talking about emotional karma and backlash from this dogmatic thinking and ... 'you must bury this deeply and never let anyone know.' We need to admit the truth. The truth shall set you free. Once you are free, you can get beyond the poison ... the evil and hate. That is the poison that people created themselves. There is no Satin that created this. It's created in your own mind and in your own hearts. It is so typically human to blame some other person or entity for all of their wrongs. Each and every person has to take self responsibility and realize that we can not blame it on the Devil. There is no Devil. There is nothing like that. There is just good and there is bad. We make that choice all of the time. It's not either right or wrong. We label this stuff but it is just there. Things just are. It takes a lot of courage to admit that first, and to understand, it takes a lot of mental understanding to keep an open mind."

Where did Christianity go astray?

"They misinterpreted many things. First of all what they tried to do was to copy Pagan rituals in order to sanctify the religion in order to get it to become sacred.

It started in Rome where there were deities all over the place. Everybody had their own personal favorite. But they had ways of worshiping where they would all get together and do things. Basically, the Christians were a sect that was driven out into the hills. They were not tolerated because they were extremely dogmatic. The problem was in the interpretation of Christ. They got so fired up about ... 'This is the only way to achieve eternal life,' that they were missing the point. Jesus is probably standing around somewhere being the immortal that he is, shaking his head saying, 'they are still not getting it.' Probably laughing, hanging out with other spirits like him that feel immortal and have moved beyond space and time. Their realities are not the same. They understand the idea of keeping one foot on the earth and one foot in heaven. They're regenerated themselves and conquering death. Human beings are just beginning to understand it. We have been fed this dogma for so long. It has been spoon fed to us since we were born so you can't help to have these preconceived beliefs. Once you move beyond them you can be free, but until then, you are not."

But Jesus seems to talk about Satin.

"Jesus was talking about Satin tempting, and he was also speaking of the dogmatic religion that he was brought up in and in how best it could be put in terms that others could understand so they could get an idea of what he meant. He understood the key. His words have been so misinterpreted and it is really because of translating languages. Anybody who is into theology will tell you that when a word is in one language and you translate it into another language, it loses some of its essence. And then if you translate it into another language, from that, you are really talking about taking something out of context, the way it was originally intended and meant by the person who spoke the word. Not to mention the fact that most of Jesus' words were not written down until one hundred years after he was dead or gone from that group of people. I think he was immortal. He suffered death but I think he regenerated himself. His spirit was very strong. He lived with the Essenes for many, many years and understood how to conquer these things."

Perhaps his energy was sent down as a high level Dominant because of the paradigm shift at that time in history.

"Sure, you bet. He had to usher in a new era of enlightenment. So did Mohammed and other people. The only problem is that Jesus' word was sent out to the European nations. The way that they perceived it, really threw it off kilter. The way the Europeans are is very different from the Eastern religions in the way they view things and the way they live their culture. We have always feared them. Actually they are much more pragmatic about life, death and rebirth. Most Europeans are very mistrustful of those kinds of ideas, so they have to mold their religion around anti-eastern thought, if you see what I am saying. The Easterners totally understand the Yin and the Yang and they are just seeing it and it is manifesting in their religious beliefs. But really is it all one energy.

Once you tap into that, there is no turning back. You can't deny it. It is there. That's what people have to understand. I'm sure that there will be people who will come to this book or come to you for counseling who already do know that innately ... that they felt some sort of movement and shift in their reality here. The explosion is going to happen and when it does ... maybe the end of the world isn't going to be 2012, and it's not like the world is going to blow up and go anywhere. It's that the way everyone perceives this place is going to change entirely."

Can you talk about this peak, the cycle change that is occurring?

"It's because we are speeding up on ourselves. Time ... there have been many different philosophies on history and on 'future.' To understand what the Peak is look at an hour glass. History does cycle. It's like a spiral. Like anything else ... like in biology there are spirals, and the way vines twist is spiral shapes. Your time also does the same thing. Time is like an hour glass, the way that space and time bends ... light bends. This all has much to do with physics as well as psychology. This is all inter-related. The peak will be like the center point there (of the hour glass). Everything will change ... the viewpoints. Then we will start moving in the opposite direction. I'm not allowed to say what that will be. It will alter the course of humanity. Whether it is for the better or for the worse, it's up to the humans on the planet to decide. Right now, many people are being decimated by many different factors and that is because it is getting closer and closer to that ... And it is happening more frequently, if you have noticed the massacre of the Indian. Say if you looked at the spiraling down, if you looked at it as a flat structure that was going around on itself like a monkey tail. It's spiraling out ... draw lines that go straight down concentrically through the center of the circle. Make where the line intersects the circle be a point in time where some atrocity occurs ... a great void in the universe. When your time spirals in on a time when that happened before, another atrocity occurs. History does repeat itself, but it manifests in a different manner. You have the Indians being massacred from the 1830's through the 1910's. You go through a period of time where there is no real mutilation and decimation of an entire population of people until Hitler when you see it happening again. Then you speed up even faster, and you see it again over in Korea and in China. Now it's in Bosnia and Russia. It's just everywhere. That's what I am talking about because time is starting to catch up with itself. It is getting tighter and tighter and tighter. It is why information is going faster and faster ... why computers are processing faster. Everything is happening much faster and people are beginning to feel it. The stress is great during this period. If you don't know how to deal with it, then it becomes very, very uncomfortable. If you are dealing with it and you understand what is happening, you are able to deal with it in a very positive manner."

This leads us to talk about the importance of each individual getting in touch with their Higher Self, their Dominant, particularly because of this paradigm shift. As previously discussed, Gary Zukav talks about the fact that we can no longer depend on our five senses. We need to become multi-sensory. Deepak Chopra has said, "It will become the survival of the wisest."

"People have to let go of the pretensions and the guilt that they carry around with them from the past. You have to start living in the now."

I would interject that it is difficult to live in the now when there is blocked off trauma that keeps being triggered and acted out in the now. This is another argument for going through this process of healing which is difficult, but allows one to live in the now and to create a vision for the future.

"Anybody who gets a grip on this understands that ... you live simultaneously in the past, present, and future. What is the future a minute from now will be the past two minutes from now. You have to understand that you are here right now and that you have the power inside to alter your state of mind in that moment, right then. Most people don't understand that power. They think that it comes from without. 'Oh God is out there somewhere' ... no, it comes from inside.

Wisdom is strength. Knowledge is strength. Knowledge is power. The more you have the more you have access to ... however, the thing that is really comforting about the peak and about the information, is that there is so much to know. More and more people are becoming important because they specialize in certain things. There is no way that you can know everything anymore. That stopped a long time ago. There is just too much. So it is spiraling in on itself and spiraling out on itself at the same time. It is hard to explain this except it is coming to a point where both the two will meet. When it all lines up correctly, this is when this Peak will happen. It will just shift everyone's consciousness. There won't be any denying it. You can call it the Angels coming down from Heaven. This destruction that people look for, if that is what you look for, that is what you will get. If you don't look for that, that is not what is going to happen to you. Your time in that era will be of enlightenment, strength, and courage and fortitude to continue on. Others may experience death and they will be sent into the nether regions ... maybe not to be reincarnated but to reabsorb as energy. To go off into the cosmos somewhere is not exactly what I had in mind. I am a little more interested in staying here and developing this species to its fullest potential in a positive light. So hopefully that is what will happen if we can all get the strength together to do that. There are many people working for that, believe it or not ... more than just me. It's going to start happening more prevalently where they (Dominants) will be coming out and saying 'I'm tired of being held back and stifled and we are going to get on with the show now. Come on, get rid of this anger and negativity and get it over with. The best way to do it is through intense hypnosis therapy where the consciousness is suspended.'"

(The Dominant is certainly referring to those individuals who have persistent psychological symptoms that were born from childhood wounds. However, the paradigm shift will force all of us to take a look within and address any unfinished psychological business and become more aware of the importance of our spiritual evolution. Hopefully this book will contribute to a dissociative/trauma/hypnosis model for healing in order to provide more opportunity for individuals to heal their unresolved traumas and stressors. None of us get through our childhoods without some scars.)

Can you talk about how you as the Dominant were seeking the hypnotherapy in order to help S clear away the blocked off emotions as well as have the setting to help the past life energies move on? Even as high level as you are, you needed to find the external helper which is me, to help with the process.

"No entity is an island. We cannot exist without the ... let's put it this way, oxygen can exist as a single atom and hydrogen can exist as a single atom. When you put the two together in a certain combination, you get water which is a totally different element. You get two gases producing a liquid. The idea being, that the manifestation occurs from change and that it takes somebody else to help manifest the change within, sometimes because the consciousness supersedes most stuff. The consciousness won't let go of certain preconceived notions that it holds on to ... which is what reality is. When our consciousness gets suspended, it certainly helps the subconscious to move into more of a guided direction."

You couldn't help Jack and Claire leave without the trance, correct?

"Exactly, they weren't willing to go. S, the conscious part of this being, didn't understand that there was something ... how was I supposed to communicate with her except through meditation and she wasn't doing meditation correctly. She wasn't having someone ask the right kind of questions of me. I try to guide her toward certain things that would help find the answers. I am there to guide. That is what I do best. It was a long, hard process to get her finally to a place in time where she could get what she needed to get over and on with ... so what, her father died. I am not saying that it is not a terrible tragedy, but it happens to a lot of people. We can not be so egotistically selfish that we share that pain with everyone around us and feel so melancholy. That's what I was trying to get rid of. She was beating herself up."

Explain to the reader that hypnotherapy is not something that I am doing to you.

"There is no post hypnotic suggestion here. You are not sitting here putting ideas or suggestions into this person and then they are coming out later, no. What the hypnosis does is suspends the consciousness. All you do is help guide the consciousness toward total relaxation where the subconscious is, which is me. I am not the subconscious. I am just a part of it."

Where do the helpers fit in with the subconscious?

"This is very confusing. They are like little concentric energy fields inside of this huge energy field which is the subconscious. Then there is the huge energy dome that binds all of us together which is the universal subconscious. The child helpers are little energies that have been present in others."

Another point about hypnosis, you said that it was important for S the conscious mind to be suspended when Jack and Claire left. You didn't want S to be aware of those feelings?

"Oh no, no, no. It's hard when the consciousness is as inquisitive as S's is to not keep some of it from seeping through. I allowed some of it to gradually come through so that she understood that Jack was suffering a lot of pain. He couldn't let go of the fact that he was in a tragic situation. Even now he feels sorry for himself. I knew that when he left, that he was going to periodically check in. He is much happier now and he is back with his family and he is revived but his energy is still subconsciously planted in S with that hurt. It's not that his energy is not gone, but every once in awhile, it will rear its ugly head."

The hypnosis allows you the Dominant and the Oversoul to release the blocked off feelings safely over time.

"Exactly. I still think the best way to do this work is to have a place where people come and they have like a home that is very comfortable and they stay for a month."

(I agree with the Dominant that a setting where the client stays may be a way to release and resolve the trauma in a shorter period of time. On the other hand, clients may not be able to tolerate this more intense process. The weekly sessions have proved effective for the most part. There are times when I wish that the client could have a few days of intense abreactive work in a controlled setting where the client could stay overnight. Residential treatment centers for adolescents would be an ideal setting for the hypnotic/ abreactive work to occur. Unfortunately these settings perpetuate a paradigm of medication and containment. Psychiatric hospitals do the same.)

Do you feel that we could have cleared away everything which took about a year on a weekly basis in a few months on a daily basis?

"If it was done correctly and if it wasn't successful in a few months, then you have them come back again on a weekly basis. You have to be flexible. Some people need this intensity and they are ready. They need to do this every day until it is all gone. That's the thing about things speeding up as well too. They want to get it over with so they can start moving. It is like being kinetic energy being held in one spot, and you are being held back by something inside of your brain in your subconscious that won't allow you to move forward with the power within you. Then you are going nowhere. That is a lot of people."

Over the years my clients who have blocked off trauma have difficulty in moving ahead.

"Actually people should be moving out in all directions. Your energy should expand everywhere. The energy shouldn't move in a straight line, that is a very narrow definition. It has to expand outward in like a concentric circle. The goal is everywhere. You need to be open to this. It is like watching ripples in the water when you throw a rock in it. They go out, out, out."

Can you talk about the importance of meditation?

"Meditation is the key to self-analysis for each individual to come into their power. That is the key right there. They are talking consciously, and that is important as well, but you also need to remember that there is something inside of you that drives you called spirit. The spirit needs to be fed with quiet time. Not quiet time in dreams, but quiet time in contemplation and meditation where you just clear the mind. You are consciously and subconsciously aware at the same time. That's what meditation is. It is like being quiet and letting both sides of your brain communicate with each other. The left brain is what controls your speech. I am speaking to you through it, through using the physical body. I know how to utilize it."

Some Dominants don't seem to be able to verbalize. They can signal or nod but cannot come out and talk. With some clients, their child helpers come out and talk but the Dominant communicates through ideomotor signals.

"It doesn't mean that they are wrong, it just means that they haven't progressed to that level where they can integrate with the left brain. S's left brain is very developed. Her brain is just like everyone else. She doesn't use nearly enough of it as she could. Humans are beginning to use more of it then they did when Einstein and other people said that we didn't use that much. We are beginning to. We are beginning to have to because we have more and more knowledge that we have to know. It's affecting children even more. They are learning more in school than we ever did.

People have to understand that meditation is the key to integrating the two halves of the brain to work together ... the concentric circles are the very heart of this whole thing. If you are integrated, if your mind works together, your inner subconscious desires are manifested out in your conscious life in a positive direction and it is not hurting anybody, then what is the problem? You are actually living your power. That's what Deepak Chopra is talking about, that's what Gary Zukav is talking about ... getting in touch with that power within. That's what meditation helps you to do because the power within can only manifest itself when the two halves of the brain work together toward enlightenment, education, knowledge, peace or whatever label you want to attach to this emotion. It's letting go of fear and accepting love.

What happens in meditation is usually ... the first few times ... let me try to give it to you in the sense of what happened to S. The first time she got into deep philosophical thought on herself and started doing real self-examination, it was terrible. You go through a couple of periods where you feel like I am a terrible awful person, the things I've done, and the things I've been. You have to let go of that negativity and realize that is your past and to forgive yourself and move on. That's what meditation can help you do but most people are unable to do that and that is where trance work comes into play because it utilizes the meditative state to contact the subconscious brain to allow it to free up parts that are being held back."

That is what the abreaction does. Don't most Dominants want to clear things up?

"No one ever wants to carry hurt and pain. Eighty-year-old women who are not whole and integrated can be rejected and feel paranoid and have pain. You build this conception around yourself when you are young. Your point about the five-year-old, or the child helper ... that is when in our conscious reality of the birth process when the child isn't born until the child "dies" as an old person. There is a formation going on of psychological thought and how the perception of this psychological thought is played out in this conscious reality is what we are trying to alter. It can either be internal or external that causes the problems. If it is internal, it is an attached energy. If it is external, it is like abuse or it can be harsh words. It can be misunderstandings. People don't understand where their child is coming from and the parents never have enough time for their children. You see this a lot."

Can you talk about why S's five-year-old helper needed to come out. What was going on at that time that might have been overwhelming?

"There was no sexual abuse. The father left and went to Vietnam. It was a huge change. He had never been gone like that for a year. It put a lot of stress on the other adults in the household. It brought out this part of her that wasn't quite ready to come out yet. It put a lot of fear ... but what happened was that S's ancestor who had been a wise woman but was burned at the stake for being a witch, Claire, was part of S. It is like a DNA strand that carries on from generation to generation. Sometimes people get it and sometimes they don't. S got Claire's. Claire had a daughter Amelia who carried on the lineage. This is the same family that lives in --------- now. They have a couple of branches ... there is one in Scotland still. These people have a gift of being able to see directly into someone and know what their problem is. Claire was burned for it because she could heal people. She could lay her hands on them and they would be well. That scares people. They don't understand how someone can be like this or how someone can understand how to utilize the energies around them. Claire didn't understand it herself. That's why she couldn't protect herself. There was a lot of fear and hypocrisy going on in those times where people didn't want to talk about it."

What time frame was that?

"It was 1673."

As I understand, Claire was connected to the five-year-old helper.

"She was a part of the soul of this person S. Her intention was to comfort at first, to be with the child ... the father was gone. She came out as sort of a helper. When you think about a child and their imagination and their playmates, their imaginary playmates, what are they really thinking of? Maybe to them that person is very real but it is just an inner world. You don't know unless you are that person. That's your perception of what you are seeing them think. You don't know what they are seeing. S needed comfort. Her father was gone. Claire tried to comfort her but it got 'sputtered' because Claire held a lot of fear about the fire, just fear period. She was a terrified entity, a terrified energy that suffered a painful end. That's not what she wanted to have happen to this person. So she also pushed a little bit in knowing that something inside wasn't right. Claire was smart enough to know that she was with the person who was going to help free her.

When we are coming together to form the human soul before we are born into the person, we are energy fields. When we came together and I guided them into this system, at birth, they (Claire, Jack and Jane) knew that I was going to do this one day ... that I was going to put them out of their misery. It's really hard because now people are drawn to S consciously knowing that there is something about her ... it can be real leery because S will have to be careful of what she gives up. She can heal people with her mind, tell them what they need to do to help themselves — whether they believe her or not is their problem."

It is really you coming through?

"Exactly, I am her essence. I'm not her, I'm not the conscious part that makes the stupid mistakes. I know better."

You knew that when you came to be Ss's Dominant that Jack, Claire, and Jane would be tagging along. Did these energies know that they were supposed to cooperate?

"They are a part that I bring with me to create a whole ... like putting the cherries in, and the flour to make the crust, and the sugar, and all the other ingredients to make this cherry pie. There are all these different ingredients that go in to make a whole thing. You can not make something out of one entity ... I'm just one soul. There is so much different energy going on in your body, just physically, different parts, different organs, and different systems. It's the same thing with the mental part except I guide it. I'm the Overpart. It's like sitting at the computer controls and controlling the computer. I'm the part that is in the mind, not the brain. The brain is what I utilize. The brain is like a giant computer. It's like the most profound computer ever. You program it to think what you want, and it will happen. There are a lot of subconscious messages that people feed themselves. They feed themselves how evil they are, how bad they are, and they have been doing it for so many thousands of years now that they can't see past it. There are so many blind people that are out there saying, 'You're evil.'

I know that to find inner peace you've got to meditate. You have to become a whole person. Read what Jesus said! Maybe his translation of 'I am the Way, the Truth, and the Life' was misconstrued just a little bit. I live the way the truth and the life. Come on think. He totally believed in himself and his own power and that is what everyone needs to have consciously. Jesus didn't just do it subconsciously; he knew how to tap into it, to God, to his father, to him. It was all one. If you are not whole, then you are not all one. The whole point is to become unified ... your whole mind to be able to utilize that power within. Now I can run this computer the way that it is supposed to be run. We have gotten rid of all the bad file commands. Look at it like that."

So you are saying that the brain is nothing without your guidance?

"Exactly. If I leave, you die or the system shuts down. Actually I do leave. I have to be refreshed. I have to go to my 'Source' every once in awhile. That's what happens when you sleep. Then your brain is left on automatic pilot. Part of what you see during sleep in dream state are images that are created for you ... sometimes they are just pure fun. Sometimes there is a message in them. Sometimes I program the message in there to be in your consciousness, because the other parts of you that are part of me go with me. Then you come back and maybe can hazily remember like something peacefully settling over you or maybe you feel like you have flown through the air on a silver cord."

You can quickly come back to protect the Host?

"Absolutely. You are connected by an energy tunnel. I can immediately vortex back into your self, into your human form."

Is that why a lot of the clearing away cannot be done when we are sleeping, because these other things are happening?

"Humans are definitely not ready to hear about that part yet. Maybe twenty years from now people will leap to where I am, and will know what I am talking about. It is like thinking that the world is flat for so long. There is only so much that we can deal with at once."

I cited a quote to the effect that time is Nature's way of not having everything happen at once.

"That is very good. That's exactly why humans create the imagery of time for themselves. They can't deal with everything all at once. That's why human nature, left brain nature ... the reason why change is so scary to it is because it means reorganizing all of your data files. Who the hell wants to go through that process? It takes a long time. If you ever deal with a heavy duty computer, if you were to have to reorganize all of your files, sometimes it takes a long time ... you sit there and defrag it or defrag your hard drive ... or system reorganize your files ... it will take 20 to 30 minutes sometimes and you can't use your computer the whole time that it is happening because all these files are being reorganized. Nothing else can be done."

That is the process of the abreaction, of having the children come out to release their feelings, having Jack and Claire resolve their trauma , and help Jane let go and forgive so she can stay and help in a positive way.

"Exactly. We weren't getting rid of them. What I was getting rid of with Jack and Claire and they knew this coming in, was that I was helping them to move on to the next level. It is like coming to class with a teacher and now Jack and Claire can become ... (helpers), I don't know about Jack ... (the Dominant directed communication toward Jack) 'Jack, I know you're out there. You have got to chill.' I think that he is going to have to go through another incarnation. 'Jack, I am sorry, but you are going to have to go through another incarnation.' Claire is ready. 'Jack, you have to remember that this time with your family is important and your energy fields will be renewed and refreshed and when you come back the next time, you may even make it. It will happen then.' Claire is beautiful. She is helping and is ready to become her own entity now ... to move into her energy field to help control others ... to help others."

Can you talk a little bit more about how the energy is transmuted through the DNA?

"You have to remember that there are a lot of eggs and sperm out there that can come together in many different combinations. That is first. When two people meet and mate and have a child physically, sometimes it brings together a genetic code that has not been seen perhaps in 250 years and it usually takes that long for another genetic code to pop up that is similar or very similar and that allows energy to reattach itself. It is like reproducing energy. I am struggling with this so that especially your scientific readers, your physicists, biologists, understand that DNA is a code. If you process the right code, you are going to tap in ... it is like processing a code on a computer, if you have the right code number, you bring it together, and your system is going to come up. That is what your DNA is. Your parents through their manifestation of love and creation, and the sexual pleasure, the physical side, bring about the code that can unlock the potential for a human. Not all humans are meant to be born. I am sorry Right to Lifers. They are not born until they are born. It's because that energy field knew that it was not going to come into that child at this time. Things are not working out the way that I wanted. We spend that time when that fetus is developing organizing all the different parts that are there genetically. We are the energy that processes that. We bring it all together and at the moment of life, when we breath in ... we are not inhabiting ... consciousness isn't inhabiting this baby when it is inside its mother. We are guiding it. We know that this is the potential. Sometimes the potential is not right and we abort the process. We abort it. But if you ask me, human beings and their religious beliefs about birth control are ridiculous. We have way, way, way, way too many people on the face of the earth right now who are suffering, needlessly I may add, because they can't control themselves. There is no enlightenment going on and people aren't thinking. We need to become wise to what is going on around us. .. what we are doing to ourselves. That is because most people are sleeping!!! They are just totally left brain. That's it. Even if they are beginning to be left brain, some people are so asleep that they can't even be that. They can't even be intelligent. They are so overwhelmed by the energy fields around them in knowing that something ... that they won't integrate. They have so much pain that they are carrying around from when they were a child and not letting go of it and not realizing their full potential and that is all that hypnosis is. That's what this trance work does, is to release that."

What happens to people who don't release the blocked off trauma and go through their life carrying these feelings and having all of the symptoms and manifestations that goes with this?

"That is their karma. If they can't overcome it, if they can't learn the lesson, then they are destined to repeat the mistakes over and over. It is only when you wake up and you stop repeating the mistakes and you start realizing the motivation behind them, that you then change your karma, that you change your energy ... when you let go. Most people won't do that."

It seems that the energies come together for that reason, for Jack to leave ... for Jane to resolve her feelings so she can help S, and for us to accept what comes our way and learn and grow from it.

"Certainly. That is part of it. There is part of it that does that and there is part of it that is us. It is not the only reason to let go of the old stuff. The Tibetans are right about the karma but I'm sure they know this. Part of the reason is to help process problems. It is like the computer. There are also the games on there that you can play, 'this is fun.' You are here to create, to enjoy the five senses ... to realize that part of our Spirit created these beings so we could enjoy these pleasures of the flesh, the physical senses ... not that we can go around and sleep with whomever we want ... not that we can drink to excess. Anything in excess is a sin, anything. Overeating, oversleeping, over-reading your Bible, etc. Anything to the point where you become dogmatic and push yourself on other people and become ugly and rude and abusive is a sin. If you want to call anything a sin, that is it. If you are not in balance, that is it. That is all that Jesus was trying to point out about evil because that is evil. Evil is the excess of something to the point where it creates hate and dogma."

When a woman is pregnant and the family is talking to the baby, is that doing anything?

"Let me put it this way, it is letting us know that the parents are looking forward to this presence in their life. We are very glad for that. Usually we choose parents who are other energies that we have missed. They have been alive ... they have been in this form and that we can only communicate with them through the dream state or during that time when the physical part is sleeping. So we want to come into the physical so we can hang around with these people again. Not always. You don't choose all of your relatives. You do choose some, your friends. A lot of times we know that these are the right parents for us."

I work with men who expose themselves and when I suggest that these men are not all bad, and that their acting out behavior is a compulsion to repeat their original trauma, my word is not generally accepted.

"People who are saying that, their minds are closed. Minds function best when open. Everybody has seen that bumper sticker. It's true. Those people have feelings. Those people have problems, very serious problems, definitely. There is something very wrong with them and they need to be kept away from other members of society who they might be able to hurt. At one point in human evolution, those people were banished. If you look at Dahmer's personality as a big pitcher of sand, the white colored sand. There were still a few sprinkles of the black sand in there. The other way around is if you are on a beach in Hawaii, there is all that black sand there. There are also pieces of white sand in there too. You can not separate bad and good and say 'You can't be all ...' It is just not possible. It's there. It exits. You have to learn how to walk in between the two and say that I choose not to be evil or I choose not to be so self-righteous that I am going to make people gag."

Why would the universe allow Dahmer to be born with all this negative energy and allow it to hurt other people?

"Why did AIDS come into existence? Why does the sky turn blue? Things just are.

You cannot ask why about things like that. It just happens. As far as his energy coming together, there was a purpose, the purpose being that this energy had to be processed. It was time. When he was caught, he was relieved. You could see it in the poor man's face. I feel so sorry for the victim's families. Don't get me wrong. It was a horrible thing. He did not deserve to be bludgeoned to death in prison. He needed to be studied. They needed to get into his mind a little bit more so we could understand."

Carrying blocked off trauma seems to cause a real energy drain.

"That's all that it is. (An energy drain.)

Let me end this with another computer analogy. If you don't have a Pentium processor, you are not going to go very fast. The more hard drive that is being used up to store stuff, the more time it takes to process your information. Your computer may seem sluggish and tired. It takes longer to get started. It takes longer to process stuff, or it crashes frequently. Of course it does. It has way too much stuff on the hard drive."

Interview Three with Dominant

Because you allude to awareness of things in S's reality, I asked how you watch TV for example. I ask this because there is a mythical sense of the Higher Self as some ethereal spirit that is up in the clouds somewhere. People will find it hard to believe that I am sitting here talking to you.

"The body is like the VGA monitor, the hardware, and the keys of the computer. Your eyes are like the mouse that points and chooses what they are going to take in. You can look at it as an analogy of that sort. Your hard drive is always aware of what is going on. It has to be. It has the counter clock in it. You have the counter clock in you too ... if you are going to live or die, it's up to your counter clock and how well you take care of it. It's theoretically possible that people could live forever, if they were to renew themselves. The counter clock would never go off. Just like a computer, it would never go off, if someone was to replace the battery. Does that make any sense to you? That is exactly what it is like. I am the hard drive. I am the Soul and I was created by my creators.

I don't want to give people the analogy that if the computer dies, it is all gone ... trash it, it is empty, there is no energy left, it is not plugged into the wall. The reader has to remember that we are not plugged into anything, not like a computer that we can control. We have the biggest co-processor and hard drive up there in our brains. We are energy. That is the Soul. That's what makes us different from computers. When we finally learn how to access and tap into that energy to create ourselves ... (is this making sense to you?)"

You exist as an energy field without being in the body?

"If you can learn to utilize cells to regenerate parts of your body, you could ... live on and on. People freak-out when that is mentioned. It is a very misunderstood concept. There are many animals in the animal kingdom that are so concentrated on survival that if they lose a limb, they will grow another one. That can happen. It doesn't necessarily happen to humans because they place their beliefs and limitations on their brains ... it is like putting things in the way of programs that you want to access, files that have been planted in your brain when you were brought into this world. They are in your system. You know that they are there but you can't access them because you are afraid. That's the fear. The fear is what is blocking access to our files. You look at the fear as a virus, something that stomps on your computer drive. It keeps you from accessing the information that is still there. It will be overwritten if given enough time until eventually you will only have the overwrite, because you have lost all access to the information that you had on there originally.

All the programming you receive sets your personality type, some programming can come from past lives ... we discussed that in different areas. The problem is that it is all set usually within the first five to ten years of your life, although the overwriting on the programs that you come into the world with, the innate wisdom of the baby to grow and change and develop is overwritten by racial hatred, negativity, fear, and stuff that you get from your parents and others around you that twists your thoughts ... it is unfortunate but it does happen. That's why you have clients come to you, because they have had trauma. That's what has happened to them. They have had so much bad programming that it has deteriorated their minds."

In reading Roger Woolger's book, *Other Lives, Other Selves*, he is sighting theorists who talk about the birth trauma and how that affects the child. You were saying that the unborn child is not recording any information. Can you talk about that?

"It's not recording anything negative. They hear their mother's voice very well. They may be able to hear some outside stimuli ... not to process it in the senses that we have. They have no understanding at that point of 'outside.' They do not conceptualize things as older humans do."

It has been suggested that the birth trauma concept may be more about the past life energy of one of the helpers.

"I agree. When the energy is set is at the time of birth itself. That is when you enter the world. You don't enter the world yet when you are inside of your mother. That's when the energies are aligning ... they are choosing, we are going to line up now. We are going to enter this child now. As the child takes its first breath, that's when the energy for the life force that we sustain as an independent body enters this life, yes! What you have before that is a fetus inside the mother."

What if there is birth trauma?

"Yes, certainly. The energies that have come in are experiencing a backlash. They are trying very hard to succeed with the birth. They want the birth to occur. A lot of times they will pull back. Maybe something wasn't right in the configuration."

So you and the helpers are aware of the trauma of the birth.

"Look at the trauma at the death. It is the exact same thing in reverse. It is like letting go of all the energies and letting go if you want to die. Most people fear death just like the energy fears birth because it is a painful process. Sometimes death is also. Sometimes birth is not painful. It is most painful for the mother, not necessarily the infant. The infant has been desensitized for the last nine months to endure that pain, pushing through. That is why some people suffer claustrophobia because they had a traumatic birth.

In fact this body, S's body ... she got stuck. Her shoulders got stuck in her mom. There was a doctor up on the table pushing ... I can see this. I wasn't there. I mean I was there as a baby, an infant trying to enter the world through this human. I can remember seeing him on the table with his butt kind of in the mother's face pushing on her stomach ... pushing the child out because the shoulder was stuck."

Were you hovering over the scene as you talked about before?

"You are waiting to enter at the first breath."

How does it feel to enter the baby's body?

"It is like being sucked in. Then when you really die and you don't go to the light, it is the same thing. When the actual moment of death occurs, when the human dies, that is the same feeling. It is like a reversal of the other way. That is peaceful. The birth process is the traumatic one for the soul entity. We know that we are going home when the human dies. For the energy part of us, we know that we are going to be renewed.   For example, Dannion Brinkley who wrote Saved by the Light reported that he left his body after being struck by lightning but returned to fulfill his mission."

(It should be noted that I have found that the Dominants are aware of significant occurrences and individuals who are making a difference on the earthly realm. The Dominant sees through the third eye, the sixth chakra, and can tune into relevant human issues. S's Dominant was aware for example of the contribution that Gary Zukav, Wayne Dyer, Deepak Chopra, to name a few, are making to the paradigm shift.)

"Basically the death process for his case was specifically related to the fact that he needed to be taught knowledge while he was out and his energy needed to absorb a certain amount of knowledge. They wanted him to go zooming back in so he could take that knowledge and help people. He was chosen. There are very few people who are chosen like that. You have to have a lot of respect on the human level for someone who is willing to change their entire life and belief system. Sometimes it has to happen in a very dramatic fashion like that in order for people to really believe it. It is beginning to happen more and more. People are opening their eyes up a little more."

Is there a separate energy that will be born out of this existence? I know that you don't take your consciousness with you.

"No. Not in the sense of ... I see what you are saying. I am it. What happens karmically to the soul is happening to me. My lessons…"

As the Dominant, you take what you learn from S's life.

"It is not conscious to me. I am conscious of S … aware that I am in that body that operates on that level during a business day or whatever and I try to help her make more decisions. But people who block me off in their own selves, not me per se, but the one that inhabits them, the people who have a Dominant guiding them, people who block their Dominant off and refuse to see things or refuse to open their eyes, they fear death, there is a lot of fear, they don't understand the concept that their consciousness is working with the higher part of their brain to guide them through driving a car, eating dinner, physical activities and even sleeping. Where do you go when you sleep? What does your consciousness do? There has been so much mystery surrounding this for so long. That's the time when we get to go on an adventure, learn a lesson, or we can kind of free form. The consciousness gets to take a rest, it has to. It is utilizing too much energy."

It doesn't seem like this system is going to be stuck here.

"L, S's daughter said something to me that struck me quite profoundly. She said if you die with a light heart, you go straight up to Heaven or straight up to the cosmos, or whatever you want to call it, climb the vine. But if you die with a heavy heart with fear and sadness, and if you are not accepting of it, that is when you get stuck. It means letting go of this life and all of its problems no matter what. Even the most terrible criminal who is sitting on death row … there are some of them who have been turned to positive thoughts and they have begged the family of the person they have murdered for forgiveness. You see these men on the TV show and they are saying, 'I feel so awful, I am so sorry,' even though they are going to die anyway. They are not trying to get out of jail. A lot of them on death row are waiting for the wheels to grind into place and they accept what has happened and they do, they die with light hearts. Are they really not going to heaven because of the bad past acts they committed? It is at that moment of death ... that's why the Catholics believe in last rights and absolution of the soul. It is sort of like a formality of letting you be able to die with a light heart so that you can go directly to the source instead of being distracted along the way and not finding that light, not finding that energy and being consumed back into the realm of existence that you came from originally."

Can a spirit leave without being attached to a physical body?

"Sure. Usually it helps if they have a guide."

What I want to talk about is how you, the Dominant, choose for the child helpers to come out when there is an overwhelming or traumatic situation.

"In my sense there is no time. For the clarification of your reader, it can happen anywhere between three-years-old and all the way to seven. Some times there is a lot of fog surrounding them. It takes a long time for concepts to get through to them. There is sometimes a disruption in the genetic code that allows somebody to take longer to learn."

I have heard from other Dominants that they knew when they entered the system that the Host would be abused or in this case that S's father would die when S was a child.

"Yes. When they say God knows all, that's what that means. It's you who has to make that decision. It's the consciousness that has to make the decision in how you are going to deal with it. If you learn to tap into your higher level parts of your brain and really begin to understand your senses and work with your soul instead of against it, those answers come to you. That's what people call prayer and meditation."

People aren't praying right ...

"They want material stuff. They are praying to be relieved from the stress of the job. They are not praying for guidance. Sometimes people do but it seems like it is convenient whenever they want to pray for guidance ... whenever things have gotten so bad. No, it has to be a continual process."

As you discussed before, meditation is the state of mind that occurs when we the conscious part are in direct link with you the unconscious part.

"Christians have the concept of prayer screwed up as though they are some little low life form of trash and that God is this great powerful thing that is high above. It is not like that. God comes from within you to speak with you. That's what people didn't understand when they set Joan of Arc on fire and they asked her how God spoke to her and she said, 'he speaks to me through my imagination.'

They thought she was crazy. She wasn't crazy. She had just saved her country from destruction."

How about the quote, "God is in you, he is everywhere."

"The interpretation of Christianity became uni-dimensional. That was mostly due to the church. Not so much the original beliefs of the Pagans. Jesus Christ was nothing more than a Pagan. He was like the greatest hippie that ever lived in that sense. If you want to talk about peace, love and light, this man had it all. People don't want to see that. They don't want to think that he lived out in the desert and lived off the land and he didn't buy into material things. When they said to him about taxes and he held the schilling or whatever it was out to the centurion and said, 'Render over Caesar that which is Caesar's, and under God that which is God's.' Don't people get it!! Material wealth is not where it's at.

You are not going to be happy if you don't have your soul right. The soul can't be right if the Dominant is being blocked off and traumas are allowed to surface and triggers are allowed to play a role in creating bad life choices. People who expose themselves, people who abuse kids ... they are doing nothing more than reacting to the bad programming they have got in their hard drive."

(Blocked off trauma is stored in the amygdala, a sort of primitive hard drive. The blocked off feelings are not tied to language or rationale, and tend to manifest in obsessional behaviors. Thus the individual can't access the more rational part of the brain during a behavioral reenactment.)

Until people clear away blocked off emotions, they keep repeating these feelings in present moment, self-defeating behaviors. The whole point of this book is to get people to see that they need to clear away blocked off, unresolved emotions from overwhelming and or traumatic experiences so that their Dominant, their Higher Self, their spirit, is free to guide them through this life journey.

"Exactly. Be healthy. It allows you to always find humor in situations. You can make decisions and you find your own power within. That is the key right there, when you can tap into your Dominant and rid yourself of the negativity and fear; you will realize how powerful you are and how much you can change your life."

Let's stay with the concept of prayer for a moment. You had said that S had tried to mediate but did not ask the right kind of questions.

"S was raised in a family where the mother's family was raised 'Christian' but they weren't real churchgoers at least not in the generations that she saw. Mostly the reason why is because that family was Scottish and they were Pagans and Witches. They had a lot of people who were involved in Masons and higher occult things. S's father wasn't like that at all. Her father was raised in a very strict southern

Baptist household down in Texas ... very, very Protestant. Southern Baptist is almost as Protestant as you can get ... no drinking, no smoking, no gambling, none of that dancing, no makeup. Of course nobody pays much attention to that anymore. The idea is that they are very strict in some of their beliefs and interpretations of the Bible. That's how the father had taken over as the spiritual guide in the house. They went to church all the time. The mother questioned these beliefs because she comes from this line of Witches, women who have had clairvoyant thoughts. The mother would ask why we were not allowed to drink wine if Jesus did. She gave S a lot of insight as a child to ask the right questions. However, the dogmatic teachings of the Baptist church overlaid that and that is how she was taught to pray, not the 'Our Father who art in Heaven,' not the Lord's prayer, although they said that every week, but it was more like ... go to a Baptist church sometime and sit there and they sing the Doxology and they pass the plate and the preacher stands up there yelling and screaming about hell fire and damnation. S didn't have the faintest clue about how to pray and how to become one with God and how to listen to his voice and to be in meditation. It was all like you see on TV ... 'Please come save my child.' It is so much of what is ingrained from the boob tube that we see or what we see around us or what we hear or feel, depending on what one of our senses is more Dominant in that particular person ... how they intake things. I'll tell you. She just didn't know how to pray. She was asking the wrong way. She was demanding. 'I know that you are up there God and you have to help me.' That doesn't work. You just can't access God that way. You have to come through the inner self." *(Remember that the Dominant is the connection between you and the universal intelligence.)*

People are trying to get in touch with God. They don't know how to get in touch with their Higher Self which is you, let alone even know that you exist within them as the guiding force.

"If you can't know yourself, how can you know God? Most people will admit readily if you ask them what they want to do. They don't know. They have no clue."

Without a vision you shall perish ...

"With S, it's not about a career anymore. What do you want to do with your life for S was always limited about being a lawyer or a fireman. She realizes now that what you do for a living is not nearly as important as what you do spiritually when you are not there at the job, or how you come to that job no matter what the job. You can enjoy it if you have your heart in the right place or your soul in the right place. You can rise far in any position if you understand your own power. That's how mere stock boys rise to become the president of the company because they know that they are powerful and that they can make the right decisions."

Napoleon Hill who wrote *Think and Grow Rich* talked about success being less about money and more about knowing what you want and sending specific messages to the unconscious mind regarding your goals.

"Exactly, that's all it is. To quit and run away and to drink yourself into inebriation, or overeat, or to put all these things into your body which we consider to be moral sins… Nothing is a sin unless it is done to a point where it breaks down your will, deteriorates your power. That's a sin."

If you are my Dominant, do you listen to me? Don't I have a right to have conscious choices about goals?

(This brings up the eternal struggle between what we want to do on a conscious level versus what we are supposed to be doing at the soul level.)

"Everybody has that. That's where the choice comes in. Whether or not you are willing to listen to the inner voice that is telling you what to do, is going to depend on how successful you are. Consciously you may say that I am really good at this and I want to do this but if something inside of you is telling you that this is not where my path lies, then you know that it is a conscious thing that is more ego. If you are going to look at a Freudian perspective of the ego, id and superego, I am kind of like the superego. The ego is the consciousness. The id is the basic instinct for survival. I guess that I can buy that but it is just a lower form of ego. That is like the superego and the ego fighting over what is best.

Teens need to be educated and not lied to about this kind of stuff from the time they are children. There is nothing shameful or harmful in the sexual act of sexual union, especially if you are in love with somebody. That's the closest you can come to actually being one with them. It's very special. Kids are taught to only heed those urges when they understand that the other person feels the same way that they do … it's a commitment type of feeling."

Children who were sexually abused tend to act out sexually at a young age.

"Adults need to be in work like this where they can clear away their trauma so they don't do that (act out blocked off feelings)."

It's back to the premise that your blocked off feelings keep getting you into situations that are reminiscent of the original trauma.

"The best thing that you can do is to get kids as soon as you can who have been abused, get them to clear that mess out of their minds so that they don't feel shameful."

That leads me to talk about the frustration in working with children under the age of 12 or 13 who do not seem developmentally ready to receive the blocked off feelings. This is not to say that children don't benefit from therapy at a younger age. Just that I don't often see that children under the age of 12 or so have major abreactions regarding their trauma.

"I do have to agree with you. The reason why is because the personality and the mind itself on the conscious level doesn't conceptualize yet. You can't put an age limit on it. Some kids who are nine are ready. Some kids at 13 are ready, but then you get some people who are 45 but are not ready, because they can't deal with it."

So you as the Dominant make that decision that S can't handle these feelings yet.

"Exactly! Say that the child is already living in a fantasy world so that none of this affects him yet ... he's not acting out or doing anything crazy to release the trauma because he doesn't remember it. It has not come into play yet. But when the anger starts surfacing, that's when you need to get them into therapy. The things to tell the parents or the reader is to look for the clues ... the withdrawal, the silences, the storming around in anger that emanates off the kid ... if you feel that, you may want to consider having them, not when they are nine-years-old, if they are just frustrated, but when they are really starting to say stuff like, 'you can't make me do this, I hate you,' or when they really start to get rebellious or angry. That's the sign that now is the time before things deteriorate to the point where you can not talk to that child and they have gone out and done something horrendous that you can't save them from."

What seems to happen is that the Dominant often can't stop this anger from coming out.

"Exactly. That's why the child is doing it ... it's telling you, the parent that it loves you more than anything, that it hates you and is angry with you because it wants you to help it. They don't know how to verbally tell you, 'please get me help, please help me.' But when you do, the child will be grateful and love you more and you will have a better bond with them. If the parent is the one who is abusing the child, they both need help. But say there is a mother in the house or a father who can notice that there is something really wrong ... say a mother who is silent and let's the things go on but she feels terrified and afraid ... first of all she needs to take a stand against that kind of violence by finding the help and support services that are offered. The second thing is that they do try to get them some clinical help but a lot of people turn away from it because of the bad wrap that counseling has gotten from just sitting there talking in an office about your problems. It doesn't seem to help anything. No, they need to get into some therapy where they are healing their soul from this terrible, horrendous experience."

By the time people get to this type of therapy, they have been in therapy so long without symptom relief, that they are turned off with the notion of therapy. Also, it seems to me that parents are pressured to go through their managed care where kids are being pumped up with psychotropic drugs and are not receiving the deeper therapy that is needed.

"How long did it take for S, about two years? This girl had been looking for therapeutic help from the time that she was 18 and went to college."

It was interesting how the eight-year-old came out right away.

"That's the one who needed the most help because she was reliving her father's death every day. It was really holding S back because she couldn't get over that feeling that 'people owe me something because the government killed my dad.' The government has killed a lot of people's dads and moms and various other relatives. It is a feeling of entitlement that had to be dismissed."

The symptoms are telling the external people, the parent even the Host to get help. I would say that even younger children can benefit from therapy in that some negativity can be released but when the anger emerges the system seems to be losing control.

"Yes. The angry teenager is about to come out and that is the last thing that the parents want to see. There are books written about how to deal with your rebellious teenager."

We need to realize that the anger is anger that was blocked off when the Host was under the age of 7 or so.

"That's why many cultures, say the native American culture, Indian cultures, and I think the Jewish culture, the Bar Mitzvah, have rituals it's symbolic ... the idea being that you pass the child through ceremonies from childhood to adulthood and usually that is what it is. It is to get rid of childhood trauma."

It is the Shaman concept of lifting of the lights to clear away the blocked off emotions in the teenager from their childhood, so that they can enter their adulthood without this emotional baggage. So what I am purporting here is not a new concept, but a concept that needs to be integrated in the therapeutic community.

"This is the easiest way for this culture that has been so engrossed in the religious concept of shame and guilt to accept the signals. We have been so demoralized. Freedom has a price. Being in a country like this where you can see and do ... there is very little censorship allowed on a certain level. Things are available readily. You become very desensitized. Those are the signals that you have to look for now instead of the ones of wisdom and knowledge that ancient peoples did because they understood.

People were smart enough to know which individuals were troubled because the quarters were so much closer. The society had to band together for survival. If

there was a Dahmer among the group, they would have known it ... which one it was, because they were all there and there weren't that many people. Now all you can see is anger, a withdrawal, or a cold silence. Sometimes it is the reverse of the angry teenager ... it's the angry teenager being extremely cold and austere ... they won't say a word. Comedians say that it is the quiet ones you have to watch. Sometimes the ones that scream the most just want the attention. They want you to help them to figure out how to get past this bad stage of feeling low self-esteem, pressure and stress. They are really beginning to understand how what we call reality works ... the real world, supposedly, and how nasty people can be to each other. Their childhood dreams of peace, love, and light, are all starting to diminish in the face of what we call reality. You need to give them the key to their soul so they can go back to the peace, love, and light, anytime they want, instead of feeling all of these angry, scared feelings all of the time."

Talk about S's development in terms of the first split off around the age of 5. Do you make that decision to block off the overwhelming feelings at the grandparent's house? You and the child helpers were going along, and then there was a major change in the family. Talk about your decision to block off the feelings that were too overwhelming for S at that developmental stage.

"Right ... It's sort of like a realization, a kind of a dawning that happens to each individual at a certain moment in their life. It's like a thunderbolt hitting you, an awakening ... people awaken at different levels. What happened there was probably the first time S's grandmother ever really got angry with her. It was something that hurt her, that made her say, 'Wait a minute, she has never been like that before.' It was something that you noticed or felt a bad feeling and the bad feeling was scary. Sure, we take a part of the soul and it is kind of siphoned off into this area because it is a fearful feeling and it is deposited there and it is imprinted on that child because it is such an overwhelming feeling. Usually it is mostly fear. There can be some excitement mingled with it because it is a change. They realize that they have had a new thought that they have never had before. You know how kids will get a concept in school. Say you are studying a mathematical equation in algebra and you are totally baffled. Then all of a sudden, you get it. 'Wow, I understand this.' That's exactly what it is. It can be an exciting feeling but at the same time it can be very scary depending on what the thing is that triggered it. So sometimes you may feel that feeling again as an adult. You will get that same equation but it was brought about by a fearful situation and it will trigger that anger or that trauma that you felt because it is attached to that fear."

You had to siphon off some of that fear from S, the conscious child.

"There was a lot of talk because of S's mom not getting along with her parents. S's mom never really got along with her mother. They were exact opposites karmically. S's grandmother is a strong willed Aires woman and S's mother is a strong willed Libra woman. If you understand the energy alignments, you don't find it to be so unbelievable. S's mother is diametrically opposite of her own mother on the karmic wheel. Aires and Libras are opposite. What is so amazing about this is that S and her daughter L are also opposite, Cancer and Capricorn. Fortunately though, water and earth make for a lot better combination than air and fire. You don't see mud slides devastate too much. Usually water and earth work together to create bounty. All four are cardinal signs. All four are very strong willed woman. The grandmother is the one who leads this quadrangle and she was an intimidating woman and she and her husband would argue a lot because he would drink. There were some really scary arguments that were witnessed by S when she was a child."

So you felt that you needed to block some of this off.

"Sure, because it was scary. She had been living all of her life up to that point with her mother and father. Her dad just doted on her. Her grandmother doted on her. It was that she was a little older child and seeing something that she had never seen before and it scared her."

The point is that this is not always about an overwhelming horrible trauma. The unconscious mind has to block off overwhelming stress because of the child's ability to deal with those emotions.

"It doesn't have to be a bad feeling. Sometimes people have good feelings but they act out in bad ways. The acting out of the bad experience is what gives them the good feelings, that is what I am trying to say."

There is excitement in acting out the bad feelings. Bessel van der Kolk talks about the fact that opiates are being released when blocked off trauma is being re-experienced. Eg. The excitement of being scared at a horror movie, the high that follows domestic violence, the thrill that criminals seem to have in acting out their rage in the anti-social behaviors.

"Yes, that is exactly what I mean by that. It raises that adrenalin level. If it is a negative action that brings about this good feeling, you are taught to feel guilt and shame in which of course with people like Gacey and Bundy ... they should. You shouldn't be allowed to go around taking the life, liberty, and pursuit of happiness away from other people. There is a respect level that has to be initiated between the forces of each human."

Talk about the five-year-old helper.

"She was there to help with fear."

So she did her job?

"Yes. She did her job but she was also attracted to the past life energy that was with her. This is where people… the reader may get a little lost."

How did Claire get connected to the five-year-old helper? I have seen with other past life energies that they tend to attach to a child helper with matching feelings and want to believe that they are helping that child helper in some way. But when it is time to deal with the feelings held by that child helper, they know that they have to leave or resolve their feelings if they are to stay for the best interest of the system.

"Claire was part of the ancestral line of these people. She was a family type entity. She passed on at the moment of trauma to S from the grandmother. I know that this is going to sound very, very strange. She was a family helper and when S's great-grandmother died, she came in … she just follows the family around … she had, until she was released. She came to S because she knew that S was going to release her one day, free her … because she didn't know how. She could see in this child right away that this child had no fear. The fear is present is everybody, just like the Yin and the Yang. If you are mainly positive, you are going to have a little bit of negative. If you are mainly negative, you are going to have a little bit of positive. You can't ever get away from that. She (Claire) knew that S walked on the line between those two. She was a family type entity."

Did you have a say in letting Claire come into the system?

"Oh yea. I knew beforehand what this life was going to be like or what more or less was going to happen with this person … that she (Claire) was going to be a gifted individual and that their fear would be overcome in this person and that she would be able to heal other people by simply allowing them to look inside themselves or take the souls around her and exorcise them through her channel to the next level. She definitely can channel spirits. That's a given. Claire attached to the five-year-old."

With many child helpers, they talk about the fact that they have a protector who usually listens but isn't able to come out and talk. The sense is that they will leave when everything is cleared away.

"It is something that attaches to each generation of a family, depending on how strong the family is …"

Sometimes these external helpers aren't there and I wish they were because then the Dominant is overwhelmed in trying to keep everything under control.

"It's the genetic line, and how strong the genetic code is … That is a low level Dominant that has to deal with everything and does not know how to communicate with other entities. If we are to use the computer analogy, their hard drives have been overwritten. That Dominant has never had any programming placed into its memory banks that has been worth any amount of good to that system. What it has had or what it was innately born with in this life that it is trying to deal with in this life. It has been overwritten by so much garbage that when they do try, and they know there is a problem and they want to get help, they are clueless. To find that one computer code that is going to allow them to access that remaining bit of information ... do you know how long that would take? It is very difficult. They do not have a strong enough ... I don't want people who are reading this to feel that they are in this category. It is not hopeless. Basically their wills aren't strong enough to overcome it. It is very frustrating; it takes a lot of patience. Try working on a computer that has crashed and try to get it back up again. You'll get so frustrated. Until you find that magic key that lets you back into that hard drive to reboot your system, to bring it back up the way that it was before, you are not going to be able to access any information at all. So these people, their programming is really screwed up and they need serious, serious calming. They are the people who need to be in a home setting for a month doing nothing but therapy."

Back to Claire ... Claire seemed to connect to the five-year-old. Do the external energies like Jack and Claire and Norma know that they are not supposed to live precariously through the Host?

"Jack and Claire are more localized in the family themselves. They are passed on through contact with other humans. They have been hovering around them. It's like, 'ah, I want to attach to them.' It's almost like waiting for another bus for them. They are waiting,...they get off the bus at this one stop and say that they are stuck on person A. Person A meets up with Person B. The soul that is attached to Person A says, 'this is the one who is going to meditate, and take me out, and I'm going to be free.' It is usually from a relative to a child type of a situation."

It seems that if you are more enlightened then your Dominant has to fight off these souls that are trying to attach.

"It happens all the time. There are so many energies that bombard this system."

I have other high level Dominants who talk about fighting off energies that are trying to enter their system.

"You ought to get Dominants together. They would love to talk to each other. It is very difficult to meet other people who understand what it is like to be constantly bombarded with energy from other people. Sometimes you have to seem almost cold. It is like you have your arm out and you built a wall around you that is invisible but it is a psychic shield that allows you to only let in what you want to let in and only give out what you want to give out because your psyche becomes bombarded with requests. It is almost like being a DJ who gets 30 million requests for different songs and doesn't know which one to play first."

Did Jack and Claire know that they were supposed to behave themselves?

"Jack liked to party. He liked the footloose and fancy free feeling. The thing is that so does S, her consciousness. So that was maybe not the best decision that I have ever made. I am not going to say that I am infallible. No, no, no. My creators may be but I even wonder about them at times. Look at nature. There are lots of problems in nature. We have to wonder if there is not a little bit of chaos that reigns.

I learn lessons just like everything else. I just happen to be a lot more advanced than most of the human intelligence. There are a lot of them who are advanced like the teenager's Dominant that you describe. I wouldn't mind meeting her because she would probably understand very well what it is like. It is very uncomfortable to be around another strong Dominant though for too long. You feel intimidated ... you try to play out some willpower stuff. If they are on the same wavelength, you can have a friend that helps you achieve a level of understanding or just feel support.

I wasn't real sure that S was going to be quite that crazy sometimes. Jack knew that S was his ticket. He just took advantage of the youthful partying atmosphere that was surrounding her. He definitely enjoyed it when S was in her twenties."

Interview Four with Dominant

I asked about a friend's sister who was dying of cancer. I was told that there was a lot of anger coming out during her lucid moments. Does the system want to resolve this before the energies move on?

"That is part of it and it is also part of what caused her cancer. If she had released the anger when she was younger, the cancer wouldn't have eaten away at her. Now she is angry because of that. Her system knows this. She probably should clear some of the anger away. Maybe if ... depends on her faith, if she is Catholic, maybe they should call a priest, perhaps a Pastor ... whoever is of her faith. She needs some faith and guidance. She needs to know that she can leave with a light heart. Everything has to be resolved."

What happens near the point of death with the system if there is one helper that is still holding on to fear or anger?

"Oh yea, they are not ready to leave. Where do you think all this stuff (energy that is stuck here) is coming from that affects for example the teenager that we helped? It is from people who die who are holding on to this negative energy and that energy gets left behind. You just transform your energy level. You come back again, maybe in a different form or maybe in a human being. When you die with a heavy heart, you remain like a ghost."

The Dominant has often stated that L S's daughter has a high level shaman guide as a Dominant.

"Her mind is not being filtered or being fed a lot of garbage. She is into classical music and a very open child. She is a wolf. She already knows her spirit and her power animal."

Say one of R's *(friend's sister)* child helpers is holding on to anger at the point of dying, is it saying, "I don't want this body to die with me holding on to this anger"?

"That is part of it. I am tuning in to some real fear. (Back to my friend's sister.) Real fear ... something maybe was said to her as a child. I'm getting that four-year-old impression ... that's where this is coming from. There is something really, really wrong there. Yes, the teenager is probably angry. The anger is coming from the fear of the four-year-old. It is being expressed right now because she is in pain. Somebody needs to exorcise the pain, clear her conscious. Hopefully if she is Catholic or something, she needs to call in a Priest, someone to console her in whatever way makes her feel the most comfortable.

All religions are valid in some ways. The point of the whole exorcising is that you are on your own in this life and you have to find your way to the plane that I am at right now. If you live your life alone without making that karmic connection in dealing with these problems, you are going to suffer immensely ... internally, externally.

Sometimes it doesn't seem fair when people seem to prosper even though they are real jerks. It doesn't seem fair. Karmically it will come around because they can't take it with them when they die. Trust me; what is most important in this life is your spiritual evolution because that is what they are looking for. That's what we are looking for when we put the energy into humans in the first place ... to see the ones who can really understand and grow and evolve as humans. Most people don't want to do that. They don't want spiritual growth. They want freedom from death. They want to know when they die ... they want that scared feeling appeased. You can't. You got to go into the fire. You got to face it. You got to face what it is that scares you and let it go. You can't walk that balance. You can't be in between the Yin and the Yang where the perfect sorcery and magic live, the perfect Avatar, the spiritual balance that lies within there. You can't obtain that without first walking through fire and water, good and bad. It's all there. It's all at once.

It is like any computer. If you go to the computer, it just is there. Like any human being, they are there, but their programming they are receiving, the programming they have received ... who used them before you used them if it is a past life type thing. We have the most brilliant computer in our own bodies and we don't utilize it. It is not for prosperity or for outward worldly purposes for destroying the planet. The purpose is for inner construction of pathways to higher levels of understanding. That is exactly what it is for.

I'm tired of this, 'let's keep people in the closet stuff,' and letting the Christians rule the world and dominate us with fear, hatred and sin. They have manifested what they have sown. The fact that they have sown such hatred, contempt and violence along with the Christian religion, is so very unfortunate. Christ is very unhappy about this ... this misuse of his word and his teachings. Believe me, he is very unhappy about that. The people who are blessed by him, know it. I'm one. I have been blessed by God and Goddess as well. Christ knew about her too. He didn't speak about his mother because of his Jewish upbringing and tradition, he was trying to co-relate to his people. Also, it has been translated a zillion times. A lot has been lost in context, believe me."

Did Jesus have a relationship?

"Sometimes people know that from the minute that they are children that giving of that energy can deplete your own. It is a union with another person, but it can create its own energy and sometimes in order to become more powerful, you have to stay away from that type of energy. Personally I think, from what I am being channeled and have been told, and what I know, Christ never did. He knew that it would diminish his power.

S has a need for someone, but that is for Jane."

Interview Five with Dominant

Why don't we talk about when S's father died when she was 8-years-old and how you had to help S with this trauma?

"Literally, I was the one who dealt with it. I still feel the pain right now of losing that man for her sake. It was very hard for her because he represented everything that was good. But what hurt him the most and what I had to deal with was that I also knew that he was very disappointed when she was first born, that she wasn't a boy. His mother wrote him a scathing letter telling him to be thankful that she was healthy and well."

I remember that the eight-year-old talked about him doing a lot of things with her and that she was angry when he left.

"It is still a very, very sad thing that happened. Especially since we really don't know what happened to him with being involved with the _____(government *agency named)* **and all of those organizations. He loved his children."**

When he died, it was a matter of you the Dominant siphoning off the bad feelings in order to protect the conscious eight-year-old.

"He came to her this week and was with her to help her through, to do the right thing regarding her job. She called upon her father's energy. He was also a Dragon, 1940. He was an Aires Dragon, another Cardinal Dragon. He gave her the fire she needed. He actually put that fire in her belly to be angry enough ... instead of being the meek and timid crab that would normally crawl away. Her dad came into her and pushed her to do the right thing and to take a stand and make a mark. His energy is with me right now in fact."

I'm sure that he is aware that S is doing OK.

"I'm getting a psychic hug from him right now. He told me to tell you that he helped the eight-year-old too. As soon as he died he went directly to her to give her the strength she needed to get through the next few weeks until he was buried. Then he had his own stuff to do. He is a very powerful man ... his energy. It's not haunting, but he can be pulled by the people who love him. His energy can be pulled. I don't know that you could pull it. He was my father biologically speaking, this body. I am able to go right to him and be with him sometimes and get his energy."

The energy of the father that is with you is his Dominant, if in fact our consciousness does not go with us.

"Yes, the Dominant always goes on. That's why there are a lot of people who are asleep because there is not a lot of Dominant energy like that. Some people pull more than others. It has the ability to pull lives that belong to it. It is like being in the solar system ... let me put it this way. Remember the circle, or the computer ... it is like being able to pull on the network. When you are the Dominant, you are on the network. You can pull in information off the web. A lot of people are walking around with their computers shut off totally. The only thing that they are going on is what they see and hear and smell ... and it is not registering anything with them. They need to turn on their computer which is their brain. When Timothy Leary said, 'tune in, turn on, and drop out,' he didn't necessarily mean LSD. He didn't necessarily mean drop out of society. He meant, tune into your brain and turn it on. Tune into it and find that higher level. Figure out what is going on inside of your head. The only person who can really do it is you. Sometimes as one progresses, one needs helpers such as yourself, an external helper who facilitates the processes.

The only way that you can change is by wanting to from inside ... turning on your computer, recognizing signals that are saying, wait a minute, 'wake up and smell the coffee.' It is like waking up and turning on that power on button and going and browsing the web.

I dare all the readers of this book to do that ... to turn on their brain literally one night and sit there with no sound, no light, maybe a candle burning and to close their eyes and literally start thinking and let their thoughts just take them wherever they go and find out what starts coming out. People are afraid to do it because they are scared. Fear rules their lives."

Let's go back to S's father. Again, it is his Dominant who remains present. His child helpers for example may have gone elsewhere.

"Yes, that part of him is no longer an issue. He knew that she needed him in that form. In his physical form, the father would have been harder for S to get along with. They would have clashed a lot. They are both Dragons. He is also an Aires Fire and she is water. They loved each other a great deal but one of them had to go so the other could facilitate the process of progress and evolution. He sacrificed himself and he gave his Dominant energy to her. He (father's Dominant) came to her one night when she was nine-years-old and she literally woke up and saw him standing there in his favorite yellowish tan striped tee shirt that he used to wear, and with his glasses on. He was telling her, 'I am here to protect you and I am going to be here for a long time and I am going to help you whenever you need me. Don't worry; you are going to be safe no matter what.' There have been some tight spots that S has gotten into and she has somehow managed to get herself out of them. It is because of the father, sacrificing his life. He is part of her now. He is also a part of S's brother, but the brother does not know him as well. He gave his Dominant energy to S. S's mother (still alive) gave her the wisdom to ask the questions. That's where the two come together to create what you see in front of you (S) as an external being. The Dominant of this being that is me."

Do you get some help from S's father?

"Yes, very much so. He has a direct link to the part that I can't talk about. I can't even describe that yet. He is directly linked to that. He is an Angel."

Are we to understand that her father's energy is the position that Christians call heaven?

"Exactly... Their (Christianity) vision is very limited. They misinterpreted Jesus' words, 'I am the vine, and ye are the branches.' (John 15) If a vine keeps growing and growing and growing, and is trimmed properly, and the population was controlled, and ye are the branches, do you know how big that bush is and how fruitful it is. It is going to continue to grow out. It is not going to stay at one level. It is going to continue to grow ... I am the vine and ye are the branches. He wanted us to evolve. Most people misinterpret what that man said. He was martyred too. The energy that flows through him (Jesus) also flows through S's dad and also through S, Christ's energy, it is there, believe me. She definitely feels a lot like he does sometimes like she is going to be held up to be a martyr and knows maybe that her life is going to be at stake. There is no fear here because she knows that if it does happen, she will just move on and she will be with L."

Describe what happened to dad.

"He was a serious Christian, a serious believer in Christ's energy. He was a Deacon in his church. Even though he may have been consciously and physically limited somewhat, his spirit was right. He was right with God and Goddess. He understood more than he knew he did. He had the belief in him consciously that Witches were evil. He knows differently now. He understands God and Goddess and the duality of nature because he is in that position. He wasn't there before. His subconscious already knew. All of our subconscious already know.

We need to turn them on. Hello, turn on your computer people. Let's boot it up and let's get going. Turn on your computer, your brain. That is the ultimate computer. It created a computer. We are the ones who started the Mathematical evolution. We are the entities ... we found you as evolutionary species to inhabit. We are created out of fantasy but we are real. It's like creating something on the computer. It is an image that you have before you even create it. Then you sit down and work with software and it comes up. If a kid has blocked off energy, or if a child needs a helper, maybe they need a new modem or maybe they need to upgrade their hard drive. Their processor can't handle the information. That's where they bring in the other software, the other technology that supports. That's where they get those other helpers.

Do you know what runs a computer? It is a silicon chip. Do you know what a silicon chip comes from? A quartz. A quartz is a crystal. A crystal is not anything more than an energy source. That's what a computer runs on. It is being powered by a crystal and electricity and a 11010 binary message codes that are produced in such a fashion so that you can understand them ... that your meager brain can comprehend what is going on inside that thing (the computer). I guarantee that 90% of the people in this world do not understand how a computer operates. They just know how to point and click their way across the internet. Your brain is like that binary code. When you imprint messages such as, 'you are bad, you are evil, you are nasty,' and you do it for so long, you destroy people's psyches, their self-confidence, their esteem, their love ... you create fear and mass hysteria. That is what has happened to most of the world's population."

Talk about how S's dad's energy will move on to higher levels and new assignments.

"Correct. More than likely he has moved on to his next karmic level. His mission

175

was accomplished. He has moved on to a higher level. He may not have to come back here again.

Wouldn't that be nice? Think about it. Would you? If you could live forever IN THE KNOW, in a different body form, that was intelligence, goodness, light and love, would you want to come back here? You are here to learn more lessons. If you haven't learned your lessons yet, yes you have to come back and do it again. Sorry, that is how it works. Hell isn't anywhere except right here what we make of it. This Christian Hell where we go to when we die is a bunch of hokey pokey. That is what has caused a lot of people to fear death."

The Dominant and I discussed working together to help others release past life energy.

"S had no direction, and you are giving it to her. This is what she needs to do to help people. She has always wanted to help people."

Let's get back to the child helpers. When did the teenage helper come out to help with the anger? Remember reader, typically the teenage helper has to come out early to help with anger. With many of my clients, particularly the sexual abuse victims, the teenage helper comes out very early, usually right after the abuse begins. It is not uncommon for me to talk to a teenage helper who is older than the conscious Host. Think about that.

"Actually, the teenager has been around all of the time. S had energy from Claire. Along with the fear was a little anger. S could throw temper tantrums when she was little. When she didn't get her way, she could stomp her foot. She had these little blond curls and she was the cutest little thing. She would put her hands on her hips and would stomp her foot.

The teen helper is the part of you that holds anger and feels injustice. The teenager itself as far as becoming aware ... that doesn't happen for most anybody until they are about nine or ten ... when their cognitive sense starts awakening. Then they really see how unfair and fair things can be. That's when children lose their sense of imagination. That's the problem."

Again, with my sex abuse survivors, the teen had to come out early.

"Yes, way too early. S's didn't come out ... her father died at the right time, as far as the timing went so that she wasn't so young that she didn't know him, but she wasn't so old that he limited her freedom of thought. He would have. In his physical form he was making S and her mother wear only dresses. Women had their place."

He doesn't get upset when we talk about this now.

"He is not a conscious being with these rigid moral codes that were planted in his consciousness. His hard drive has been erased of all that bad stuff. All that he is now is just perfect love, thought, and understanding, and gentleness and kindness ... all the things you associate with love. When you die, you go into the light; the white part of the Yang ... there is a little bit of Yin, because there is a way to communicate. But when you are alive, usually you are in that Yin, where it is dark, and there is a little bit of light. You have to find that light. That is where the Yin Yang comes from. Our consciousness thinks the evil thoughts usually. Unless it is some subconscious entity coming through, but our consciousness is the one that carries it out ... not our subconscious. Our subconscious may be prompted to do this by a subconscious trigger, but it is our consciousness that feels the shame and anger. The evil and goodness just are. There is no moral or amoral about it. It just exists. The triggers, the psychic triggers that cause conscious beings to act in such a way that they rape children, expose themselves or whatever ... yes, their teenage helper came out when they were little, and they were disillusioned at a very young age. They've had no imagination, no thought left, and their consciousness is shameful, guilty, and angry. Look how sorry Dahmer was, how tragic his life was, how guilty he felt ... because somebody abused him as a child. (I agree with the Dominant that Dahmer was abused in this lifetime but as the Dominant said before, he also had some past life energy which gave impetus to the evil behaviors.) There was definitely past life energy there, but he was definitely abused by somebody as a kid. Somebody got to him. Perhaps his parents should investigate whether he had a male baby-sitter or something like that.

With a serial killer, you are dealing with someone who has no illusion. They have no imagination. They have nothing. When they are doing what they are doing, they are just totally shut off from everything that we know of as humans, as conscious beings. Their programming is so messed up that they are like a virus that just attacks another system and just totally shuts it down. They become like a virus.

This is the Truth with a capital T."

Interview Six with Dominant

The only child helper that we have not covered is the ten-year-old. When did the ten-year-old come out to help?

"The ten-year-old part of the brain holds the growing intelligence of the child. It's the curiosity part. When the ten-year-old helper kicks in, around age 9, it creates an excitement and a stimuli in the brain to learn more, understand more. Just as they start seeing things around them that their curious nature really wants to understand in a more detailed way. Each person processes this information in a different way."

Did the ten-year-old have to come out early to help with the aftermath of the father's passing?

"Yes, it was coming out early and was rationalizing in helping S deal with her father's death. It was rationalizing what her (the ten-year-old) role was. It came out right away. The eight-year-old child questioned whether the paternal grandparents would be her grandparents anymore. It was the ten-year-old asking the questions because she knew that there was something terribly wrong in that the paternal grandparents would be around awhile but that they would not play a major part in their life anymore like they had. She was saddened by that.

The ten-year-old helper was aware of the four-year-old and Claire and the fear and knowing that this comes from the mother's side of the family. The women on this side of the family have never been responsible with the power up until this point. They have not broken the chain of madness that has occurred by driving themselves crazy. Do you understand what I am saying?

S has broken that chain and she is not going to let it happen to her daughter. She keeps contact with those people to a minimum. L can spend time with the grandmother and great grandmother but she wants her to understand that they are not all there. They are still very much asleep in some ways. They won't wake up and smell the coffee. S's mother is trying and is very anxious to read this book. She is a very curious woman and is the one who gave curiosity to S. That is why there is that love there, that bond S has with her mother. There have been a lot of problems. It is a complicated relationship.

The ten-year-old came out early to help differentiate from the mediocre and the banal and what was really going on. When the eight-year-old saw the pictures, the ten-year-old understood what this meant. (S at age eight saw the pictures of the father's crime scene.) **The intelligence level was there with the ten-year-old."**

Had she come out early to help?

"She had already come out to help, sort of … not to where she came to full play as a teenager when they come into their own power. She did come out to help a little bit and had some anger. It did add fuel to the fire. We were ready for a timber explosion, a forest fire, when this child turned 14 or 15, which the Dominant me, has been able to control for the most part."

Often there is not the high level control that this Dominant has and often many of my trauma victims display a lot of rage and destructive behaviors. Remember for most of my sex abuse survivors, the teenage helper has to come out early to deal with the anger and rage. Understand that the extreme behaviors we see in teenagers are the explosion of the built up anger and rage from the earlier traumas. Often why a system goes completely haywire is because the Dominant can't control the rage from exploding. Even some higher level Dominants speak of their concern of controlling the anger. Often anger can be on two levels, the middle helper, and with the teenage helper. One Dominant spoke of great concern that if both levels of anger were triggered at the same time, the results could be disastrous. The Dominants are often overwhelmed in trying to control the blocked off feelings.

"I have kept processes logical and very well organized."

The ten-year-old had to continue to deal with the aftermath of the father dying and the changes that followed, i.e. moving in with the grandparents.

"That is exactly what happened to S and I can explain why. She was OK when she lived down in Texas with the family name that was accepted there. Nobody thought twice about the name. They had lived there for years. (The last name which I can't give is a name that could easily receive teasing from school kids.) That name becomes extremely unusual when you live somewhere else. You become the butt of jokes and criticisms on yourself that you are not responsible for. It was a name given to you. Why blame someone for a label? The family rejected S when she took on her step-father's name. He played an important role in helping her deal with ... telling her the truth about some of the things in life ... telling her some honesty, giving her some direction, at least some guide posts that she could go by so she wouldn't get in trouble. The paternal family couldn't understand why she took on the stepfather's name because she wasn't going to live in Texas by all of them.

As far as most people go, there is so much blocking in them. It can be a past life experience or it can be a trauma from their recent life that is blocking them to the point where they feel asleep, they feel that there is something wrong. It doesn't mean that their Dominant isn't strong. It means that their Dominant is not able to break through to the other side. Maybe Jim Morrison (rock singer 70's) was trying to say that when he said 'break on through to the other side.' That is what he meant. Get rid of those illusions. Get rid of those blockages that you have and open the doors of perception. It has been coming for a long time and people need to know that it doesn't mean they are not intelligent. This Dominant was already pretty much aware of that because of the life that it had led before. It doesn't have anything to do with anybody in particular, it's just that this person happens to have this Dominant, because she was right for it, and it was right for her."

It is important for the reader to understand that everybody has a Dominant. The conscious Host has to meditate to get in touch with that Dominant. I want it to be clear that this Dominant who is talking to me is not the exception ... that I have not found some isolated freak thing where some higher part of the mind is talking or channeling through S's physical body for whatever reason.

"I am the rule. It is nothing more than I am the thing that controls that computer.

I am the timer clock on your computer. I know what processes to perform. I don't have to die soon. If people wouldn't put road blocks in the way, we could learn more from our lives and extend our lives more in this lifetime … if we need to. Sometimes we don't want to. The Dominants inside … they just give up. They can't fight anymore and are just not going to bother to try."

I have worked with some clients whose Dominant became very overwhelmed with the blocked off feelings and all of the problems, that they were giving up hope that the system could ever be functional.

"Basically that is where they need somebody who is like me. Edgar Cayce was like this person (S). He could literally look at someone and know what was wrong with them when he was conscious. S is not like that yet but she is heading in that direction."

(The Dominant can scan others and know what exactly is going on in terms of past life energy, physical problems, chakra energy, and know the nature of the trauma from this life time.)

Now that S has cleared things away and you, her Dominant is coming through, S will be more secure and trusting of those gut feelings.

"It is because of the ten-year-old and the self-esteem. It all comes back full circle if you understand gentle reader. The problem lies in the self-esteem issues that were attached to this ten-year-old personality who was also harboring a past life entity. *(Jack from the Titanic.)*"

Why did Jack attach to the ten-year-old?

"The intelligence part of this brain spoke to him somehow. He knew that if he attached to this system, that he would be cleared later. He knew that this person was real, real, real … the one that was about to be born, the energy that was being put together, was going to be very powerful and even though he (Jack) wasn't able to sense on that level but when she was born and he found her, he attached to her because he knew right away this was the one. I know what it is. Jack saw S as an opportunity to get out of the Titanic disaster."

You have said before that you were a part of Jack's system as a helper and that you as S's Dominant permitted him to come into this person.

"He wasn't some wandering peasant spirit that attached on to S like a crazy man. He knew that this was his opportunity and that this was the person that he had been waiting for … that he was 'undead' if you want to call it that. So were a lot of other people who have died … haunted houses and all this other stuff. You hear about it all the time and nobody wants to believe it, nobody wants to think that it is true. If they don't want to believe it, I don't really care. I know what it is. I know when Jack showed up. When you talked to him before he was cleared away ... I can't talk to him now, but you knew his name and address. This guy worked on the Titanic. He went down with it."

Where was Jack from 1912 to 1960 when S was born?

"He was hanging around. He was waiting for his opportunity. He may have gone into another person to be cleared away, but more than likely he just hung around."

Were you aware that he was around when S's energies were coming together?

"Yes he was hanging out in the area ... he was in the waiting line to be expelled, whatever you want to call that."

Remember that Jane is an incarnate. After her death, she went into the light and has returned to resolve some feelings from her past life. She will remain with S to help her with matters of love. Jack's energy needed to be guided out. The Dominant has said that Jack's energy will probably have to come back to resolve some things and S to learn some lessons.

"Jane is reincarnation. Jack was just hanging around waiting for his opportunity to catch the train to the light. He saw that opportunity when he saw this person was being formed. He knew that this was someone who was also a relative of his, by the way, very distantly ... but we are all related somewhere along the line."

You have said that the past life energies are coming down through the ancestral lines through the DNA. The reader may ask what S has to do with someone who was killed on the Titanic.

"In some way, his energies are connected to S's because it is like matching up the right parallel port to the computer to get the printer to work. If you are going to use computer lingo, that is the best way to put it. Jack interfaced well with this system. Let's say that some African spirit is hanging around, and maybe it doesn't interface well with S's system, because maybe she does not have a lot of Afro-centric background. There may be some from 200 hundred years ago, but not enough to pull in any strong force that is left hanging around. There are African people who do that. There are Eurasian people who do that. Race is really silly. It is a differentiation in bio-chemistry. It doesn't mean that they are more powerful or less powerful. Yes, there are certain differences in outlook. That is all it is. It is perspective. It is like being on the top of the building and looking at a tree and being in the middle of the building and looking at the tree down below, and being on the street and looking at the tree. Everybody sees it from a different perspective. Everybody is on a different level. That doesn't just apply to race. That applies to things in general. Period..."

Back to the ten-year-old ... she has cleared away her feelings and is doing OK.

S will now consciously be able to understand why she has self-esteem issues because of some of the problems she has been having in conscious reality.

Let's start to review now. When the child helpers come out to hold feelings, say for example when the eight-year-old helper's feelings were triggered, S would feel these feelings, even as the adult.

The reader needs to understand that regardless of which child helper, when those feelings are triggered and or just compulsively need to get expressed, the conscious Host will be affected by those feelings.

"Exactly… When S's self-esteem would be affected as she got older, she would get really angry. When she was a teenager, she would get out of control a little bit when the teenager came out."

Did the ten-year-old hold anger too?

"It's more the self-esteem. The teenager holds the anger. This is why you have to get the teenager in on this a little bit to get a little backbone to that ten-year-old and say, 'wait a minute now, you are not stupid, you are not a fool.' Quit letting other people around you who can't see what you see, make you not believe in yourself. That's where the teenager comes into play. The intelligence is there for the ten-year-old to pull on the teenager's backbone because that is the part of the brain that holds the intelligence. When the intelligence is put down, sometimes the whole system can shut down. That is where I came in and said no. This child is too good and has too much to offer to let these fears and inhibitions mask her true achievements and accomplishments. No, I'm not going to let that happen."

I have discussed in part two how the teenager helper's job is to give fortitude and backbone to the system. However the teenage helper that has to come out early to hold the rage and anger from severe trauma can really explode and be destructive to self and others as the Host approaches teenage years and even younger.

"The intelligence was attached enough to the ten-year-old to pull on that ... and say, 'you think I'm evil or ugly,' or whatever somebody would say that would be cruel or hurtful that would trigger this. The teenager would help that ten-year-old be wise enough about it to be angry but yet be helpful. It wasn't until the teenager came into her own though that the anger toward the mother started to come out. That is a whole other matter."

As I discussed in the part two, the teenage helper is often a helper and protector for the younger child helpers. When someone triggers one of the younger child helpers and upsets them, the teenage helper will come out often aggressively to protect that system.

"Absolutely… It has to. Intelligence and self-esteem are very closely related. It has to be understood that they function from the same area. The intelligence is the whole brain, but the bottom of the brain where you hold your emotions … if your emotions tell you that you are bad, then the rest of your programming is going to be screwed up. Your intelligence is going to be messed up. You won't think clearly."

If you examine most developmental theories, from ages 6 to 11 is a big stage that is based on competence. Erik Erikson's psychosocial stages of development which describes polarities of success versus failure for each stage, depicts an industry vs. inferiority through the middle childhood. The child either has developed a sense of duty and accomplishment or takes with them a sense of failure and a lack of value for accomplishment. So the correlation between accomplishing tasks, using your intelligence and how you feel about yourself is quite important.

"School is the only thing that validated this child. Her intelligence was great, extreme. However, self-esteem can ruin the greatest intelligence. People telling you that you are fat, lazy, or ugly, or whatever they are saying that is hurtful and hateful because of something that is their problem.

Paul, in talking about what Jesus was saying, 'Get the plank out of your eye before trying to remove the splinter from your brother's.' Take a good hard look at yourself first. See what you can do to improve yourself before you start in on somebody else, especially a child who is within that age group (5-11). They need your support, guidance, and wisdom at this point, not your jealousy, anger, hatred and your fear. No!"

Can you stay with this concept of children and give the reader some more advice?

"Basically you have to try to get into your child's head and understand how they feel. If you can't do that, then you have no business being a parent. End of statement. Most people have no business being parents. They are not passing on their intelligence. They are just passing on their gene pool to feed their own unsatisfied, egotistical and selfish needs. They think that they can live precariously through their kid. Kids are not for you to live precariously through. They are for you to treasure and you need to realize that they are their own human beings, entities that were created out of love first. If they are not and the person chooses to keep the child anyway, give it a loving home. The child isn't born until the child is born. That is when the personality comes into play. It has no personality while it is in the womb. It is part of the mother.

I really hate to jump on the band wagon of the pro-choicer, but the life may decide to abort itself. There is a real relevancy here. We have too many people on the planet right now to support life the way that it is going. Most people are so asleep, and so intimidated by the thought of changing their own mind, and their own thought processes, that they raise children who are just as stupid as they are. They breed like rabbits and don't think about what they are doing.

You can not humiliate children to get them to do what you want. If you do humiliate them to get them to do what you want, they will hate you the rest of their lives. It will always be there somewhere. I will tell you, you don't want that. If you love your kids and when you're an old person and you see that your kids can't stand you ... they treat you condescendingly, or they stick you in a nursing home. Why do you think they do that to you? It's because of what you did to them."

Talk about some examples of adults who still have resentment toward parents for the way they were treated.

"That's getting back to the nitty gritty here. You have to be responsible for your own actions once you become an adult. Most people are walking around in 30- to forty-year-old bodies thinking they are (adult) but they are not. They are not taking responsibility for their actions. Most of it is ego-driven, sanctimonious and selfish. It hurts their kids. I don't want to get on the parents too hard. It is because their Dominant has been shut down ... some inner voice that they hear when they are yelling at their kids that would be telling them this is not right is not heard. They have it but they don't hear it because it was shut down by their parents and their parents before them. It perpetuates itself from generation through generation."

You need to clear away the blocked off stuff, so that you can be in touch with your Dominant as well as free your Dominant from having to deal with the blocked off stuff, so that your Dominant can come through and guide you through this life without interference. Remember the Dominant is overwhelmed and overburdened on a daily basis when it has to put energy into the child helpers who are holding old fear, sadness, shame, and anger.

"Yes, guide you through this life, and if you choose to have children, to guide them too. You can bond with a child even when you have done things that are terrible to that kid, even if you are sixty and your kid is forty. There is no reason why you can't go to that child if you do this work and if you clear things away ... basically you reconfigure your brain system so that it is thinking properly and is working like a computer should work, not chaotic and shut down. Then you will have the strength and peace of mind to be able to go to your children and say that I was terrible. I see what you are doing to your kids and it is terrible too, and it is my fault. I want to break this now. Let me help you. It is never too late people. It is never too late until you are dead. Then you are in the part where you have to go and stand ... it is like tallying up. That is if you make it through the light. Then you can regroup and come back as an incarnate. Most people don't make it that far. They get stuck. That is why we have so many people walking around sleeping."

Let's talk about Jack for a moment. It seemed that he connected up with the ten-year-old.

"They partied a lot. The intelligence knew how to get away with partying when she got older. She wrote for a fake student ID saying that she was from France because she could speak French."

Jack wasn't supposed to live vicariously through S, correct?

"No, but he did anyway. He was enjoying the heck out of it. It was free and loose times. He enjoyed it. He thought it was great. That is probably why S had trouble with men."

Jack got to the point where he knew that for S to integrate, and for the child helpers to clear away their feelings that he needed to leave.

"Jack, Claire, Jane and me had been looking for this kind of help. Everything happens for a reason. When S was in college she was starting her quest. From the time she got out of her mother's influence and until just recently when she met up with you and started doing hypnosis work ... you knew right away that she needed this kind of work. She had been looking for this kind of work for a long time."

I asked about one of the Jesus quotes to get further interpretation.

"'I am the vine and ye are the branches.' The Bible likes to interpret that as Jesus being the son of God and you are all extended from him. He was misquoted. Really what he is saying is that he is living proof that you can become like God. You just have to believe in yourself and trust in that inner voice that says peace, and wisdom, and love and light. When you do that and when you get rid of the negative influences, and the back pictures, and you clear away the bad programming, you become part of the vine too. You may be a branch, but we are all like that. We can become a part of the major vine."

Isn't "unless ye become as children," implying a rebirth?

"What he is saying is that you have to have faith as little children. Look at your life like a child. Imagine yourself as God, and you are a little kid and you can rule the world and you could rule it benevolently, and kindly, and gently, and with love. Or, would you rather rule it with fear, anger and hatred, and prejudice. You decide.

What did he really mean when he said this? *(Referring to the Jesus quote.)* What

does the Christ inside say when you listen to this quote? Doesn't it sound somewhat egotistical for Jesus to be standing around saying, 'I am God.' I don't think
that I would have liked this guy if he said that to me. I don't think that he would
have had a big following of people if he was ... 'I am God, You aren't.'

Come on, he was trying to tell people, 'you can be like this.' Listen to the Sermon
on the Mount where he talks about, 'Blessed are the Peacemakers, Blessed are the
Hungry in Spirit, Blessed are those who Seek.' Think about this for a minute; really think about it, not just from the perspective that this is Jesus, the son of God.
I'm the daughter of God, and so are you and so is every other person who walks
on this planet. It is how you choose to process the information. What about all of
those lost years of Jesus' life that they don't know about? There are a lot of people
who speculate that he went with the Essenes. They are very much into finding the
inner power. He was an intelligent young man and he could argue Jewish law with
the elders because he already knew that there was something wrong here. People
were living piously and sanctimoniously in these great houses and everyone else
was starving. He saw the problems and tried to do something about them and he
was persecuted for it. The reason why there was a religion that sprung up around
this man is because he knew the secret between life and death. He may be walking
the face of the earth right now if he is an avatar or guru or he may be the re-born
spirit into someone else. I'm not the one to say that ... in fact I'm not allowed to
say that."

In summary, the purpose of this book is to get people who are walking around with
all of these symptoms and manifestations because of some trauma, or overwhelming
feelings, and maybe because of some energy that needs to live or resolve something
from the past. The reader has to understand that not everyone has a complicated system like S with past life energies, incarnates etc. I have seen a number of clients who
have a past life energy that needed to be guided out. Many of my clients have child
helpers who have leftover feelings from a past life which have to be resolved. Many
clients just need to resolve the feelings from this life. Perhaps two or three child helpers had to come out and deal with some feelings, albeit fear, sadness, self-blame, and
anger. Once those feelings are resolved through the abreaction, the client's symptoms
are alleviated. Yes the conscious Host has to work at catching up with learning how
to respond to and deal with the normal frustrations and stressors of life, but it is certainly easier without all of the old emotions coming out. Remember the theory; there
is a compulsion for blocked off feelings to come out in reality, which causes you the
Host to experience symptoms.

"That is why you have so many people in prison right now."

I believe that the way we have helped S in using the trance state to allow you the
Dominant to safely release and resolve the old stuff and to help Jack and Claire to be
guided out is the way to go. Remember reader, S was not really aware of what happened when Jack and Claire left. As powerful as that was, S did not have to feel the

impact of those sessions. This work is about clearing away the blocked off emotions from the child helpers so they can go back inside to do the job that they were supposed to do (review roles of child helpers) which gives the Host certain characteristics that have been missing, such as creativity, sense of humor, moral fortitude and back bone. It also frees the Dominant from having to baby-sit the upset child helpers which is an energy drain.

"Exactly! That's the goal."

Then S the Host becomes more in touch with you, her Dominant. Remember, S is not hearing this conversation. When the old stuff is cleared up, the Dominant is freer to help the Host. It works both ways. Being open to and in touch with your Higher Self, the Dominant, is the ultimate goal. Once the childhood wounds are resolved, the Dominant is freer to let the light shine through S's consciousness.

"Certainly ... and to not be violent, to not be cruel, but to be patient, to be kind. What did Jesus say or Paul say in Corinthians that love was ... 'love is patient and kind, love is understanding.' These are basic tenets that people live by. Think about them very deeply for a moment. It is not the Bible, the Jewish Bible, the Old Testament ... I don't even count that. It's the Jewish laws mixed in with a lot of their history, if you can call it that because they really didn't write a lot of this stuff down until years after it happened. It was handed down orally. Then later it was written by scribes when they had the ability to write. But it doesn't necessarily mean that it is all facts."

Can you talk about that?

"They don't want to believe in Goddess. Nobody does. Come on, there is day and night, there is dichotomy in everything. The Jews don't like to see that. They refuse to see that. They only worship what they can't see. The laws that they have given themselves to live by in reality are so complex and so detrimental to them as people from being able to see Goddess and nature around them. The Druids were hated because they believed in both God and the Goddess. The Easterners too ... they have always had the sanctimonious belief that they are more powerful than any other ... their Cabala system is extremely powerful. I will admit that. Go to any Jewish Bar Mitzvah and tell me that young man understands Cabala, that they are being trained in Cabalistic thinking. They don't allow that very much anymore ... only in the Ascetic communities and then only in very special cases. They know that it is there. They want to fool themselves. Why have this pretentious attitude?

Who is right? Everybody is right. What is right for you is that you get inside your own mind and clear the negativity away so you can find your own truth for yourself so you can emerge successfully into the light. Get in touch with your own truth and live a decent life. You don't have to be perfect. You can live in poverty.

You can live in a mansion with servants. As long as you are doing the right thing and your heart is in the right place, and you understand that you have God and Goddess and that you have power inside of you and it comes from within, you don't have to worry about all that other stuff."

Talk about God and Goddess being a higher universal energy.

"Where we come from is energy. Dead energy is non-existent. There is something inside of me that is going to go away if this body dies. Like everybody else, when they die, there is something in them that leaves them ... that animation that spark of life that energy continues. You can't have dead energy. The body dies, the soul does not."

For example, you talk about S's dad who went into the light and he is in that stage or level perhaps that is referred to as the first Bardo state, where his energy can watch out over S and even help her.

"Exactly. He comes to help her."

That is his Dominant, because you said you don't take your consciousness with you.

"He doesn't judge himself like he did when he was alive. The Dominant isn't as harsh. It understands that those were lessons, those were problems, and they were related to symptoms. It's the knowledge. The Dominant is knowledge."

They may be there for awhile or move on to a different level.

"And if they want to move on from that point, they will either come back here as an incarnate or a helper ... because you have to, because you are not ready to move on. Certain boundaries ... we can even take this back to the parenting thing. There are boundaries set even for afterlife. If you don't meet certain rules, your parents don't let you go beyond those boundaries.

This system is becoming ready to integrate and there are some people when they leave this plane and they 'die,' they move past that first Bardo state ... they may stay there awhile to comfort others, then they move on to another level that I am not allowed to speak of. That first Bardo state is just in general to help comfort people who are alive today."

Jane needed to come back to heal her emotional scar.

"Jane came back because of a life time of agony that needed to be healed. Jane is OK now. Her emotional scar is healed. She is able to move on and help S."

Remember, the Incarnate stays after resolving some old scars to help the conscious

Host in some way. Jane will help S with matters of love.

"Jane is a part of S. She is from her bloodline ... familiar ancestral line. Jane looks like S. S looks like Jane. She is a direct ancestor. Jane is more direct than say Jack, who was an uncle's son of an uncle's son but was just able to interface with this system. Say somebody buys a new PC that looks like the same PC they had twenty years ago but it is just an updated version. That is what Jane is with S."

When S dies, you the Dominant may go on to help L and her children. Jane may go on to help someone else.

"Sure. Maybe it will be S's brother's, child's, child ... something that they could trace back to a great, great, great, aunt. That may be what Jane is for S. That is who Jane may attach to if she needs to incarnate and work on this again in a future life."

You had said that Jack will probably have to come back to work on some things.

"Jack definitely has to come back to work on some things."

After you go through your rejuvenation period and come back say as a Dominant, you don't remember or aren't allowed to remember the conscious memories of where you lived, what the person did and all of that. Most child helpers can express a sense of knowing that they were here before but don't remember the what and where. I would think that you bring the previous lessons learned, the knowledge and wisdom, to the current incarnation.

"Exactly... I do remember some ancient Egyptian thing, some kind of ceremony."

What time frame are you talking about?

"It was about 7 or 8 thousand years ago."

So you have been around a long time. *(Stupid statement.)*

"That is why I am like this. There is another male that you see that has a high Dominant too. He has been around for awhile. S's husband has been around for awhile. He has only been around for about three thousand years as far as his Dominant. His Dominant is pretty good. There are Dominants walking around who are older than me. I am a baby compared to some of them."

Are you saying 7000 B.C.?

"B.C.E., whatever you want to call it. It was maybe 10,000 years ago from now."

So you have been through a number of rejuvenation periods?

"Oh, yes! It is all 'Vampiric' in a certain sort of way. We kind of come into the bodies and try to work things out. Consciously though, you are not aware of us. Consciously, you don't try to tap into it, and you are not aware of it. I have been fortunate in that I have had some of the same helpers with me. Claire is here this lifetime because I was with her before. She has survived. She got a little out of control and was burned. She was very, very intelligent and very wise."

What about Norma?

"She attached. She was somehow related back into the family line back to the 1850's or 1860's. I believe that Norma was born in the mid-west or Kentucky, Tennessee, Arkansas, or somewhere in that area where some of her family may have moved to. She was able to interface with this system rather quickly right away, because she had died so recently. Her life had been so tragic that she wanted peace and resolution."

Had she gone into the light?

"She couldn't. Her fear was so great of everything."

It seems to be the fear that keeps people from going into the light.

"They are scared. They don't want to leave this earth. They are scared because they don't want to die. They are afraid of the death. They don't want to accept it.

There is mass terrorization and lots of evil before the coming of the light. We are moving in a constantly moving galaxy which is in a constantly moving star system which is in a constantly moving universe. Accept change a little bit more gradually and understand that this does not have to be evil. It is not evil. It is the part of the mind that is in touch with God. There is no quick soul healing."

This was a complicated case that involved a high level Dominant, child helpers, incarnates, past life energies. Not all of us have such a complicated system. Yes, we all have a Dominant along with the six helpers and some external helpers that assist and guide us through this incarnation. Don't be spooked by what you have read but perhaps be comforted by the fact that we are surrounded by a conglomeration of soul helpers who are here to guide and protect us.

Hopefully this case example, as well as the others, shows the importance of healing our childhood wounds. I also hope that S's Dominant has helped dispel the myths that surround hypnosis. Again, scientific investigation has shown that the combination of hypnotic/abreactions and cognitive restructuring is an effective approach to the healing of these childhood wounds. If a high level Dominant doesn't convince the world that all the power and resources that we have are accessed through this natural state of hypnosis, I give up or at least feel sorry for you.

What has come to me through this work is the confirmation that healing is at the soul level. We need to believe that we have the power within to heal as well as to help us with our purpose and mission. As Gary Zukav reminds us in The Seat of the Soul, we are evolving to a higher level of consciousness that requires us to align our personality with our spirit.

S made the difficult decision to go through a tedious process in order to heal her childhood wounds. Now she can move on in life, certainly with adversities and tribulations that we all face, but without the heavy burden of the negative energy that so encompassed her.

"What is most important in this life is your spiritual evolution."

S's Dominant

Part V

To Heal or Not to Heal

More and more individuals recognize that they have to resolve the underlying source of their symptoms. They are listening to their Dominant. More and more clients do not want to depend on psychotropic drugs. The reality is that for many trauma victims, the medicines don't often help and can often exacerbate symptoms. Many individuals come to me and believe that they may have a carryover energy that is manifesting in reoccurring dreams, ruminating thoughts and obsessive behaviors that can't be explained in this lifetime. Individuals are recognizing that their relationship problems are symbiotic of unresolved childhood problems. Our Dominant's are going to force us to go inward and resolve our childhood wounds. Healing involves a commitment to a process that can be difficult at times because the abreactions involve the release of primary emotions. As I tell my clients, these are the intense feelings that you are feeling when you are triggered and are symptomatic. Choose to do the hard work in a therapeutic setting in order to release and resolve the childhood feelings once and for all. Retrieve the parts of yourself and move toward wholeness.

Not to Heal

For those who choose not to resolve their childhood wounds, the likelihood that your symptoms and manifestations will persist is quite high. The blocked off emotions will continue to produce an array of symptoms and manifestations such as:

> **depression, anger, despair, panic attacks, withdrawal, anxiety reactions, powerlessness, flashbacks, sleep disturbance, compulsions, obsessions, trust issues, self-esteem problems, triggers vulnerability to self-medication and addictions, decision making problems, relationship problems, remaining a victim, becoming the victimizer, emotional and sensate triggers**

Most importantly, childhood wounds keep you living in the past. Our current reactions and perceptions are colored by the past. As Eckhart Tolle states in *A New Earth*, **"You look at the present through the eyes of the emotional past within you."** This is too often seen in relationship problems. One spouse raises his or her voice which triggers a primary emotion from a childhood experience which results in an intense exchange. They don't even realize that the deep emotions that have just been triggered are mainly from their past.

Just as important, the unresolved parts of the self continue to make decisions for us. It's the part of you that holds your anger and rage that seeks relief through drugs and alcohol. It's the part of the self that holds the blame and shame from abuse that eats to feel good. It's the part that holds the memory of the abuse that acts out sexually. It's the hurt boy or girl in you who wants you to treat your kids like you were treated or draws you to dysfunctional relationships. Remember, sheer willpower can not win out over the blocked off emotions. When the feelings are resolved you will gain conscious control over your impulses. As S's Dominant stated, **"When feelings are released, the power they had over you is diminished."**

Remember, the blocked off feelings don't fade away as we get older. Anger may turn to depression or physical problems. Panic attacks may be replaced with sleeping problems and night sweats. Intimate relationships continue to be marred by the repetition of old patterns that remain unconscious. Carrying emotional pain keeps you living in a world of blaming, projecting and denying, believing that some thing or some person will come along and make you happy. As Ceanne DeRohan stated in *The Right Use of Will*, **"Unpleasant experiences have not come to punish but to point out that you have the denial."** These experiences serve to release the feelings that we are blocking.

Don't let fear or ignorance (e.g. false assumptions about hypnosis) keep you from the spiritual balance that your soul is seeking. Your spiritual presence will come through when you accept and release your unresolved emotions. For those who are not ready to clear things up, be careful in believing that medicine alone is the cure. You are still carrying the blocked off feelings which may eventuate in more physical problems. Enter counseling with the courage and conviction of releasing your emotional pain, safely and tolerably over time. Seek a therapist who understands that there is an underlying source to your emotional pain and in order to feel natural feelings, this pain needs to be extinguished.

To Heal

I would now like to share the benefits for those clients who have chosen to commit to healing. I have to do much convincing to have my clients bare with the abreactions in the office, the vivid dreams and sleep disturbance, and the periods of moodiness that may be a generalized anxiety or a frustration whereas everything and everyone gets on your nerves. The blocked off feelings have to be processed and released over time. When my clients work through the initial phase of intense abreactions, there is a threshold when symptom relief begins to occur. As I tell my clients, there are no epiphanies, no quick healing. The strong message that I send to them is to trust their unconscious mind because it knows what to do; it knows how to take care of them; it knows how to protect them when this work is being done. Accept the feelings that come through as feelings that are being released once and for all.

What begins to happen is that clients report that if they get upset, they recover quicker. As time goes on, the emotional reactions aren't as intense. As the primary emotions are released, the repetitive, compulsive behaviors begin to subside and will eventually stop. Clients stop drawing themselves to situations that repeat the childhood patterns. When the juvenile offender resolves his blocked off trauma, he will no longer act out. Clients become more conscious of the red flags of dysfunctional relationships and begin to make better choices in this area. As the negative energy is released, emotional and sensate triggers subside. Sleeping problems begin to improve.

What gets tricky is helping people understand that as they feel better; there may be more layers of unresolved emotions that have to come through. I have to reinforce in my clients that they are not going backwards or getting worse. Sometimes the deepest emotions i.e., anger/rage will have to be released after the upset hurt feelings are resolved. Remember in S's case, Jane was the last helper to come forward. Her letting go of the hurt, pain and grief was very difficult for the Host.

Most of the emotional work is done from the heart chakra. When the blame, shame, envy and jealously of childhood wounds are resolved, the natural feelings of trust, love, and compassion start to emerge. No matter what you do or try to think, it is hard for you to feel good about yourself if you are holding a hurt little boy or girl inside filled with blame and shame. It is exciting to see clients start to feel good about themselves, sometimes for the first time.

Just at the right time, the Dominant begins to open up the throat chakra which helps the client with expressing feelings, asserting themselves and speaking up. This is the energy center that is about personal power and faith in ourselves. This is when some of the cognitive/restructuring can benefit the client in expressing feelings in appropriate ways and at appropriate times. Communication skills are addressed at this time. Yes, there is a time and place for talk therapy which comes after a significant level of balance is achieved in the system. Because rage despair and panic are lower frequency and heavy emotions, clients describe feeling lighter as they clear this material away. They report having more energy and more enthusiasm for life.

On the physical level, nobody is claiming that hypnotic/abreactive work is the cure for all ailments, but certainly carrying emotional pain throughout your life will have detrimental effects on the physical body. More and more doctors are referring clients with reoccurring stomach problems, for example, to psychotherapy. Many of my clients who do the hard work have gotten off of their stomach medication and blood pressure medicine. More and more research is correlating unresolved emotional pain to physical problems. Do your body a favor and heal your childhood wounds. As His Holiness the Dalai Lama states in *Ethics for a New Millennium*, "**Not only do negative thoughts and emotions destroy our experience of peace, they also undermine our health.**"

On a spiritual level, clients begin to see the nature of things more clearly. Often they are overwhelmed by the flood of insights that come to them. I explain to them as they clear up the old stuff that their Dominant comes through more. Remember that our Dominant talks to us through hunches, intuitions, and gut feelings. If we are filled up with negative energy, we can't tune in to what our Dominant is telling us. Although we don't reach the level of our Dominant, we can draw from the essence of our Dominant which helps us with finding our purpose and mission in life. My clients become more goal oriented with regard to career and educational choices.

If carrying trauma keeps us living in the past, then certainly the healing of childhood wounds affords my clients the potential to live in the present moment. This is clearly a challenge for all of us, to be alive in the present moment. As Deepak Chopra writes in *Ageless Body, Timeless Mind*, "**Live in the present; have your attention on what is here and now. Look for the fullness in every moment.**" Too often we destroy the present moment by feeling guilty about the past and worrying about the future or believing that some future event will come along and make us happy. As Rollo May states in *Man's Search for Himself*, "**To try to live in the 'when' of the future or the 'then' of the past always involves an artificiality, a separating one's self from reality; for in actuality one exits in the present. The past has meaning as it lights up the present, and the future as it makes the present richer and more profound.**" May points out that confronting the present produces anxiety because it forces us to make decisions and take responsibility for one's life. He goes on to say that our future is made by confronting the present courageously and constructively.

As time goes on, vivid dreams with negative emotions are replaced with dreams in which the client feels empowered versus powerless. Remember what S's Dominant purported; the conscious mind has to assimilate the bad thought patterns. They have to be neutralized. "**Messages die hard in the conscious mind.**" Even when the blocked off trauma is resolved, we have to change the conscious blueprints that were set because of the trauma. Cognitve/restructuring techniques such as future pacing help the client visualize reacting in new ways. They learn that feelings are signals that are telling them to take action, respond, and do what has to be done. Ultimately through conscious choice, the client must practice and learn to react from authentic power and make good choices in their current realities.

It is important to understand that the resolving of childhood wounds doesn't guarantee a stress free, blissful life but gives that individual a level playing field so they can confront the challenges of life that we all must face. Certainly the healing process stops the immobilization that comes with carrying childhood trauma. I inform my clients that life will continue to present them with experiences that will require them to use their power to make better conscious choices and to take new actions toward achieving their goals. As David Reynolds writes in *Playing Ball on Running Water*, "**Happiness, peace, and a life of ease would destroy us. Without anxiety and trouble, we could not survive. So don't seek anxiety-free living: don't strive for constant bliss. Choose rather to continue your struggle. Resolve to react forceful to the challenges of reality. Hold to your goals. Fight your fight. And live with** purpose." When you resolve your childhood wounds, you can begin to live with this present moment purposefulness.

The healing of childhood wounds opens us up to our essence. The following traits start to emerge as my clients move toward wholeness:

Emotional Balance, Reverence, Faith, Personal Power, Forgiveness, Improved Self-Esteem, Present Moment Living, Confidence, Improved Relationships, Goal Oriented Behavior, Improved Decision Making, Trust, Compassion , Gratitude, Spiritual Awareness and Authentic Power

The healing process is not about recovering memories but about releasing the negative energy and filling that space with positive energy so that you can achieve a spiritual balance. It is about moving from external power to authentic power. It is about making the unconscious conscious and achieving a greater sense of awareness. Most importantly, it is about fixing a fragmented system and moving toward a sense of wholeness and integration.

Does That Work?

This is perhaps the most often asked question when individuals know that I do hypnosis as part of the therapy. I would like to share with the reader what that process involves to dispel any myths that would keep a potential client from participating in this effective healing process. Remember, the two hypnotic or trance states are natural states of mind that connect us to all of the power and resources we have to heal. The following is the approach that I use in my practice. Keep in mind that I am describing the hypnotic aspect of the therapy, that there is an equally important conscious, cognitive restructuring aspect that comes into play as the healing process unfolds.

Imagine sitting back in a chair in a safe, quiet setting with the lights down and a candle burning. An Indian flute CD is playing softly in the background. After a few deep breaths, I ask you to pay attention to your body, your face, your shoulders, and then your legs. I remind you clients that trance is focused attention. I then get you to imagine walking down steps and sitting in a comfortable chair. The safety, security and comfort of the chair is enhanced. I remind you that you can get back to the chair whenever you need to. I then suggest that you let your awareness drift or float away to a favorite place. You may already have a favorite place from your meditation. Otherwise I will ask you to let your unconscious mind take you to a safe setting. It can be a real place or an imaginary place. The sights, sounds, and feelings of a favorite place are then enhanced. You can always get back to your favorite place as well. I inform you that your unconscious mind takes over and will protect you as the work is being done. I then become an external helper. Sometimes you will remain in an alpha trance that half asleep on the sofa state of mind. Sometimes you may feel that you fall asleep but there is no sleep during the sessions. This is call theta trance.

This is the trance state that allows me to communicate with the non-physical helpers. The work is done with both trance states. I will tell you that it is not up to me or you but that your unconscious mind knows exactly what to do. Neither you nor I make anything happen. I will remind you not to try to think back on anything. That which needs to be remembered for healing will be brought to you. I simply ask your unconscious mind to help you remember what you need to remember to heal. The difficult work that must be done first requires abreactions. As discussed, an abreaction is a controlled release of blocked off feelings, sensations, and images. This release occurs safely and tolerably over time. You must trust that your Dominant (*your Higher Self*) knows exactly what to do and how to take care of you when this work is done.

The unpleasant memories that you have to remember are feelings that are familiar to you. The fear in your panic attacks, the deep hurt and sadness that may be triggered in your relationships, and the rage and anger that may erupt, are the feelings that have to systematically be released and resolved in order for you to move on. As each child helper is freed of its negative energy, that helper returns to a positive position in the system, giving you back a trait, a gift, and or a special quality that has been missing. Yes, between sessions, I remind you that you may experience vivid dreams, some periods of moodiness, and sleep disturbance as this work is being done. This is a small price to pay to achieve a release from the symptoms of childhood wounds. There is no random chaotic release of old feelings but a clear schema that is followed over time to move your system toward a balance and wholeness. Many of your sessions will be unremarkable because the work is being done at a deeper level. Many sessions will involve the intense release of emotions that come with the abreactions. I monitor the energy/chakra patterns and will inform you what to look out for during the week. For example, when the work is done with the heart chakra, you may experience some dreams with upset feelings or you may become easily triggered by little things in your daily life. When the deeper work is done you will come out of the trance feeling drained. Certainly time is spent on a conscious level processing the abreactions. In time, the benefits of doing this hard work will pay off in the ways described above.

There are no spinning wheels, swinging watches or suggestions or consultations with the devil with this approach. Again, the trance states are natural states of mind that connect us to the universal intelligence, the inherent wisdom available to all of us. Remember, when you are in trance, your unconscious and conscious mind are matched up at the same frequency allowing the blocked off material to be released as well as to connect you to the power and resources you have within. This is what prayer and meditation are supposed to do for us. I suggest to my clients that they find ten to twenty minutes a day to sit back in a chair, put on some light music, take some deep breaths, and close their eyes to allow their unconscious mind to do some work for them. In *Ageless Body, Timeless Mind*, Deepak Chopra tells us, "Take time to be silent, meditate in the silence. You are connecting to your source of pure awareness." This is what hypnosis does for you.

The healing of childhood wounds cannot be accomplished by talking about your problems. As Malidoma Patrice Somè purports in *The Healing Wisdom of Africa*,

"The pain of abuse that someone carries within, the trauma of unfulfilled dreams, and the sorrow of loss are not the kind of feelings that go away over time. Whether we deny them or not, they remain as part of the weight that keeps our bodies tensed and our spirits constricted. They fuel our drive to violence, and they eat our spirit. When they are addressed in ritual, we get the chance to heal them."

Healing at the soul level requires a deeper process. Don't let your fear keep you from engaging in a natural process that will release the negative energy, get your helpers back to a positive role and move you toward integration and wholeness.

A Shift in Consciousness

We are currently in the midst of a paradigm shift. A paradigm is a set of beliefs, a concept that is accepted by most people. We used to think that the world was flat. That belief was questioned and eventually there was a shift in thinking toward a collective belief that the world was round. Galileo lived in exile after his book proclaimed that the earth was not the center of the universe. The church with their dogma and power considered him a heretic. It is now generally accepted that the earth rotates around the sun. As S's Dominant and many others are talking about, we are coming to a close of three major astrological cycles. The universe is becoming less dense, thus more particles, energy, and information will move through. This is why is seems that everything is speeding up. Just as an individual has to release negative energy in order to evolve, so do cultures, societies, and countries need to discharge the culmination of centuries of blocked off anger and rage. This is why things are happening right now. The planet as a system needs to release its collective negativity in order to evolve. The universe will no longer allow us to deny the blocked off parts of ourselves. Those aspects of our life that we are avoiding and ignoring will come to light. Our deepest emotions must be accepted and expressed. When we deny, we tend to project, displace and externalize. We see the world as a projection of what we are denying in ourselves. Rollo May states in *Man's Search for Himself,* "**The more a person lacks self awareness, the more he is prey to anxiety and irrational anger and resentment.**" Anxiety and anger block us from sensing the truth. These emotions cut us off from the power and resources we have available to us.

Unresolved traumas and dissociated stressors are surfacing for healing. More and more carryover energy is coming through and manifesting in symptoms. This is why everything seems so discombobulated at this time. Just watch the news. Mothers are drowning their kids, Amish children abused and murdered, spouses murdering their spouses, teachers abusing their students, and kids being kidnapped, raped and murdered. Remember, one of the basic tenets of Dissociation theory is that blocked off feelings will continue to manifest in compulsive behaviors. His Holiness the Dalai Lama writes in *Ethics for the New Millennium,* "**Where denial and suppression occur, there comes the danger that in so doing, the individual stores up anger and resentment. At some future point they may find they cannot contain these feelings any longer.**"

199

We are currently in an "extraordinary science phase" of a paradigm shift which is always filled with uncertainties, questions, and soul searching. It is about letting go of old beliefs that no longer work or are needed for the emerging paradigm. Those in power tend to dig their heels in and resist change. Many will continue to think in error and dismiss certain truths to maintain their current viewpoints. Despite our fear of change, humans can not stop the impending shift. As S's Dominant has previously discussed, this paradigm shift is not necessarily the end of the world or a doomsday. The geographical changes and terrorism are not the wrath of God but necessary phenomena that has to occur before a shift in consciousness can happen. Just as the individual has to resolve the negativity before moving to a higher level, so does the planet.

Psychology. Although there is some movement in the psychology field as evident in more training in hypnosis and trauma, psychology generally remains stuck in a five sense cognitive mindset. Talk to your client about their symptoms and pump them up with medication seems to be the treatment plan. On the other side of the peak, healing at the soul level which will require the resolution of traumas from this lifetime and past times through deeper energy work, will be necessary in order for individuals to move toward authentic power. Children need to be better assessed for trauma and treated accordingly versus being labeled hyper and put on medications. Adolescence is the time when trance work should begin because of the increase and intensification of symptoms. Remember, the dissociated feelings from childhood really begin to surface at this time, particularly the anger. Medicine may still be used but not to perpetuate denials. It's a sad commentary on psychology that more people are going to psychics as well as to Peru for Shaman healing because they are not satisfied with Western psychological practices. Again, more and more people are coming to me because they know they need the deeper work. The work of Brian Weiss and Roger Woolger has helped advance the reality of carryover energy as a phenomena which needs to be addressed in psychological healing. The writings of Wayne Dyer, Gary Zukav, Eckhart Tolle, and Carolyn Myss have contributed to a Transpersonal viewpoint.

Medicine. At some levels the medical field seems open to the use of Reiki therapy prior to and after surgeries. They have become accepting of acupuncture and chiropractic. I receive many referrals from physicians who are more understanding of the mind and body connection. The emerging paradigm will require the medical profession to see that we are more than blood and chemistry that we are also about energy. Deepak Chopra has single handedly promoted and advanced the notion of mind, body, and spirit through his books and lectures. It seems to me lately that more medical doctors are open to hypnosis than are the mental health professionals.

Relationships. As a marital therapist, it remains shocking how many couples do not realize that they are replaying their childhood struggles in their relationship. Unfortunately, these symbiotic relationships only trigger each partner's wounds and perpetuate the negativity. We tend to unconsciously draw ourselves to others who are at the same level of differentiation as we are. The notion that someone will come along to make me happy, secure, and fulfilled is an illusion. Work on being someone who has something to bring to the party. When we blame our partners for our unhappiness, nothing changes. If you happen to be in a symbiotic relationship, understand that you own the feelings that are triggered. These feelings are telling you that you have a part of you that needs to be healed. Studies of successful relationships show that individuals who have worked on their childhood baggage, worked on their sense of self, as well as their individual goals, will have a better chance of connecting in a conscious, inter-dependent relationship.

In the emerging paradigm, partners will help each other become the best person they can be. Each person will help promote psychological healing and spiritual growth in the other. Remember, love is about giving, not getting. Knowing yourself and being able to communicate your wishes and desires to your partner is imperative in a conscious relationship. Take responsibility for what makes you feel loved and cared for and share that with your partner.

We are in the midst of a great dichotomy. There is an incredible amount of information coming forth, while at the same time there is much negativity. Never has there been a time that we will have to display an enormous amount of humility in order to be open to new learning and the discovery of new truth. In reality it's the awakening to the absolute truth that has always existed but to which so few have connected. According to S's Dominant, **"We have placed our faith in outdated concepts. The dogma keeps us from finding the self within."** In *A New Earth*, Eckhart Tolle writes, **"What is arising now is not a new belief system, a new religion, spiritual ideology, or mythology but a new dimension of consciousness."**

S's Dominant proclaimed, **"everything will change ..."** *(implying viewpoints).* The emerging paradigm will no longer allow man to live in external power, a world that has been based on projecting and displacing our fears, anger, and resentments onto other individuals, groups, and nations. This remains the plight of mankind. The emerging paradigm will not support religious, spiritual, or psychological perspectives that allow us to escape our fears, avoid confronting our childhood wounds, or allow us to perpetuate a dependency and powerlessness. It will support a view that freedom and integration is achieved through confronting one's developmental crises.

"It's time for humans to wake up and take responsibility for their lives."

S's Dominant

Seek the Truth

Rollo May writes, **"For to seek the truth is always to run the risk of discovering what one would hate to see."** This forces us to be conscious of ourselves, conscious of the denials, judgments, and false assumptions that limit and distort our view of the world. To seek the truth forces us to heal the parts of ourselves that keep us living in the past, repeating old patterns, and making bad choices. When we release the old blockages, we get back the parts of ourselves that give us compassion, fortitude, and faith. We come into our power and begin to live with purpose. When we break away from the old patterns we open ourselves to a greater spiritual awareness. This is what Jesus meant when he proclaimed, **"Except a man be born again, he cannot see the Kingdom of Heaven."** Spiritual growth presupposes that we first do the psychological healing. Release the denials and judgments and connect to your Spirit. This is about **getting your soul right.**

We are here to evolve, to grow, and learn lessons. You have a "guiding force" which I have called your Dominant which is with you to protect you and take care of you during this incarnation. However, it will force you to go within to heal your wounds so you can open yourself up to the power and resources you have in order to pursue your purpose and mission in life. Take quiet time and listen to your Dominant. As in S's case, as she resolved her carryover energy and her childhood wounds, I saw her transform and become like her Dominant. According to S's Dominant the most over-looked message brought forth by Jesus is in the following statement; **"You can be like this."** *(Implying that the inherent wisdom of the universe is available to all of us.)*

Deservedly, I would like to end with a few words from S's Dominant.

"Tap into your power and rid yourself of the negativity and fear. You will realize how powerful you are and how much you can change your life and other people. Tap into your spiritual side and be grateful!"

Our unwillingness to see our own faults

and the projection of them onto others

is the guarantee that injustice, animosity, and persecution

will not easily die out.

Carl Jung

References

American Psychiatric Association (1980). *A Psychiatric Glossary.* Washington D.C.: Author.

Ansari, Masud (1982). *Modern Hypnosis: Theory and Practice.* Washington D.C.: Mas-Press

Breton, Denise & Largent, Christopher (1996). *The Paradigm Conspiracy.* Center City Minnesota: Hazelton

Buscaglia, L. (1982). *Living, loving and Learning.* New York: Random House Inc.

Chopra, Deepak (1993). *Ageless Body, Timeless Mind. The Quantum Alternative to Growing Old.* New York: MacMillan.

Chu, James A. (1991) *The Repetition Compulsion Revisted: Reliving Dissociated Trauma.* Psychotherapy, 28, 327-331.

DeRohan, Ceanne (1996). *Right Use of Will.* Santa Fe: Four Winds Publications.

Dyer, Wayne (1992). *Real Magic.* New York: Harper Collins.

Erikson, Erik H. (1963). *Youth: Change and Challenge.* New York: Basic Books.

Gibran, Kalil (1951). *The Prophet.* New York: Alfred-A-Knopf.

Hammond, D. Corydon (1995). *Clinic Hypnosis and Memory: Guidelines for Clinicians.* ISSMP& News 13, 1-6.

Herman, Judith L. (1992). *Trauma and Recovery.* New York: Basic Books.

Hill, N. (2005). *Think and Grow Rich.* New York: Penguin Group.

Janet, Pierre (1925). *Psychological Healing (vol 1-2)* &. Paul & E. Paul, Trans). New York: MacMillan.

Judith, Anodea (1987). *Wheels of Life.* St. Paul Minnesota : Llewellyn Publications.

Jung, Carl G. (1970). *Psychological Reflections.* New York: Princeton.

Lama, Dalai (1999). *Ethics for the New Millennium.* New York: Basic Books.

Levine, Peter (1991). *The Body as Healer: a Revisioning of Trauma and Anxiety.* In M. Sheets-Johnstone (Ed.), *Giving the Body its Due* (pp. 85-108). Stonybrook, NY: State University of New York Press.

Myss, Caroline (1996). *Anatomy of the Spirit.* New York: Three Rivers Press.

May, Rollo (1953). *Man's Search for Himself.* New York: Dell Publishing.

Phillips, Maggie & Frederick, Claire (1995). *Healing the Divided Self.* New York: W. W. Norton & Company.

Putnam, Frank W. (1989). *Diagnosis and Treatment of Multiple Personality Disorder.* New York: Guilford.

Reynolds, David K. (1984). *Playing Ball on Running Water.* New York: Quill.

Ross, Colin A. (1994). *President's Message.* ISSMP & News, 12, 1-3.

Segroi, Suzanne M. (1982). *A Handbook of Clinical Interventions in Child Sexual Abuse.* Massachusetts: Lexington Books.

Some, Malidoma Patrice (1998). *The Healing Wisdom of Africa .* New York: Penguin Putnam Inc.

Terr, Lenore (1991). *Childhood Traumas. An Outline and Overview.* The American Journal of Psychiatry, 148, 10-20.

Teicher, Martin H. (2002). *The Neurobiology of Child Abuse.* Scientific American, (cap A) March, 68-75.

Tolle, Eckhart (2005). *A New Earth. New York:* Penguin Group.

van der Kolk, Bessel A. *The Compulsion to Repeat the Trauma: Re-enactment, Revictimization, and Masochism.* Psychiatric Clinics of North America. 12 (2), 389-411.

van der Kolk, Bessel A., McFarlane, A. C., & Weisaeth, L. (Ed's) (1996). *Traumatic Stress. The Effects of Overwhelming Experience on Mind, Body, and Society.* New York: Guilford Press.

Watkins, John G. (1995). *Hypnotic Abreactions in the Recovery of Traumatic Memories.* ISSMP & News, 13, 1-6.

Weiss, Brian (1992). *Through Time into Healing.* New York: Simon & Schuster

Woolger, Roger J. (1988). *Other Lives, Other Selves.* New York: Bantam Books.

Zukav, Gary (1989). *The Seat of the Soul.* New York: Simon & Schuster.

Zukav, Gary (2001). *The Heart of the Soul.* New York: Simon & Schuster.

About The Author

©Cynthia Lawson Photography

William Jump is a clinical psychotherapist and hypnotherapist. In his two decades of private practice, he has utilized Ericksonian Hypnosis techniques for the treatment of child, adolescent, and adult survivors of childhood traumas. His work has aligned him with both Dissociative and Transpersonal perspectives. He formerly worked for a State CPS Child Sexual Abuse treatment team. Special interests include couples and family therapy and parent-child discipline.

Bill currently maintains a private practice in Maryland and is available for presentations, consultations, and media interviews: www.wmjump.com.

Printed in the United States
205082BV00005B/58-60/P

9 781934 588376